Also by Nancy Silverton

Nancy Silverton's Sandwich Book
(with Teri Gelber)

Nancy Silverton's Pastries from the La Brea Bakery
(in collaboration with Teri Gelber)

The Food of Campanile
(with Mark Peel)

Nancy Silverton's Breads from the La Brea Bakery
(in collaboration with Laurie Ochoa)

Mark Peel and Nancy Silverton at Home: Two Chefs Cook for Family and Friends

Desserts
(with Heidi Yorkshire)

A TWIST OF THE WRIST

QUICK FLAVORFUL MEALS WITH INGREDIENTS FROM JARS, CANS, BAGS, AND BOXES

NANCY SILVERTON

WITH CAROLYNN CARREÑO

PHOTOGRAPHS BY AMY NEUNSINGER

ALFRED A. KNOPF · NEW YORK 2007

THIS IS A BORZOI BOOK

PUBLISHED BY ALFRED A. KNOPF

COPYRIGHT © 2007 BY NANCY SILVERTON

PHOTOGRAPHS COPYRIGHT © 2007

BY AMY NEUNSINGER

PUBLISHED IN THE UNITED STATES

BY ALFRED A. KNOPF,

A DIVISION OF RANDOM HOUSE, INC.,

NEW YORK, AND IN CANADA BY

RANDOM HOUSE OF CANADA LIMITED,

TORONTO.

WWW.AAKNOPF.COM

KNOPF, BORZOI BOOKS, AND

THE COLOPHON ARE REGISTERED

TRADEMARKS OF RANDOM HOUSE, INC.

LIBRARY OF CONGRESS CATALOGING-

IN-PUBLICATION DATA

SILVERTON, NANCY.

A TWIST OF THE WRIST:

QUICK FLAVORFUL MEALS

WITH INGREDIENTS FROM JARS,

CANS, BAGS, AND BOXES /

BY NANCY SILVERTON WITH

CAROLYNN CARREÑO.

P. CM.

ISBN: 978-1-4000-4407-8

(ALK. PAPER)

1. QUICK AND EASY COOKERY.

2. CONVENIENCE FOODS.

I. CARREÑO, CAROLYNN.

II. TITLE.

TX833.5.S555 2007

641.5'55—DC22

2006049557

MANUFACTURED

IN CHINA

FIRST EDITION

CONTENTS

A
TWIST
OF
THE
WRIST

INTRODUCTION

While writing this book, I felt as if I were on a mission. It came about as the result of a sort of reality check on my part, an awakening that started a few years ago, after I read a review by Amanda Hesser in the *New York Times* of a cookbook in which the author used packaged ingredients to create quick, easy meals. As Amanda pointed out in the review, the author's premise was to get people in and out of the kitchen as quickly as possible so they could do something *enjoyable*—like talk to their husbands or play with their children. Anything but cook! I happen to enjoy cooking and feeding the people I love, so I was disappointed—although, I admit, not terribly surprised—to realize that this was where Americans' heads were in terms of cooking. It was as if we were back in the fifties, before women were "liberated" from the kitchens that enslaved them.

The truth is that many people—at least the majority of the people I know— really don't cook much at all. Home Meal Replacement (HMR), better known as takeout, is the fastest-growing segment in the food industry. I see it in L.A., among my friends, for whom stopping by the grocery store to pick up a piece of fish that was grilled twelve hours ago or roasted vegetables that have been sitting out half the day has become the modern version of "cooking at home." We've moved so far from the kitchen that I felt that what people needed was a gentle, realistic way back.

Enter the jar! And enter *A Twist of the Wrist,* a collection of recipes that takes advantage of quality premade ingredients to create entrées that have the same complexity of flavors and textures as ones you'd be served in a restaurant. Not that a meal always needs to be "complex." There's nothing wrong with a simple grilled fresh fish fillet on a bed of arugula finished with a squeeze of lemon juice and sea salt. It's just that eating that way night after night could get a bit boring. And besides, it's so easy to make it better than that nowadays.

About the same time that I read the *New York Times* article I had begun to take note of the abundance and variety of quality jarred, bottled, canned, and otherwise packaged goods available these days. In the past (even the not-so-distant past) canned food in America meant soggy tamales, mushy ravioli, and overcooked, tinny-tasting vegetables. And cookbooks touting jarred or other packaged products were terribly compromised because the products they used in their recipes were really substandard and, as a result, so were the dishes made with them.

But today it's a whole different story. Many delicacies are imported from Europe that weren't available even ten years ago: marinated tuna from Italy and Spain; marmalades, jams, and butter cookies from France; and tapenades, capers, pesto, and pasta (not to mention a million wonderful olive oils) from Italy. And things have also changed here at home, where many American chefs bottle the same pasta sauces, salsas, and dessert sauces that they serve in their popular restaurants. By using these products in the right way in these recipes I was able to layer different flavors and textures in delicious, satisfying ways without having to make every component from scratch.

I realize that for many people, preparing a dish of pasta that takes advantage of jarred tomato sauce or a chicken salad that starts with jarred mayonnaise and a rotisserie chicken or a dessert in which neither the cookie nor the ice cream is made by hand might not seem like a big deal, but for me, it was a total anomaly. Some might even say a fall from grace. I come from a school of cooking in which anything that is viewed as less than fresh from the farm; anything that is not straight from the earth; anything prepared, frozen, packaged, or preserved; anything not made with the very best ingredients, by loving hands, is considered if not downright evil, a total cop-out. Which means that in the past, if I were writing a recipe for chicken salad, the first step would be "roast the chicken," followed by "make the mayonnaise." For me to write a book in which a jar of mayonnaise is even mentioned is revolutionary. But it's a revolution that I felt had to happen.

The goal of my so-called mission is to show people a way to create satisfying meals with a minimum of effort and time so that they will be encouraged to cook at home more often. I think there's a level of satisfaction and pride that comes from preparing a meal for yourself and your family and friends— even if it is helped along by premade ingredients—that you can't possibly get from dumping a container of food out on a plate. (The simple act of squeezing the orange juice for my youngest son, Oliver, to drink with his cereal every morning before school makes me feel like I'm contributing something to his day and to him.) If I had to use packaged foods to help make everyday cooking a reality, it was a compromise I was willing to make, and to promote.

I don't want you to get the wrong idea. *A Twist of the Wrist* is not meant to offer an antidote to cooking from scratch. At the height of summer, when basil is at its peak and you have the time, I still recommend that you break out the mortar and pestle and make pesto the old-fashioned way. I still believe in making a tremendous effort when you have the time to entertain, and in preparing elegant, labor-intensive desserts when the inspiration hits, and, of course, that there's nothing like warming the house with slow-cooking meats on a winter weekend afternoon.

But this isn't a book for those times. It's a book for typical evenings when you get home from work, don't feel like going out, but want (or need) to have dinner on the table within an hour—or less—of walking in the door. It is a book for when you're hungry and even a trip to the grocery store is more than you can bear, and for dinner parties when you want to have friends over but you don't have the half a day it takes to go all out in preparing the food. Thus, dressing up a store-bought corn soup with a homemade bacon and Cheddar crouton, composing a Niçoise salad using canned tuna and jarred potatoes, or serving dinner guests a dessert of jarred prunes doctored with brandy and served with premium vanilla ice cream is not the alternative to slow cooking. It's the alternative to *not* cooking. And the alternative to takeout.

This book is more than just my invitation and "permission" to open up a jar. It is an invitation to think in a totally different way about cooking. It is my welcome into a world where packaged and fresh items, combined in creative ways, are not compromises, but inspirations. And it is my invitation to you to get back in the kitchen.

Guest Chef Contributors

In the beginning stages of conceiving this book, I was concerned that people in my field whom I respect might think I was crazy. We're cooks. And we're the kind of cooks who make everything from scratch. I've been a long-standing proponent of sustainable farming and locally grown food. Back in the early eighties, I was one of the first chefs to start shopping at the Santa Monica Farmers' Market—a ritual now for Los Angeles chefs (and for chefs all over the country at their respective farmers' markets). But as I've explained, I knew a book of dishes that come together much more quickly and easily than those we cook in our restaurant kitchens but that are still cooked with love and a great attention to detail was a good idea. I kept thinking that I couldn't be alone; I couldn't be the only one impressed by the products available now. And I also kept thinking: Well, every chef loves Piquillo peppers!

Besides, I know from having been there for so many years that nobody is under more time constraints than a restaurant chef. When we get home after a long day, we're exhausted and our creativity is spent. At the same time, we're not going to just throw a chicken breast on a plate. We're going to do something to it. It's who we are.

With this in mind, I decided to invite those very chefs and editors whose judgment I feared to contribute a recipe to the book. I sent out letters soliciting recipes from these friends, assuring them that I had not given up on the idea of slow cooking or shopping at farmers' markets when the time allows. I just want people to cook more, I told them.

And in came the recipes, along with honest stories of how these people really cook at home. Here was Gale Gand, one of America's top pastry chefs, baking turnovers for her little girls by filling packaged puff pastry with apple butter and applesauce (and apples!). Here was Mario Batali tossing up a pasta dish with all the bold flavors for which he's known—all with ingredients straight from the pantry. And here was Ruth Reichl, editor of *Gourmet,* telling me about her emergency dessert solution: a pie made with frozen blueberries baked in a frozen piecrust.

Inviting these contributions turned out to have another advantage in that many of these chefs use ingredients that I don't normally use. My friends Mary Sue Milliken and Susan Feniger, aka the Two Hot Tamales, sent me a recipe for chilaquiles that makes delicious use of a bottle of salsa and a bag of tortilla chips. Jimmy Shaw, another great Mexican restaurateur here in L.A., makes a casserole starting with a jar of Doña María mole sauce. In a hundred years, with a hundred bags of groceries filled with jars and cans of things to taste, I'm absolutely certain I never would have entertained the idea for a recipe like the one from Tom Douglas, one of the foremost chefs in the Northwest, for stir-frying pot stickers he buys at Costco. Naturally, they were delicious.

Shopping

One of the first things I did when I began writing this book was to go shopping. And I kept shopping for the next year, until the book was finished. I went all over town, to gourmet stores, import stores, and regular supermarkets, buying jars, cans, bags, boxes, and tubes of foods—some familiar, some foreign, and many that were very weird. I wanted to taste everything. I figured there was no other way I would know what was out there. As with any recipe, those in this book are dependent on the quality of the ingredients used to make them, and in this case that means the quality of the packaged ingredients as well as the fresh ones.

I knew I could rely on some fancy producers whose products I was familiar with, such as Rustichella d'Abruzzo pastas and sauces and anything else imported by Manacaretti or KL Keller—the stuff that lines the walls of La Brea Bakery and other upscale food shops around the country. But I knew I needed to reach beyond those items for a few reasons: they're expensive, they're limited in range and scope, and, most important, I didn't want this cookbook to be a precious collection of how finally to use the infused oils, tapenades, and pestos that come in an expensive gift basket. (Although there are uses for those products here, too!) I wanted *Twist* to be a working cookbook, one used by regular people with busy lives who want to get back to the kitchen but who might be discouraged by the time it takes to prepare a meal. I wanted it to be the kind of cookbook that gets stained from wine spills and spotted from olive oil–covered fingers. I wanted it to encourage and inspire the hesitant would-be home cook. And in order for this book to be effective in meeting these goals, I knew I had to use ingredients that are available at regular grocery stores.

In tasting what seems like basically every jarred, canned, bagged, and boxed ingredient ever made, I had many surprises—both good and bad. I was pleasantly surprised at how delicious a can of beans in tomato sauce was. The beans were cooked to a perfectly creamy texture, and the savory tomato sauce tasted superb, with no hint of the can. I was equally surprised by how many jars of pesto I had to open before I found one that didn't taste as if the nuts it was made from had gone rancid. And I was disheartened by the fact that I couldn't find one vinaigrette that was good enough to be worth the time saved by not making it from scratch.

To help you with your shopping, in the introductions to each chapter I give you insights about how I shopped for the ingredients used in that chapter. I talk about the products I like in the headnotes to the recipes in which they're used and for those used more than once, in "Twist Essentials." And I also provide sources where you can buy the items used in the book.

Equipment

There is no special equipment necessary to make these recipes, just the basics: a good skillet, two good sharp knives (one large, one small), mixing bowls, and, of course, a can opener. But in trying to cut down on prep times I did discover a few handy tools that, now that I know about them, I don't think I could ever live without.

I find an inexpensive Japanese-made **mandoline** by Benviner to be a huge time-saver when it comes to thinly slicing vegetables.

A **microplane grater:** My favorite version is a long, thin, fine-grated plane that looks more like something you'd find at a hardware store than a cookware store. (They also come with a handle and a wide rectangular plane.) It's such a must for grating things such as garlic, shallots, and lemon zest that I thought about asking our publisher if we could sell the book with a microplane attached. Mincing garlic is every home cook's nemesis and yet I couldn't bring myself to call for jarred, minced garlic, which tends to be brown and rancid. I also don't like to use a garlic press because it's so hard to get the garlic out of it, and I never feel like I really get the gadget clean. I'd seen cooks use a microplane to grate garlic in the past, but I'd never considered anything but hand chopping it. Then I tried it for this book, and I couldn't believe how easy and how effective it was; you can grate a garlic clove or a shallot in seconds; once you're done, just tap it against the side of a bowl to release the gratings. No knife, no cutting board, no cleanup. Trust me—get one.

A **Mexican citrus juicer** is my favorite tool for squeezing lemons or limes. It's a little handheld tool that works like a garlic press (only it's easy to clean): you open up the two parts of the handle, put the halved lemon or lime in, and use the handle to press down on the fruit to squeeze out the juice (there are different tools depending on the size of the citrus you're squeezing). It's really effective for getting all the juice out and it also filters out the pulp and seeds.

An **immersion blender** is a fantastic tool for puréeing. It's a small hand-held device that goes straight in the pot or bowl with the ingredients you're purée-ing, so you avoid spilling all over the counter as you would if you were transferring a pot of liquid to a blender. Besides its ease of use, I like that you can see what you're doing, so if you want to leave whatever you're puréeing slightly chunky, you can stop when it's the texture you want.

You'll notice that in these recipes (with a few exceptions), I call for chives (and sometimes basil) to be snipped with **scissors.** To do this, bunch up the chives and cut them directly over the dish you're adding them to. I like the way they fall naturally when they're cut this way, but, more important, it is *really* easy to do. You can find kitchen shears at all cookware stores, but any pair of sharp, clean scissors will work.

A good **pepper grinder** is essential. If you get a not-so-good one, it often won't do the one task it was designed to do: grind pepper. I usually don't call for specific amounts of pepper because I rarely measure it. I use only freshly ground pepper, which means that I grind it directly over whatever I'm seasoning.

I like to keep **two small bowls** in my work area, one for sea salt and the other for kosher salt. It makes seasoning so much easier when you can pinch and sprinkle without having to open any containers. (And I *never* use a salt-shaker.)

What Makes a Meal

In order to simplify the process of making easy meals at home, we need to rethink what makes a meal. When we were growing up, a proper dinner required a meat, starch, and vegetable. Although we don't eat like that anymore, we're still rigid in our thinking. For some odd reason, eggs are not considered proper dinner (in this country anyway). Soup is a starter, as are salads, and crostini, which is essentially toast, is for sandwiches, which are exclusively for lunchtime. When you're using this book, forget about all that.

The recipes in this book (with a few noted exceptions) serve four people and are meant to stand alone as complete meals. Salads and soups as a main course are just right for those times when you crave something lighter. Heartier dishes such as the Boneless Pork Chops with Yam Purée and Polenta with Sausage Ragù are just the kind of warm, comforting dishes you want when it's cold outside. I included two recipes for side salads, a Tri-Colore Salad and Jonathan Waxman's Zucchini Crudo with Hearts of Palm and Pecorino Romano. Both of them take just a few minutes to prepare, and they're the perfect things to serve with some of the lighter entrées, such as any of the frittatas or crostini, to make a heartier meal or for those people who invariably just *have* to have a salad with dinner.

A Note on Seasoning

I'm always encouraged when I see a cook in a restaurant tasting as she cooks because I know she's paying attention and that she will adjust the final seasonings so that they're just right. Those last little touches—a squeeze of lemon juice, a drizzle of balsamic vinegar or olive oil, another sprinkling of fresh chopped herbs, and, perhaps most important, a little more salt—are often what make the flavors of a dish really pop. It's called "seasoning" and I think it's one of the most important steps in cooking.

The success of these recipes (and of any recipe, for that matter) depends a lot on how the dishes are seasoned. I've given fairly detailed instructions for seasoning in this book, specifying amounts of rubs for chicken and lamb and even telling you how much salt to use on a steak or a piece of fish. I also specify what kind of salt to use throughout the recipes. I call for kosher salt for cooking or any time the salt is going to be mixed into a dish, and I call for sea salt for seasoning (the flavor is more pronounced)—for sprinkling on tomatoes or greens, or on a finished piece of meat or fish. Still, the best way to season your food is to taste it to determine what it needs.

There are so many wonderful salts available now, I urge you to taste them and keep a few of your favorites—different sizes and textures—on hand for seasoning. My very favorite seasoning salt is Maldon sea salt. In addition to having a wonderful flavor, it has big flakes, which are nice because you can feel the crunch of the salt, but they're also soft enough that they can be crushed between your fingers when you want a finer consistency. Fleur de sel or "flower of the salt" is the most expensive variety. If using brands of sea salt other than Maldon, you may have to grind them with a mortar and pestle if the granulation is too coarse. There are also many good salt blends out there. The two that I use are *sale erbe,* an Italian blend of sea salt and dried herbs that is delicious for seasoning meat and fish, and a recent discovery, truffle salt—sea salt with little bits of black truffle mixed in. Because it has actual truffle bits in it, truffle salt allows me to add a hint of true truffle flavor to dishes without any of the odd taste that truffle oil imparts.

SALADS

When I was working full-time at Campanile and La Brea Bakery with three children at home, I often served salad as a main (and only) course for dinner. Salads are so easy to throw together that as long as I had some leftover meat or a whole roasted chicken in the refrigerator, which I almost always do for just that reason, it seemed I could improvise with whatever I had on hand—and the results were always delicious. For all the same reasons, salads turned out to be ideal items to feature in this book.

With the exception of boiling hard-cooked eggs, none of these recipes requires you to even turn on the stove. Tuna and beans come from a can; ham, prosciutto, and salami are naturally flavorful just as they are; and rotisserie chicken, a ubiquitous grocery-store item these days, is the start of all the chicken salads.

Bottled vinaigrettes were the one premade condiment I wanted to use but couldn't. I tried a lot of them and they all tasted artificial. So all the vinaigrettes for these salads are homemade, but they're all very simple to make, stirred by hand and not emulsified. Their flavor is dependent on the quality of the olive oil, aged balsamic vinegar, fresh lemon juice, sea salt, and freshly ground black pepper from which they're made.

When serving salads as an entrée, I prefer to serve them individually on large plates (I *hate* cramped salads!) rather than tossing them. I layer them so it's almost like I'm building two or three identical salads on top of one another. Layering the salads keeps the lettuce from getting soggy or weighted down from the other ingredients. And with the ingredients evenly distributed and artfully placed, I think the salad feels more satisfying than a pile of lettuce in which you have to dig around for a tomato or a slice of cheese. The salads are certainly more beautiful this way.

There are exceptions, such as the "Garbage" Salad (so named because I created it as a way to clean out my refrigerator), which I like to serve family style. Because it has so many different ingredients, their proportion to one another doesn't really matter, and I think in this instance it's fun for people to dig around and see what other little treats they might find amid the lettuce. When I serve salads family style, I do it in a big, wide-mouthed salad bowl. I recommend you invest in such a bowl, as the wide-mouth really makes a nice presentation.

When you're making these salads, keep in mind that no matter how much detail I go into about how to plate them, I never mean for the ingredients to be carefully placed or arranged. Although each salad is assembled in a very intentional way, I like them to look organic, as if the ingredients just grew from the plate or fell from the sky. So I might scatter olives or nuts, spoon cherry tomatoes in clumps, break hard-cooked eggs open with my hands, or rumple a piece of prosciutto before laying it on a bed of greens. But I do not worry about symmetry—except to make sure things are not symmetric!

Whether plated or tossed, the advantage to any salad, of course, is that no matter what ingredients go into it—cheese, dates, salami, prosciutto—it's always healthier than the same ingredients when they're not accompanied by greens. Or at least it seems that way!

When shopping for the items in this chapter, I paid special consideration to the lettuces I used. I avoided those that need to be washed (especially those that need to be washed two and three times) and instead took advantage of those greens that require little or no preparation and of the prewashed greens that are so widely available now. Leaves are pulled from the cores of endive, radicchio, and romaine. Sprouts are taken straight from the container in which they're packaged. And I chose live watercress or pepper cress and live Bibb lettuce, which are grown hydroponically (they're sold in plastic boxes with the roots still attached) because they don't need to be washed, and the watercress doesn't need to be trimmed with the same meticulous care as the watercress from farmers' markets.

Many of the prewashed greens available in supermarkets are organic and now are even sold at some farmers' markets. When buying prewashed greens, I recommend you look for those that are sold loose in bulk. Their containers are refilled by the produce department all day long, so the greens are generally fresher than those in bags. Plus, you can see what you're getting. If you do buy bagged greens, look inside the bag. Avoid those with dark, soggy-looking leaves. Go for leaves that look bright green and fresh.

I don't call for any greens to be washed in this book because I figure everyone has their own way of doing it. Some people wash even the prewashed stuff. I don't, nor do I wash fresh herbs, radicchio, or endive unless they're visibly dirty.

Except for the Tri-Colore Salad, Jonathan Waxman's Zucchini Crudo with Hearts of Palm and Pecorino Romano, and Traci Des Jardins's Garbanzo Bean Salad, which are meant as side dishes or starters, all of the salads in this chapter are meant to be served as full meals. A big hunk of country bread served with a slab of lightly salted European-style butter is a welcome addition to any salad meal.

Butter Lettuce and Herb Salad with Borlotti Beans, Asparagus, Artichoke Hearts, and Feta

This salad is so easy to prepare, going out and getting the right ingredients—lettuce, artichokes, and feta—is the only effort you'll have to make. In general, fresh, tender, sweet lettuce is very important to the texture of a salad: I prefer the butter lettuce you can find at grocery stores that comes in a plastic box with the roots still attached. Alternatively, small heads of red or green leaf lettuce are a good substitute.

40 MINUTES

To make the vinaigrette, pour the lemon juice into a small bowl. Add the shallot. Stir in the olive oil, kosher salt, and freshly ground black pepper.

Combine the parsley, chervil, chives, and dill in a medium bowl. Divide them in half and set one of the halves aside. Finely chop the other half of the herbs and stir the chopped herbs into the vinaigrette.

Snap the stems of the asparagus off one at a time at the natural break to remove the tough ends and discard. Starting at the tip end, cut the spears diagonally 1/8 inch thick and put them in a large bowl. Add the borlotti beans and artichoke hearts, drizzle with the vinaigrette, and toss to coat. Season with kosher salt and freshly ground black pepper and add the remaining herbs.

Place one lettuce leaf on each of four plates, and scatter a quarter of the beans, vegetables, and herbs over the lettuce, and sprinkle lightly with a quarter of the crumbled feta. Continue layering the salad in the same way until you've built four layers on each plate and all the ingredients are used. Drizzle any vinaigrette remaining in the bowl over the salads and sprinkle them with sea salt.

FOR THE VINAIGRETTE
1/4 cup fresh lemon juice
1 medium shallot, grated or minced (about 2 teaspoons)
1/2 cup high-quality **extra-virgin olive oil**
1 teaspoon kosher salt
1/2 teaspoon freshly ground black pepper

1 cup loosely packed fresh Italian parsley leaves
1 cup fresh chervil leaves
1 cup 1-inch cut fresh chives
1 cup fresh dill leaves
4 asparagus spears, preferably pencil asparagus
1 cup canned borlotti **beans** (or cannellini beans or navy beans), rinsed and drained
4 whole marinated **artichoke hearts,** quartered
Kosher salt and freshly ground black pepper
16 large leaves butter lettuce (not the outermost leaves)
4 ounces **feta,** crumbled into large chunks (about 1 cup)
Sea salt

Spicy Beets with Aged Goat Cheese, Arugula, and Horseradish Vinaigrette

The combination of beets and horseradish is a classic in Jewish cooking. Beet-stained freshly grated horseradish is a staple of any Passover meal and the inspiration for this bold, spicy salad. When you're shopping for prepared horseradish, look for one that contains just horseradish, vinegar, and salt.

25 MINUTES

Adjust the oven rack to the middle position and preheat the oven to 325°F.

Spread the walnuts on a baking sheet and toast them for about 15 minutes, until they're golden and fragrant. Remove the walnuts from the oven and transfer them to a small bowl. While they're still warm, drizzle them with the walnut oil, sprinkle with kosher salt, and toss to coat.

Change the oven setting to broil.

To make the vinaigrette, stir the horseradish, vinegar, mustard, shallot, 1 teaspoon of the kosher salt, and the freshly ground black pepper together in a medium bowl. Place the beets in the bowl with the vinaigrette, season them with the remaining teaspoon of kosher salt, drizzle with the canola oil and olive oil, and stir to coat the beets with the vinaigrette.

Mound 2 cups of arugula on each of four plates. Season them with sea salt. Spoon the beets in the center of each mound, scraping the remaining dressing out of the bowl and onto the beets. If you're using the fresh horseradish, finely grate about 2 tablespoons over each serving of beets and use scissors to finely snip about 1 teaspoon of chives over each serving.

Place the disks of goat cheese on a baking sheet and cook them under the broiler for about 1½ minutes, until they just begin to brown and melt. Remove them from the oven and place one disk of cheese on each plate to the side of the beets. Drizzle walnut oil over the cheese and scatter the walnuts over the salads.

1¼ cups walnut halves (about 4 ounces)

2 teaspoons **walnut oil**, plus extra for drizzling

Kosher salt

FOR THE VINAIGRETTE

¼ cup plus 1 tablespoon **prepared horseradish**

1 tablespoon plus 1 teaspoon apple cider **vinegar**

1 tablespoon Dijon **mustard**

1 medium shallot, grated or minced (about 2 teaspoons)

2 teaspoons kosher salt

1 teaspoon freshly ground black pepper

1 15- to 16-ounce can or jar whole **beets,** cut into ¼-inch cubes (about 2 cups)

1 tablespoon plus 1 teaspoon canola oil (or other neutral-flavored oil)

1 tablespoon plus 1 teaspoon high-quality **extra-virgin olive oil**

8 cups loosely packed arugula leaves

Sea salt

Fresh washed and peeled horse-radish for grating (optional)

20 fresh chives

8 ounces aged goat cheese, cut into 4 2-inch-thick disks

Arugula with Hard-Cooked Eggs, Artichoke Hearts, Tuna, and Charred Tomatoes

If you have an oversized salad bowl that's wide and shallow, then this is one of the salads I recommend serving family style. I'm very particular about hard-cooked eggs. I like them cooked just to the point of solidifying, so that the yolks are bright yellow. Once they turn lighter yellow and almost powdery, they're overdone and will be dry and tasteless. And if they're cooked to the point where the yolks have a gray ring around them, forget about it. Because I'm so specific about the way I like my eggs, I always put an extra egg in the water as a tester. After five minutes, I take one egg out, peel it, and break it open to see if it's done.

25 MINUTES

Adjust the oven rack to the highest position and preheat the broiler.

Toss the tomatoes in a medium bowl with the olive oil, sugar, and a generous sprinkling of kosher salt. Scatter them on a baking sheet and place them under the broiler for 5 to 7 minutes, shaking the pan occasionally, until they're charred and burst in places.

To hard-cook the eggs, place them in a medium saucepan with enough water to cover, salt the water generously, and bring it to a boil over high heat. Reduce the heat to low and simmer the eggs for about 5 minutes, until the yolks are bright yellow but still wet looking. While they're cooking, fill a large bowl with ice water. When the eggs are done, drain and immediately plunge them into the ice water to chill. (This prevents the eggs from cooking any further before they're peeled.) When the eggs are cool, peel and slice them thin with an egg slicer or cut them into quarters with a large knife.

32 small, sweet **tomatoes** (about ½ pint), cut in half (or 16 cherry tomatoes, quartered)

2 tablespoons **extra-virgin olive oil,** plus more for thinning the tapenade if necessary

Pinch of sugar

Kosher salt

4 large eggs

To make the vinaigrette, stir the balsamic vinegar and lemon juice together in a small bowl. Add the garlic and shallot. Stir in the olive oil, kosher salt, and freshly ground black pepper.

To slice the onion, take apart the layers, stack them on top of one another, and slice them lengthwise into very thin strips (about 1/16 inch thick). Place the strips in a colander, rinse them under cold water, drain, and pat them dry with paper towels. (This process helps take the bitterness out of raw onions so you're left with only the sweet, pure onion flavor.)

If the tapenade is thick and pastelike, put it in a small bowl and stir in a tablespoon or two of olive oil until you obtain a loose, spoonable consistency.

Place the arugula in a large bowl, season it with sea salt and freshly ground black pepper, and toss. Drizzle the arugula with 3 tablespoons of the vinaigrette, reserving the remaining vinaigrette to drizzle over the finished salad. Add the cucumbers and onion and toss gently to just combine.

Mound a third of the arugula salad in the bottom of a large serving bowl (or on four plates). Crumble a third of the tuna over the arugula and spoon a third of the tomatoes over the salad in clumps. Scatter a third of the artichoke hearts and then lay the egg slices or quarters over the salad. Top the eggs with a dab of olive tapenade and repeat, beginning with another layer of arugula and piling the salad high until you've used all of the ingredients in three layers. Drizzle the remaining vinaigrette over the salad and sprinkle it with sea salt.

FOR THE VINAIGRETTE

2 tablespoons aged **balsamic vinegar**

1 tablespoon fresh lemon juice

1 small garlic clove, grated or minced (about 1/2 teaspoon)

1 small shallot, grated or minced (about 1 teaspoon)

1/4 cup high-quality **extra-virgin olive oil**

1 teaspoon kosher salt

1/2 teaspoon freshly ground black pepper

1/2 large red onion (cut through the core)

1/4 cup black **olive tapenade**

1–2 tablespoons **extra-virgin olive oil,** for thinning the tapenade, if necessary

12 cups loosely packed arugula leaves

Sea salt and freshly ground black pepper

2 small cucumbers (such as Persian or Japanese, or 1 thin hothouse cucumber; if a larger cucumber is your only option, cut it in half and scrape out the seeds), sliced 1/8 inch thick diagonally (about 1 cup)

8 ounces olive oil–packed **tuna,** lightly drained

4 whole marinated **artichoke hearts,** quartered

Tuna Niçoise Salad with Aged Sherry Vinaigrette

Niçoise salad is a classic dish composed of tuna, olives, anchovies, green beans, and potatoes. It was a natural for this book, since the tuna, olives, and anchovies are all canned. And green beans cook quickly, so they weren't a problem. The only challenge was the potatoes. No matter how you slice them, literally, potatoes take a long time to cook, so I was pleased when I tried jarred potatoes and found they had good flavor and texture. I marinate them in the vinaigrette while I'm preparing the rest of the ingredients, so they really absorb those flavors.

35 MINUTES

To make the vinaigrette, pour the vinegar into a bowl large enough to toss the salad in. Stir in the garlic and shallot. Stir in the olive oil, kosher salt, and freshly ground black pepper.

Place the potato slices in the bowl with the vinaigrette and allow them to marinate while you prepare the other ingredients.

To hard-cook the eggs, place them in a medium saucepan with enough water to cover, salt the water generously, and bring it to a boil over high heat. Reduce the heat to low and simmer the eggs for about 5 minutes, until the yolks are bright yellow but slightly wet looking (see page 16 for additional egg information). While they're cooking, fill a large bowl with ice water. When the eggs are done, drain and immediately plunge them into the ice water to chill. (This prevents the eggs from cooking any further before they're peeled.) Peel the eggs when they're cool.

To cook the haricots verts, bring a small pot of water to a boil over high heat and add a generous amount of kosher salt. Fill a large bowl with ice water. Blanch the beans in the boiling water until they're bright green and just tender but still slightly crisp, about 2 minutes. Drain and immediately transfer the beans to the ice water bath to stop them from cooking and to maintain their green color. As soon as the green beans are cold, drain them to prevent them from getting waterlogged and pat them dry with paper towels.

Transfer the potatoes to a small bowl, leaving the vinaigrette in the bottom of the large bowl. Add the lettuce leaves to the bowl with the vinaigrette, season them with sea salt and freshly ground black pepper, and toss to coat. Remove the lettuce from the vinaigrette (there should still be vinaigrette left in the bowl) and fan the leaves out on four plates. Scatter the potatoes over the lettuce. Toss the tomatoes in the bowl with the vinaigrette and then scatter them over the salads. Put the green beans in the vinaigrette, toss to coat, and scatter them on the salads.

FOR THE VINAIGRETTE

3 tablespoons aged **sherry vinegar**

2 large garlic cloves, grated or minced (about 2 teaspoons)

1 medium shallot, grated or minced (about 2 teaspoons)

1/3 cup plus 1 tablespoon high-quality **extra-virgin olive oil**

1 teaspoon kosher salt

1/2 teaspoon freshly ground black pepper

6 medium canned or jarred **potatoes,** sliced 1/4 inch thick (about 1 1/2 cups)

4 large eggs

Kosher salt

1/4 pound haricots verts (or any green beans), trimmed of stem ends only

16 butter lettuce leaves (not the outermost leaves)

Sea salt and freshly ground black pepper

28 small, sweet **tomatoes** (scant 1/2 pint), cut in half, or 14 cherry tomatoes, quartered

16 ounces olive oil–packed **tuna,** lightly drained

28 Niçoise olives or other small **black olives**

1–2 tablespoons **extra-virgin olive oil,** for thinning the tapenade, if necessary

1 tablespoon plus 1 teaspoon black **olive tapenade**

8 **anchovy fillets**

20 fresh chives

Crumble the tuna into roughly 1½-inch pieces and add it to the salads, then scatter them with the olives.

If the tapenade is thick and pastelike, put it in a small bowl and stir in a tablespoon or two of olive oil until you obtain a loose, spoonable consistency.

Break each egg in half with your hands and place both halves in the center of each salad. Spoon ½ teaspoon of the tapenade over each egg half and top each with an anchovy fillet. Use scissors to finely snip about 1 teaspoon of chives over each salad and sprinkle with sea salt and drizzle any remaining vinaigrette around the salad.

Tuna and White Bean Salad with Radicchio and Red Onion

Ventresca is canned tuna belly packed in olive oil. It is an Italian delicacy. Fabio Picchi, the chef at Cibrèo, one of the most famous (and one of my favorite) restaurants in Tuscany, gave me a piece of advice about serving ventresca: "Only with beans!" he said. You probably won't be able to resist eating ventresca on its own and using it in other dishes, but with his advice in mind, if you're ready to splurge on ventresca (which in addition to being delicious is also very expensive), this classic Tuscan salad is the reason to do it. The salad tastes better the day after it's made, when the beans have had a chance to absorb the vinaigrette, so I like to double the recipe and have some left over for the next day. Note that this recipe has a lot of onion in it, which is how I like it. If you think it might be too much for your taste, you may want to use less.

40 MINUTES

Halve the onion through the core. Take apart the layers, stack them on top of one another, and slice them lengthwise into very thin strips (about 1/16 inch thick). Place the strips in a colander, rinse them under cool water, drain, and pat them dry with paper towels. (This process helps take the bitterness out of raw onions so you're left with only the sweet, pure onion flavor.)

Heat the olive oil, garlic, shallot, and a pinch of kosher salt in a large skillet over medium-high heat for about 1 1/2 minutes, until the shallots soften and the garlic is soft and fragrant, stirring constantly so the garlic doesn't brown. Turn the heat up to high, add the cannellini beans and borlotti beans and cook, stirring often, until the beans are warmed through, 2 to 3 minutes. Turn off the heat, stir in the onion, radicchio, and lemon juice, and season with additional kosher salt if necessary.

Spoon the beans onto four plates, dividing them evenly, and drizzle them with the sauce remaining in the skillet. Crumble the tuna over each serving, drizzle the tuna with the lemon-infused olive oil, and sprinkle with sea salt.

1 small red onion

3 tablespoons **extra-virgin olive oil**

2 large garlic cloves, grated or minced (about 2 teaspoons)

1 medium shallot, grated or minced (about 2 teaspoons)

Kosher salt

1 cup canned cannellini **beans,** rinsed and drained

1 cup canned borlotti **beans,** rinsed and drained

8 large radicchio leaves, very thinly sliced (about 2 1/2 cups loosely packed)

1/2 cup fresh lemon juice

12 ounces ventresca (or any olive oil–packed **tuna**), lightly drained

Lemon-infused olive oil (or high-quality **extra-virgin olive oil** combined with a pinch of fresh grated lemon zest), for drizzling

Sea salt

Spinach Salad with Lentils and Crispy Warm Goat Cheese

I love to cook lentils from scratch, but for the purpose of this book, I needed to find a ready-made alternative to preparing dried lentils. I tried a few different types of unusual canned varieties, such as beluga lentils, that can be bought from specialty food stores. While the belugas are my favorite (I love their black color), they're hard to find. I wanted something more readily available, so I tried Progresso Lentil Soup (drained of its broth); it was a long shot, but I was pleasantly surprised to find it worked. Panko, the Japanese breadcrumbs used to coat tempura, gives the goat cheese in this recipe a nice, crunchy exterior. When you pour the oil in the skillet to shallow fry the cheese rounds, it may look like a lot, but don't worry, the cheese doesn't absorb the oil; you'll discard most of it.

25 MINUTES

Lay a sheet of parchment paper on a flat work surface or have a large plate ready.

To make the goat cheese rounds, lightly pack the cheese into a 1/3-cup measure and tap the cup against the counter to release the cheese out onto the parchment or plate. Flatten the round, being careful to retain its shape, until it's about 3/4 inch thick. Repeat with the remaining goat cheese.

Put about 1/4 cup of flour into a small bowl. Lightly beat the egg in another bowl and pour the panko into a third bowl. Dredge one goat cheese round in the flour, coating it all over, and pat off any excess flour. Next, dip the cheese round into the egg to coat it, then into the panko, pressing the panko onto the cheese to coat all sides. Repeat with the remaining goat cheese rounds.

To make the lentils, heat 1/2 cup of the olive oil, the garlic, and a pinch of kosher salt together in a medium saucepan over medium-high heat until the garlic is soft and fragrant, about 1 1/2 minutes, stirring constantly so the garlic doesn't brown. Add the lentils, turn the heat up to high, and cook them for about 5 minutes, stirring occasionally, until they're warmed through. Season with kosher salt, turn off the heat, and stir in the remaining 1/2 cup of olive oil and the parsley.

While the lentils are warming, heat the canola oil in a large heavy-bottomed skillet over high heat for 2 to 3 minutes, until the oil's almost smoking (you will begin to smell the oil at that point). Place one goat cheese round in the skillet and fry it until it's golden brown, about 30 seconds per side, tilting the pan while the cheese cooks so the oil flows underneath it and keeps it

FOR THE GOAT CHEESE ROUNDS

11 ounces fresh goat cheese

All-purpose flour, for dredging

1 large egg

1/2 cup **panko** or **breadcrumbs**

FOR THE LENTILS

1 cup **extra-virgin olive oil**

4 large garlic cloves, grated or minced (about 1 tablespoon)

Kosher salt

2 15-ounce cans **lentils** or 1 19-ounce can lentil soup, rinsed and drained (about 3 cups)

1/2 cup finely chopped fresh Italian parsley leaves

1/2 cup canola oil (or other neutral-flavored oil)

4 cups loosely packed baby spinach leaves

High-quality **extra-virgin olive oil**, for drizzling

Sea salt

from sticking to the pan. Remove the cheese round to a paper towel to drain and repeat with the remaining cheese rounds.

Spoon the lentils into mounds on four plates, dividing them evenly. Drop a handful of spinach in the center of each serving, drizzle with high-quality olive oil, and sprinkle with sea salt. Top each with a round of goat cheese.

Garbanzo Bean Salad
Traci Des Jardins • Jardinière, San Francisco

I developed this recipe as a quick, easy-to-make, nutritious lunch or side dish for my son, Eli. It's very convenient to make and the ingredients are all easy to find. Naturally I prefer that the parsley and scallions come from a farmers' market and that they're organic. As tasty as this salad is for a last-minute meal, it's even better a few hours after you make it—or the next day—when the beans have been marinated and have absorbed the other flavors.

•

I love this recipe of Traci's. It's so simple and so good. Also, garbanzo beans make an ideal side to many main dishes, such as lamb or fish.

—Nancy

10 MINUTES

Combine the garbanzo beans, scallions, olive oil, vinegar, parsley, cumin, and chile flakes (if desired) in a medium bowl. Season with kosher salt and freshly ground black pepper and stir to combine.

1 15-ounce can garbanzo **beans,** rinsed and drained (about 1½ cups)

1 bunch scallions, very thinly sliced (the white and halfway up the green parts; about 1 cup)

¼ cup plus 2 tablespoons **extra-virgin olive oil**

¼ cup red wine **vinegar**

¼ cup roughly chopped fresh Italian parsley leaves

1 teaspoon ground cumin

½ teaspoon dried chile flakes (optional)

Kosher salt and freshly ground black pepper

"Garbage" Salad with Lemon Vinaigrette

The inspiration for this recipe was to clean out my refrigerator, which is how the salad got its name. In keeping with its informal nature, I urge you to pick and choose from this ingredient list and to add other ingredients you have that you think might go well here. I like to serve this salad family style. Since there are so many ingredients, their proportion isn't that important and somehow plating doesn't seem right for "Garbage."

40 MINUTES

To hard-cook the eggs, place them in a medium saucepan with enough water to cover, salt the water generously, and bring it to a boil over high heat. Reduce the heat to low and simmer the eggs for about 5 minutes, until the yolks are bright yellow but slightly wet looking (see page 16 for additional egg information). While they're cooking, fill a large bowl with ice water. When the eggs are done, drain and immediately plunge them into the ice water to chill. (This prevents the eggs from cooking any further before they're peeled.) When the eggs are cool, peel and slice them thin with an egg slicer or cut them into quarters with a large knife.

Put the shredded chicken in a medium bowl, drizzle it with the balsamic vinegar, and toss to coat. Set the chicken aside to marinate while you prepare the other ingredients.

Put the tomatoes in a small bowl. Drizzle them with olive oil, season with kosher salt, and toss to coat.

4 large eggs

Kosher salt

1 1½-pound **roasted chicken,** meat shredded and skin and bones discarded (3–4 cups)

¼ cup aged **balsamic vinegar**

28 small, sweet **tomatoes** (scant ½ pint), cut in half, or 14 cherry tomatoes, quartered

High-quality **extra-virgin olive oil,** for drizzling on the tomatoes and adding to the balsamic marinade

To make the vinaigrette, pour the vinegar and lemon juice into a small bowl. Add the garlic and shallot. Stir in the olive oil, kosher salt, and freshly ground black pepper.

Put the greens in a very large, wide-mouthed salad bowl and season them with sea salt and freshly ground black pepper. Add the chicken, salami, provolone, and beans. Drizzle the vinaigrette, and gently toss to combine.

Arrange the egg slices on top of the salad and sprinkle them with sea salt. Spoon the tomatoes (along with any liquid remaining in the bowl) over the salad in clumps of 3 to 5 tomatoes. Scatter the olives over the salad. Use a sharp knife or a vegetable peeler to cut or shave 15 to 20 very thin slices from the wedge of Parmesan and scatter them over the salad.

FOR THE VINAIGRETTE

2 tablespoons aged **balsamic vinegar**

1 tablespoon fresh lemon juice

1 small garlic clove, grated or minced (about 1/2 teaspoon)

1 small shallot, grated or minced (about 1 teaspoon)

1/4 cup high-quality **extra-virgin olive oil**

1 teaspoon kosher salt

1/2 teaspoon freshly ground black pepper

12 cups loosely packed mixed baby greens

Sea salt and freshly ground black pepper

2 ounces thinly sliced Italian hard salami (about 10 slices), cut into 1/4-inch-wide strips

2 ounces thinly sliced provolone (about 4 slices), cut into 1/4-inch-wide strips

1 15-ounce can cannellini **beans,** garbanzo beans, or borlotti beans, rinsed and drained (about 1 1/2 cups)

28 small pitted **black olives**

Parmigiano-Reggiano wedge, for shaving

Fennel, Treviso, and Prosciutto Salad with Anchovy-Date Vinaigrette

Radicchio is an Italian chicory commonly found in the United States. There are two types: radicchio di Verona, which we know simply as radicchio, and radicchio di Treviso, which goes by the name treviso here. They both have the same crunchy texture and slightly bitter flavor. Treviso's leaves are elongated and pointed rather than round. If you can't find it, radicchio works fine in its place. A slice of prosciutto can vary greatly in size depending on what part of the ham it's cut from. If yours are very large, you may want to rip one slice in half and use it for two servings and snack on the rest. When you're looking for dates, look for a soft variety, such as medjool, and avoid those that are dry, hard, and crystallized.

20 MINUTES

To make the vinaigrette, stir the dates, anchovies, orange zest, lemon zest, and garlic together in a bowl large enough to toss the salad in. Stir in the olive oil and vinegar.

Remove and discard the outer leaves of the treviso. Carve out and discard the cores, separate the individual leaves, and add the leaves to the bowl with the vinaigrette.

Cut out and discard the core of the fennel. Halve the fennel and cut off the stem end so that just the bulb remains. Separate the layers of fennel, stack them on top of one another, press down to flatten, and slice them lengthwise into very thin strips (about 1/16 inch thick). Add the fennel to the bowl with the treviso and toss to coat them evenly with the vinaigrette.

Divide half of the treviso and fennel evenly among four plates. Lay a slice of prosciutto over the salads, rumpling it so that it doesn't completely cover the treviso. Grate a thin layer of Parmesan cheese to cover the prosciutto and pile the remaining leaves and fennel on the salads, reserving some of the tiniest leaves to top them. Rumple another slice of prosciutto over the salads and grate another thin layer of cheese over the prosciutto. Top each of the salads with the remaining small leaves and freshly ground black pepper.

FOR THE VINAIGRETTE

8 large soft dried dates, pitted, smashed with the flat side of a knife, and chopped (about 1/3 cup)

12 **anchovy fillets,** chopped (about 3 tablespoons)

Grated zest of 2 medium oranges (about 1 heaping tablespoon)

Grated zest of 2 large lemons (about 1 heaping tablespoon)

4 large garlic cloves, grated or minced (about 1 tablespoon)

1/2 cup high-quality **extra-virgin olive oil**

1 tablespoon plus 1 teaspoon red wine **vinegar**

4 heads treviso

1 large fennel bulb

8 thin slices **prosciutto** (about 4 ounces)

Parmigiano-Reggiano wedge, for grating

Freshly ground black pepper

Zucchini Crudo with Hearts of Palm and Pecorino Romano
Jonathan Waxman • Barbuto, New York City

My friend Jonathan Waxman wasn't very cooperative about getting a recipe to me, so I just stole one from him. He serves a version of this salad at his wonderful Greenwich Village restaurant, Barbuto, all year long, changing the vegetables with the seasons—asparagus in the spring, zucchini in the summer, and fennel in the winter. The hearts of palm (which was my addition) give the salad another dimension—but more important, because they come from a jar, they gave me an excuse to include this easy-to-make recipe here. Hearts of palm is one of the rare vegetables that most people are used to eating canned. Until recently, when it started popping up on menus of nicer restaurants in Hawaii and Florida, I'd never even seen fresh hearts of palm. If you're one of those people who have to eat vegetables with every meal, this is just the thing. It makes a great alternative to the Tri-Colore Salad for something to boost up a meal. —Nancy

20 MINUTES

Using a mandoline, slice the zucchini lengthwise into very thin slices (about 1/8 inch thick) and place them in a large bowl. Using a knife, slice the hearts of palm lengthwise into very thin slices and add them to the bowl with the zucchini. Drizzle the vegetables with the olive oil and sprinkle them with the pecorino, parsley, and a generous amount of sea salt. Toss to thoroughly coat the vegetables and season with more salt if necessary.

2 medium zucchini

1 14-ounce jar hearts of palm

1/3 cup high-quality **extra-virgin olive oil**

5 tablespoons grated Pecorino Romano (about 1 ounce)

2 tablespoons finely chopped fresh Italian parsley leaves

Sea salt

Tri-Colore Salad

I decided to include this recipe even though it's a side dish, while most of the other salads in this book are stand-alone meals. For a hearty eater, or people who just have to have a salad with their meal, it's just the thing to go with soups, pastas, frittatas, or crostini.

15 MINUTES

To make the vinaigrette, pour the lemon juice into a medium bowl, whisk in the olive oil, and stir in the kosher salt and freshly ground black pepper.

Tear the radicchio leaves off the core, discarding the core, and break them into 1-inch pieces into a large salad bowl. Tear the endive leaves off the core, discarding the core, and break them into 1-inch pieces into the bowl with the radicchio. Add the arugula, sprinkle with the sea salt and Parmesan, and drizzle three quarters of the vinaigrette over the salad. Toss gently and add more vinaigrette if desired.

Divide the salad evenly among four plates, drizzle them with a little olive oil, and sprinkle them with more Parmesan.

FOR THE VINAIGRETTE

1/4 cup fresh lemon juice

3/4 cup high-quality **extra-virgin olive oil,** plus extra for drizzling

1 teaspoon kosher salt

1/2 teaspoon freshly ground black pepper

1 head radicchio

1 head Belgian endive

4 cups loosely packed arugula leaves

Sea salt

1/2 cup fresh grated **Parmigiano-Reggiano,** plus more for sprinkling

Chicken Salad #1: Tarragon Chicken Salad with Avocado and Bacon over Arugula

I always keep a roasted chicken in the refrigerator at home. It's so handy to have around to make quick, last-minute meals. I'm lucky to live near a place in Los Angeles, Pollo alla Brasa, that roasts chicken over a wood fire. If you have such a place where you live, it's worth a special trip to go there for your chicken. You can really taste the wood and the fire flavors in the meat, and chicken cooked this way has a nice, firm texture. Because the amount of chicken you get from a whole chicken varies, I suggest you add the mayonnaise to the chicken gradually, using only as much as you think necessary.

35 MINUTES

Adjust the oven rack to the middle position and preheat the oven to 350°F.

Place the bacon on a baking sheet and cook it in the oven for 17 to 22 minutes, depending on the thickness of the slices, until it's done but stilly chewy, not crisp. Remove the bacon from the oven, transfer it to paper towels to drain, and allow it to cool slightly before tearing it into irregular pieces.

Combine the shredded chicken, chopped tarragon, and ³/₄ cup of the Garlic Mayonnaise in a large bowl and toss to coat the chicken with the mayonnaise. (Add more if necessary to coat the chicken thoroughly.)

Halve the avocado, remove and discard the pit, and peel off and discard the skin. Cut the avocado into uneven chunks about the same size as the bacon and season them with sea salt. Put the arugula, avocado, and bacon in a large bowl. Drizzle with the olive oil, season with sea salt and freshly ground black pepper, and toss gently.

Mound the arugula salad onto four plates, dividing it evenly. Mound the chicken salad on top of the arugula and sprinkle with the whole tarragon leaves.

8 strips thick-cut applewood-smoked **bacon**

1 1½-pound **roasted chicken,** meat shredded and skin and bones discarded (3–4 cups)

½ cup finely chopped fresh tarragon leaves, plus ¼ cup whole leaves (about 40)

1 cup Garlic Mayonnaise (recipe follows)

1 ripe Hass avocado

Sea salt

8 cups loosely packed arugula leaves

¼ cup **extra-virgin olive oil**

Freshly ground black pepper

Garlic Mayonnaise

In life, I believe everyone, *especially* those of us who are serious about food, is entitled to one food vice—something they love even though they have a hard time admitting it, whether it's Oreo cookies, Fritos corn chips, or Lipton onion dip made with onion soup mix. Mine, if I had to choose just one, is Best Foods mayonnaise (called Hellmann's on the East Coast). As many others as I tried and as much as I wanted to choose an organic brand for this book, I kept returning to my old favorite. The other mayos just didn't have that familiar, well-balanced flavor that says "mayonnaise" to me. This recipe uses Best Foods mayonnaise as a base to make a quick aïoli (garlic mayonnaise). It takes minutes to make and is a delicious way to finish so many dishes.

MAKES 1 CUP　　　　　　　　　　　　　　　　　　10 MINUTES

Stir the mayonnaise, olive oil, lemon juice, garlic, and kosher salt together in a small bowl and season with more lemon juice, garlic, or salt to taste.

1 cup **mayonnaise**

2 tablespoons **extra-virgin olive oil**

1 tablespoon plus 1 teaspoon fresh lemon juice, or more to taste

4 large garlic cloves, grated or minced (about 1 tablespoon), or more to taste

1/4 teaspoon kosher salt, or more to taste

Chicken Salad #2: Chicken Salad with Chipotle Mayonnaise, Avocado, and Watercress

This mayonnaise-bound chicken salad has chipotle added to give it a Mexican twist. I serve it over watercress because I like the peppery flavor of watercress with the chipotle. I like the live watercress sold at grocery stores in plastic boxes with the roots still attached. It doesn't have quite the same boldness of flavor as the watercress you find at farmers' markets, but when you're in a hurry, it's worth the small compromise in flavor for the time saved in not having to trim off tough stems. Because it's hydroponically grown (which means it's grown in water, not dirt), I don't feel it needs to be washed; you might feel differently. Because the amount of chicken you get from a whole chicken varies, I suggest you add the mayonnaise to the chicken gradually, using only as much as you think necessary.

25 MINUTES

Place the shredded chicken in a large bowl. Add ¾ cup of the mayonnaise and toss to coat. Add more mayonnaise if necessary to coat the chicken thoroughly.

Divide the watercress evenly among four plates and sprinkle with sea salt. Mound the chicken salad on top of the watercress. Halve the avocado, remove the pit, and cut each half crosswise into quarters. Remove and discard the peel and place one quarter on top of each mound of chicken. Drizzle lemon-infused oil and squeeze a few drops of lime juice over each avocado. Sprinkle with sea salt and freshly ground black pepper, and top each salad with a sprig of fresh cilantro.

1 1½-pound **roasted chicken,** meat shredded and skin and bones discarded (3–4 cups)

1 cup Chipotle Mayonnaise (recipe follows)

10 cups loosely packed live watercress or pepper cress, roots trimmed and discarded

Sea salt

1 ripe Hass avocado

Lemon-infused olive oil (or high-quality **extra-virgin olive oil** combined with a pinch of fresh grated lemon zest), for drizzling

Lime, for squeezing over the avocado

Freshly ground black pepper

4 long cilantro sprigs, for garnish

Chipotle Mayonnaise

Canned chipotle peppers have such a distinct, deep flavor, it's hard to believe they're actually jalapeño peppers that have been smoked. Added to mayonnaise, they make a wonderful condiment for many dishes, especially those with a hint of Mexican influence. To purée the chipotle peppers, dump the entire can, liquid and all, into a blender. If you can stand the heat, you can use more chipotles than I call for in the recipe.

MAKES 1 CUP   10 MINUTES

Stir the mayonnaise, cilantro, olive oil, lemon juice, garlic, chipotle peppers, and kosher salt together in a small bowl. Season with more lemon juice, chipotle peppers, garlic, or salt to taste.

1 cup **mayonnaise**

1/4 cup finely chopped fresh cilantro leaves

2 tablespoons **extra-virgin olive oil**

2 tablespoons fresh lemon juice, or more to taste

4 large garlic cloves, grated or minced (about 1 tablespoon), or more to taste

1 1/2 teaspoons puréed **chipotle peppers** in adobo, or more to taste

1 teaspoon kosher salt, or more to taste

Smoked Salmon Salad with Cucumbers, Yogurt, and Fresh Dill

When you're buying salmon for this recipe, the important thing is to get a whole fillet of smoked salmon, not the thinly sliced variety of salmon (like lox or Nova) you'd put on a bagel. I like to build this salad in concentric circles so you can see the different colors and textures of the different layers of ingredients.

25 MINUTES

Place the cucumber slices in a medium bowl. Add the yogurt, dill, lemon juice, and garlic and stir to thoroughly combine.

Take apart the layers of the onion, stack them on top of one another, and slice them lengthwise into very thin strips (about 1/16 inch thick). Place the strips in a colander, rinse them under cool water, drain, and pat them dry with paper towels. (This process helps take the bitterness out of raw onions so you're left with only the sweet, pure onion flavor.)

Break the salmon into large flakes into a medium bowl. Drizzle the salmon with the lemon juice and olive oil, season with kosher salt and freshly ground black pepper, and toss to combine.

Spoon the cucumber-yogurt mixture onto the center of four plates, dividing it evenly. Mound the onions in a little tangle on top of the cucumbers, leaving a border of cucumbers showing around the edges of the onions. Pile the salmon on top of the onions, leaving the onions showing around the edges of the salmon. Lay a whole dill sprig at the edge of each plate and use scissors to finely snip about 1 teaspoon of chives over each serving.

FOR THE CUCUMBERS

4 small cucumbers (Persian or Japanese, or 2 thin hothouse cucumbers; if a larger cucumber is your only option, cut it in half and scrape out the seeds), sliced diagonally 1/8 inch thick (about 2 cups)

1/2 cup strained whole-milk **Greek yogurt**

1/4 cup fresh dill sprigs, plus 4 long sprigs for garnish

2 teaspoons fresh lemon juice

1 large garlic clove, grated or minced (about 1 teaspoon)

1/2 small red onion (cut in half through the core)

16 ounces **smoked salmon fillet**

3 tablespoons fresh lemon juice

3 teaspoons **extra-virgin olive oil**

Kosher salt and freshly ground black pepper

20 fresh chives

Belgian Endive with Almonds, Apples, and Whole-Grain Mustard Dressing

White Belgian endive is the most common variety, but if you can find red endive, it's nice to use both to add some color to this simple, elegant salad.

35 MINUTES

Adjust the oven rack to the middle position and preheat the oven to 325°F. Spread the almonds on a baking sheet and place them in the oven for 15 to 20 minutes, shaking the pan occasionally for even toasting, until the nuts are lightly browned and fragrant. Remove the almonds from the oven, drizzle them with olive oil, sprinkle them with sea salt, and toss to coat. Set the almonds aside to cool slightly, and then coarsely chop them.

To make the dressing, stir the Garlic Mayonnaise, mustard, vinegar, and kosher salt to taste together in a small bowl until it's thoroughly mixed. Reserve 1/4 cup of the chopped almonds and stir the remainder into the dressing.

Pull the leaves of endive from the cores and place them in a large bowl, discarding the cores. Drizzle the endive with the dressing and toss, massaging the dressing into the leaves. Cut the apple into four segments around the core. Discard the core and thinly slice the apple segments. Combine the chives, tarragon, and parsley together in a small bowl.

To assemble the salad, build it in three layers, starting by placing the largest leaves of endive on each of four plates. Top with a layer of apple slices and continue layering the salad in this way until all the endive and apple slices are used. Scatter the mixed herbs and the remaining almonds over each salad and sprinkle with sea salt.

1½ cups whole almonds, with their skins on
Extra-virgin olive oil, for tossing with the almonds
Kosher salt

FOR THE DRESSING

½ cup Garlic Mayonnaise (page 33)
3 tablespoons whole-grain **mustard**
2 teaspoons red wine **vinegar**
Kosher salt

6–8 heads Belgian endive (depending on their size)
1 large, tart, crisp apple (such as Fuji or Granny Smith)
1 heaping tablespoon finely chopped fresh chives
1 heaping tablespoon finely chopped fresh tarragon leaves
1 heaping tablespoon finely chopped fresh Italian parsley leaves
Sea salt

Bellavitae's Piquillo Peppers with Tuna
Rolando Beramendi • Bellavitae, New York City

My grandmother in Italy originally made this recipe. She would start by roasting a huge batch of peppers on one day, either on the grill or in the oven. She would never peel them. Some she would marinate in olive oil, some were used for making pepperonata, and in the hot summer days when the peppers were in season, the day after she roasted them, she would stuff the peppers with tuna and serve them as an appetizer before a pasta lunch. We now serve these peppers at Bellavitae—to my customers' joy. They are delicious as an appetizer, and you can also put one between two pieces of crusty Italian bread to eat as a panino. Either way, you will want to enjoy them with a glass of youthful red wine, such as a Rosso di Montepulciano. In this recipe, we start with Piquillo peppers from a jar to make it easier for you and to fit the concept of Nancy's book, but if you would like to roast your own, you should: that's the only way my grandmother would have done it, and it's how we do it at Bellavitae. I prefer tuna packed in water to that packed in olive oil. I drain the tuna and then add a good olive oil to it.

•

I didn't feel I could turn in a manuscript for a book based on quality packaged ingredients without a recipe from Rolando. His restaurant in New York City, which is one of my favorites—I go every time I am there—is a relatively new venture for him. I have known Rolando for a long time as the owner of a company, Manacaretti, that imports some of the best Italian products available in this country, all from small, artisanal producers—many of which line the walls at La Brea Bakery (and also Bellavitae, of course). These products, such as Rustichella d'Abruzzo pastas and sauces, pestos, tapenades, capers, anchovies, and many different olive oils, were some of the inspirations for this book. In addition to serving amazing food in exactly the style I like—rustic and simple and often served at room temperature—one of the things I really love about Bellavitae is that they use different olive oils depending on what they're drizzling it on. I asked Rolando to recommend the specific olive oil he would use for these peppers. Obviously if you don't have it, any good olive oil will do, but I do urge you to taste different oils and keep a few on hand to use for seasoning in different places. —Nancy

15 MINUTES

Combine the tuna, olive oil, capers, parsley, lemon zest and juice, scallions, and kosher salt and freshly ground black pepper to taste in a medium bowl and stir to thoroughly combine. Add more olive oil if necessary: you want to have enough so that it is not all absorbed by the tuna but a ring of oil remains around the edges of the bowl.

Place three peppers in a clover pattern on each of four plates. Carefully unfold the peppers, turning the insides out to create a beautiful flower-like shape, and mound 1 cup of tuna in the center of each serving of peppers. Drizzle the tuna and peppers with olive oil, sprinkle them with sea salt, place a lemon wedge on each plate, and serve with crusty Italian bread.

4 4-ounce cans high-quality water-packed Italian **tuna,** drained well

½ cup Olio Verde **extra-virgin olive oil,** plus extra for drizzling

1 cup **capers**

¼ cup finely chopped fresh Italian parsley leaves, plus whole leaves for garnish

Grated zest and juice of 2 lemons

2 scallions, finely chopped (white and green parts)

Kosher salt and freshly ground black pepper

12 jarred roasted **Piquillo peppers**

Sea salt

4 lemon wedges

Crusty Italian bread

Italian Antipasto Salad with Bocconcini and Spicy Green Olive Tapenade

This is an upscale version of the sort of antipasto salad we all grew up eating at Italian-American restaurants. To keep the lettuce from wilting, I toss only half of the dressing with this shredded salad and spoon the remainder around it. Pepperoncini are pickled Italian peppers. I like Mezzetta, a Tuscan-style brand from Napa, California, which is sold at many supermarkets.

35 MINUTES

To make the vinaigrette, stir the lemon juice and vinegar together in a small bowl. Add the garlic and oregano. Stir in the olive oil, kosher salt, and freshly ground black pepper.

To make the tapenade, stir the green olive tapenade, pepperoncini, and olive oil together in a small bowl.

Toss the lettuce and salami together in a large bowl. Drizzle half of the vinaigrette over the salad and toss gently.

Pile the salad onto four plates, dividing it evenly. Arrange five bocconcini close together, like eggs in a bird's nest, in the middle of each pile of lettuce. Spoon the tapenade around the cheese, evenly dividing it. Stick a basil leaf upright between the bocconcini and scatter the olives over the cheese. Sprinkle each of the salads with a pinch of oregano and spoon the remaining vinaigrette around them.

FOR THE VINAIGRETTE

1 tablespoon plus 1 teaspoon fresh lemon juice

1 tablespoon plus 1 teaspoon red wine **vinegar**

4 large garlic cloves, grated or minced (about 1 tablespoon)

1 heaping tablespoon **dried oregano**

1/4 cup high-quality **extra-virgin olive oil**

1 teaspoon kosher salt

1/2 teaspoon freshly ground black pepper

FOR THE TAPENADE

2 tablespoons plus 2 teaspoons green **olive tapenade**

1/4 cup finely chopped pepperoncini

1/4 cup **extra-virgin olive oil**

4 cups very thinly sliced iceberg lettuce

1/2 pound thinly sliced Italian hard salami (about 40 slices), cut into 1/4-inch strips

20 bocconcini (see "**Mozzarella**")

4 large basil leaves

12 **green olives**

Pinch of **dried oregano**

Crispy Hearts of Romaine with Ham, Pickled Jalapeño Peppers, and Creamy Avocado Dressing

This salad is based on a sandwich of ham, pickled jalapeño peppers, mayonnaise, and avocado that Edgar Lopez, who worked at Campanile, used to make every day as his own lunch. Matt Molina, who was the chef de cuisine at Campanile at the time, liked it so much he often ate half of Edgar's—and eventually put the sandwich on the lunch menu. It's the perfect example of how, by taking advantage of a few really flavorful ingredients—the distinct flavor of pickled jalapeño peppers, ham, and a good lemon-infused olive oil—you can make a delicious dish with minimal effort. Since the salad is made with whole romaine leaves, eat it as I do, by picking them up with your hands. (You can buy whole romaine hearts, packaged, to make this especially easy to prepare.) Note that I specify the weight of the avocado used for the dressing. I did this because if the avocado you use is too small, the dressing may not emulsify.

25 MINUTES

To make the dressing, purée the cilantro, avocado, lemon juice, garlic, shallots, and kosher salt in a blender. With the blender still running, add the canola oil and olive oil in a thin, steady stream through the feed tube of the blender until all of the oil is incorporated.

Pull the romaine leaves off the cores and put them in a large bowl; discard the cores. Season the leaves with sea salt and freshly ground black pepper, drizzle them with 1 cup of the dressing, and massage the dressing into the leaves.

Halve the avocados and remove and discard the pits. Scoop the avocado out of the peel in spoonfuls onto a plate and discard the peels. Season the avocado with sea salt.

Divide the largest lettuce leaves evenly among four plates. Top the leaves with a few scoops of avocado, a few strips of jalapeño pepper, a few strips of ham, and a sprinkling of cilantro. Repeat, building two more layers in the same way, and drizzle the finished salads with the lemon-infused olive oil.

FOR THE DRESSING

1 cup loosely packed fresh cilantro leaves

1 large, ripe Hass avocado (about 7 ounces), cut in half, pit removed, and peeled

1/3 cup fresh lemon juice

4 small garlic cloves

2 small shallots

2 teaspoons kosher salt

1/2 cup canola oil (or other neutral-flavored oil)

2 tablespoons **extra-virgin olive oil**

2 heads hearts of romaine

Sea salt and freshly ground black pepper

2 ripe Hass avocados

8 **pickled jalapeño peppers,** halved, seeded, and julienned

7 ounces thinly sliced cured ham (such as Black Forest or other quality cured ham), torn into irregular strips

1/4 cup loosely packed fresh cilantro leaves (about 30 leaves)

Lemon-infused olive oil (or high-quality **extra-virgin olive oil** combined with a pinch of fresh grated lemon zest), for drizzling

Cumin Shrimp and Garbanzo Bean Salad with Roasted Carrots

Using precooked shrimp can be a great shortcut in many recipes as long as you get it from a reliable source. Sometimes you can find baby peeled carrots with a portion of the tops on in sealed plastic bags in the produce section of grocery stores, which is also a time-saver.

35 MINUTES

Adjust the oven rack to the middle position and preheat the oven to 500°F. Place the carrots on a sheet pan. Drizzle them with the olive oil, sprinkle them with kosher salt and freshly ground black pepper, and toss to coat. Roast the carrots until they are lightly browned and tender, shaking the pan occasionally for even cooking, about 15 minutes. Remove them from the oven and set aside to cool slightly.

To make the vinaigrette, pour the vinegar and lemon juice into a small bowl. Add the cumin and garlic. Stir in the olive oil, kosher salt, and freshly ground black pepper.

Combine the shrimp, garbanzo beans, and roasted carrots in a large bowl. Drizzle them with 1/4 cup of the vinaigrette, season with kosher salt and freshly ground black pepper; toss to coat, and set aside to marinate for about 5 minutes.

Divide half of the baby greens among four plates and season them with sea salt. Pile half of the shrimp–garbanzo bean mixture over the greens, drizzle half of the remaining vinaigrette over the salads, and spoon 2 teaspoons of the Garlic Mayonnaise over each. Repeat, piling the remaining greens in a second layer over each salad, then the rest of the shrimp mixture. Drizzle the salads with the remaining vinaigrette and top each with 2 more teaspoons Garlic Mayonnaise. Sprinkle the salads with a pinch of cumin and a pinch of sea salt and use scissors to snip about 1 teaspoon of chives over each.

12 baby carrots, trimmed with about 1 inch of the tops left on and cut in half lengthwise

2 tablespoons **extra-virgin olive oil**

Kosher salt and freshly ground black pepper

FOR THE VINAIGRETTE

1/4 cup red wine **vinegar**

2 teaspoons fresh lemon juice

2 tablespoons plus 2 teaspoons ground cumin

4 large garlic cloves, grated or minced (about 1 tablespoon)

3/4 cup **extra-virgin olive oil**

1 teaspoon kosher salt

1/2 teaspoon freshly ground black pepper

10 ounces cooked large shrimp (31–35 count), peeled and tails removed

1 15-ounce can garbanzo **beans** (about 1 1/2 cups), rinsed and drained

8 cups loosely packed mixed baby greens (or baby spinach)

Sea salt

1/4 cup plus 1 tablespoon Garlic Mayonnaise (page 33)

Ground cumin, for sprinkling

20 fresh chives

Bombay Bhel Poori
Crunchy Indian Snack with Fresh Tomatoes and Onion
Suvir Saran • Devi, New York City

On Chowpati Beach, the busiest beach in Bombay, hundreds of vendors walk around with their amazing array of foods, including this, Bhel Poori, the quintessential Bombay street food. It's a homemade snack that starts with a packaged snack mix of puffed rice, garbanzo beans, and noodles called bhel. In this version, the bhel is tossed with chopped onion and fresh tomato and seasoned with coriander and tamarind chutneys. (If I have a boiled potato in the refrigerator, I'll chop that up and throw it into the mix, too.) I have friends who call me from the street to tell me they're on their way to my house and could I please have some Bhel Poori ready for them when they arrive. You can buy the bhel mix (as well as the chutneys to make this) at Indian supermarkets and some specialty food stores. One of the delights of this "salad" is its contrast of crisp and soft textures, so it must be eaten immediately, before the bhel mix turns soggy. Add more of either chutney if you crave more heat and flavor. Serve it as a snack or side dish. And enjoy this little taste of Bombay.

•

This isn't exactly a salad—it's more a snack—but I put it here because it is unusual and delicious, and it didn't fit anywhere else in the book. And you can eat it while you're cooking other things. —Nancy

10 MINUTES

In a large bowl, combine the bhel mix, potatoes, onion, tomato, tamarind chutney, and mint chutney. Toss gently to combine and serve immediately.

10 cups bhel mix (from 2 8-ounce packages)

1 15-ounce can whole **potatoes,** chopped

1/2 small red onion, finely chopped

1 medium tomato, chopped

3 tablespoons store-bought tamarind chutney

2 1/2 tablespoons store-bought mint chutney, cilantro chutney, or **green masala paste**

SOUPS

We've all had times when only a bowl of soup will do: when you're tired or cold, when it's late and you're hungry but don't want anything too heavy, or when you just need a little TLC. Unfortunately, the one thing soups usually have in common is that they take a long time to make. But not these.

Soup is probably the one canned item that people turn to the most—with the least feeling of compromise. And with good reason: there are some good products out there in cans and boxes, and many grocery stores sell "homemade" soups in their deli cases. But simply warming up a can or box of soup and dumping it into a bowl does not make a satisfying meal. With this in mind, after finding a few soups I like, what I set out to do in this chapter was to find a way to elevate and personalize each. I found that with even this little bit of involvement, you feel like you're eating a homemade meal.

The concept of dressing up a premade product is perfect for soup because one of the things that makes soup special is that it's easy to transform from something to start a meal with into *the meal,* just by finishing it with some extra elements. With the exception of clam chowder, where the soup itself is doctored with bacon, corn, and fresh spinach, each of these soups is topped with something: Tuscan Bean Soup is enlivened with prosciutto, shaved Parmigiano-Reggiano, and fruity olive oil. Spicy Black Bean Soup has a cool shrimp ceviche–style salad on top. And warm, chewy farro and wilted spinach turn a creamy Butternut Squash Soup into a warm, comforting meal. Not only do these toppings provide different components in terms of texture, flavor, and color, they make the soups infinitely more satisfying than they would be without them.

If you eat a lot of soup, I think it's worth it to go out and buy large soup plates—shallow bowls with wide rims like those used at nice restaurants. Because they're so wide, they make it easy to float other ingredients on the soup—and I think easier to eat as well. No matter what kind of bowl you use, one thing to note when you're serving these is to serve no larger than two-cup portions. It's preferable to leave the remaining soup in the pot for second helpings than to overfill the bowls, because when the bowl is filled too high, it makes the soup difficult to eat, especially if it has something on top. As you go to bite in, the soup spills over the sides.

I tasted a lot of soups before I decided on some I like enough to include here. And I threw a lot away, like a funky-tasting potato soup, and a broccoli purée that tasted like chemicals. But I also found some really great-tasting soups. Progresso Lentil Soup was so good I couldn't think of anything to do with it besides swirl some good olive oil on top and dig in, so I didn't include it. (I do drain the soup and use the lentils in other dishes.)

In "Twist Essentials," I give you the brand for the soups I use in this chapter, all widely available. But in case you can't find them or you want to choose your own, the first thing you should do is look at the ingredients list. In all the soups I chose, the ingredients don't list anything I wouldn't put in the same soup if I were making it from scratch, things such as stabilizers, sweeteners, and MSG. Once you get the soup home, especially with those where all you do is warm them up (such as the purées), you'll want to taste it before using it in a recipe. You may have to throw away a box or can or two before you find a product you like, but that's a small price to pay for a future of warm, comforting, last-minute soup meals.

I like to serve soup with a big hunk of country bread to sop up what's left in the bowl, and also to make sure nobody will leave the table hungry. And if you're big on having fresh vegetables with every meal, serve these with a Tri-Colore Salad or Jonathan Waxman's Zucchini Crudo with Hearts of Palm and Pecorino Romano.

Creamy Corn Soup with Bacon and Cheddar Crostini

The tanginess of the sourdough crouton that tops this is the perfect contrast to the sweet corn soup. I use a bâtard—a long white loaf about three inches in diameter (much thicker than a baguette). When sliced, it makes a crostini that fits perfectly on a big bowl of soup. If you can't find a bâtard, a baguette will work fine, but because of the smaller size, you'll want to put two croutons, side by side, in each bowl.

30 MINUTES

Adjust the oven rack to the middle position and preheat the oven to 350°F.

Place the bread slices on a baking sheet, brush the tops with olive oil and bake them for 15 to 20 minutes, until they're lightly toasted and golden brown. (You can also toast the bread in a toaster, but *without* the oil. Then brush the toast with oil after they're done.)

While the bread is toasting, place the bacon on a separate baking sheet and cook in the oven until it's done but still chewy, not crisp, 17 to 22 minutes, depending on the thickness of the slices. Remove the bacon from the oven and transfer it to paper towels to drain. (Or if you want to avoid washing a second baking sheet, put the bread on half of the baking sheet, line the other half with foil, and put the bacon on it; cook the bread and bacon together. Remove the baking sheet from the oven when the bacon is done. Remove the foil and bacon from the baking sheet and return the baking sheet to the oven to finish toasting the bread.)

Rip each strip of bacon in half and place the two halves on a piece of toast, arranging them so the ends hang over the edges of the toast. (If you're using a baguette, rip the bacon into four pieces and proceed as above.) Cover the toast with an uneven layer of the Cheddar cheese, allowing the edges of the toast to show through. Repeat for the remaining crostini.

Place the crostini on a clean baking sheet and bake them for 3 to 5 minutes, until the cheese melts. Remove the crostini from the oven and use scissors to snip about 1 teaspoon of chives over each.

Meanwhile, heat the soup in a large saucepan over medium heat, stirring occasionally to keep it from scorching, until it comes to a low boil.

Divide the soup evenly among four large soup plates or bowls, filling them to just below the rim. Place the crostini on top of the soup and drizzle high-quality olive oil around the crostini.

---

4 ½-inch-thick slices from a bâtard (or 8 slices from a baguette or 2 slices from a large round rustic white loaf, cut in half)

Extra-virgin olive oil, for brushing the bread

4 strips thick-cut applewood-smoked **bacon**

2 ounces aged white Cheddar, grated (about ½ cup)

20 fresh chives

2 1-quart boxes puréed corn **soup**

High-quality **extra-virgin olive oil,** for drizzling

Chilled Corn Soup with Adobo Swirl
Barbara Fairchild • Editor in Chief, *Bon Appétit*

This recipe is from a column called "Fast, Easy, Fresh" that debuted in the October 2004 issue of *Bon Appétit*. The column was an instant success with readers, and it has become one of my favorites to cook from, too. I particularly like this recipe because the soup is so refreshing—and colorful—and it all comes together in less than thirty minutes. Originally it called for fresh corn, but for Nancy's book—and to make it a year-round dish—I call for frozen corn here. Adobo sauce is the spicy, smoky sauce that canned chipotle peppers are packed in.

•

Naturally, if you have bottled onions around from making my recipes, you could use those in place of the fresh onion here. I hope Barbara won't mind! This is intended to be a chilled soup but it's also delicious warm. —Nancy

15 MINUTES, PLUS CHILLING TIME

Heat 1 tablespoon of the olive oil in a large saucepan over medium-high heat. Add the onion and sauté until it's soft, about 4 minutes. Add the corn kernels, chicken broth, and 1 tablespoon of the lime juice and bring to a boil. Reduce the heat and simmer until the corn is just tender, about 3 minutes.

Working in batches, purée the soup in a blender or use an immersion blender to purée it in the pot until it's almost smooth. Stir in the remaining tablespoon of lime juice and 1 cup or more of water, until the soup is the consistency you desire. Season the soup with kosher salt and freshly ground black pepper. Transfer it to a large bowl and refrigerate it for at least 2 hours or up to overnight to chill.

Whisk the remaining 2 tablespoons of olive oil and the adobo sauce together in a small bowl.

Divide the soup evenly among four large soup plates or bowls, filling them to just below the rim. Drizzle with the adobo oil and sprinkle the cilantro leaves over the top.

3 tablespoons **extra-virgin olive oil**

1 cup chopped sweet onion (such as Vidalia, Maui, or Walla Walla)

3 cups frozen corn kernels

2 cups chicken **broth**

2 tablespoons fresh lime juice

Kosher salt and freshly ground black pepper

1 teaspoon adobo sauce (see "**Chipotle peppers**")

Fresh cilantro leaves

Butternut Squash Soup with Sautéed Farro and Pancetta, Wilted Spinach, and Pumpkin Seed Oil

Farro is an ancient Tuscan grain similar to barley or wheat berries. Like all grains, it takes a while to cook, so using cooked farro from a jar is a great shortcut. The jarred farro I found from Radici of Tuscany is as good as any just-cooked farro I've ever had—and it takes about 30 minutes off the cooking time of a dish. The pumpkin seed oil drizzled on the finished soup gives it another layer of flavor and complexity. Pumpkin seed oil is one of those little extravagances that you won't use often, but it's nice to have some around for special dishes like this. I store it in the refrigerator and always taste it to make sure it hasn't gone rancid before using it. Pancetta is unsmoked Italian bacon; for this recipe, ask your deli counter person to slice it into very thin rounds. If you can't find pancetta, use bacon instead and rip up the cooked pieces before adding them to the farro-spinach mixture.

20 MINUTES

Adjust the oven rack to the middle position and preheat the oven to 350°F.

Put the pancetta slices on a baking sheet and bake them for about 8 minutes, until they're curled up at the edges and done but still chewy, not browned or crispy. Remove them from the oven and transfer to paper towels to drain.

Heat the olive oil, garlic, and a pinch of kosher salt in a large skillet over medium-high heat and sauté for about 1½ minutes, until the garlic is soft and fragrant, stirring constantly to prevent the garlic from browning. Add the farro and cook, stirring often, for 2 to 3 minutes to warm it through. Add the spinach in handfuls and cook it with the farro for 2 to 3 minutes, until the spinach just wilts. Add the lemon juice and season with kosher salt.

Meanwhile, heat the soup in a large saucepan over medium heat, stirring occasionally to keep it from scorching, until it comes to a low boil.

Divide the soup evenly among four large soup plates or bowls, filling them to just below the rim. Place a pancetta slice in the center of each serving of soup and top with the farro and spinach mixture. Drizzle a small amount of pumpkin seed oil over each serving and add freshly ground black pepper.

4 thin slices **pancetta**

¼ cup **extra-virgin olive oil**

2 large garlic cloves, grated or minced (about 2 teaspoons)

Kosher salt

1 cup cooked farro

4 cups loosely packed baby spinach leaves

2 teaspoons fresh lemon juice

2 1-quart boxes puréed butternut squash **soup**

Pumpkin seed oil (or high-quality **extra-virgin olive oil**)

Freshly ground black pepper

Roasted Tomato and Red Pepper Soup
with Pesto Croutons

*I never slice the bread when I'm making croutons. In fact, there's some-
thing that really annoys me about perfectly square croutons—it's too
fussy and they look almost machine-made. I prefer to pull the loaf into
small pieces so the croutons are chunky and irregular. Not only are they
more beautiful this way, but the thin parts of the ripped edges get
browned and crispy, which makes for a crunchier crouton overall.
When making the croutons, use the center of the loaf.*

35 MINUTES

Adjust the oven rack to the middle position and preheat the oven to 350°F.

Rip the bread into twenty-four 1- to 1½-inch pieces, using only the inside of
the loaf; discard the crust.

Toss the bread chunks in a large bowl with 1 tablespoon of the olive oil.
Scatter them in an even layer on a baking sheet and toast them in the oven for
about 20 minutes, shaking the pan occasionally for even cooking, until they're
light golden on all sides. While the croutons are cooking, stir the pesto and
the remaining 3 tablespoons of olive oil together in a small bowl. Remove the
croutons from the oven and allow them to cool slightly. Drizzle them with the
pesto mixture and toss to coat.

Adjust the oven rack to the highest position and change the oven setting to
broil.

Toss the tomatoes in a medium bowl with the olive oil, sugar, and a generous sprinkling of kosher salt. Scatter them on a baking sheet and place them
under the broiler for 5 to 7 minutes, shaking the pan occasionally, until they're
charred and burst in places.

Meanwhile, heat the soup in a large saucepan over medium heat, stirring
occasionally to keep it from scorching, until it comes to a low boil.

Divide the soup evenly among four large soup plates or bowls, filling them
to just below the rim. Pile croutons in the center of each serving and spoon
the tomatoes and their juices around the croutons.

FOR THE CROUTONS

1 medium round loaf sourdough
bread cut in half

¼ cup **extra-virgin olive oil**

3 tablespoons **basil pesto**

32 small, sweet **tomatoes** (about
½ pint), cut in half, or 16 cherry
tomatoes, quartered

2 tablespoons **extra-virgin
olive oil**

Pinch of sugar

Kosher salt

2 1-quart boxes roasted tomato
and red pepper **soup**

Creamy Clam Chowder with Smoked Bacon and Wilted Spinach

After tasting a few canned clam chowders, I didn't think I was going to be able to include one in this book—they were all too bland. I was about to give up on the idea altogether and was getting ready to throw away a can of organic clam chowder I'd tasted cold when Matt Molina stopped me. He convinced me to let him turn it into something good. By adding smoked bacon and corn—and the basics, garlic and shallots, of course—he made the soup really come alive. Fresh spinach wilted into the soup at the end freshens it up even more. My preferred brands for canned clam chowder are Gordon's and Trader Joe's. If you can't find either of those, buy one that looks good to you and taste the soup before using it. To get an accurate idea of what it will taste like, though, you'll want to warm it up first.

25 MINUTES

Cook the bacon in a large saucepan or soup pot over medium heat for 8 to 10 minutes, stirring often, until it's done but still chewy, not browned or crispy. Pour off all but 1 tablespoon of the fat. Remove enough bacon to garnish each serving with a few pieces.

Add the garlic and shallot to the saucepan with the bacon and cook over medium heat until they soften, about 1½ minutes, stirring constantly so the garlic doesn't brown. Add the clam chowder, milk, corn, tarragon, and Old Bay Seasoning and bring to a boil over high heat, stirring occasionally to keep the soup from scorching. Add the spinach in handfuls, reduce the heat, and simmer until the spinach wilts, about 5 minutes.

Divide the soup evenly among four large soup plates or bowls, filling them to just below the rim. Squeeze a few drops of fresh lemon juice and use scissors to snip about 1 tablespoon of chives directly over each serving. Top with freshly ground black pepper and the reserved bacon and serve with oyster crackers on the side.

16 strips thick-cut applewood-smoked **bacon,** cut diagonally into ¼-inch pieces

3 large garlic cloves, grated or minced (about 1 tablespoon)

1 large shallot, grated or minced (about 1 tablespoon)

3 15-ounce cans clam chowder

6 cups whole milk

3 cups frozen corn kernels

3 tablespoons chopped fresh tarragon leaves

1–1½ teaspoons **Old Bay Seasoning**

12 cups loosely packed baby spinach leaves

Fresh lemon juice to taste

40 fresh chives

Freshly ground black pepper

Oyster crackers

Tuscan Bean Soup with Prosciutto and Grated Parmigiano-Reggiano

This is a take on pasta e fagiole, the classic Tuscan bean and pasta soup, but without the pasta. Where the homemade version is thickened as a result of the beans being cooked for hours, I created a rich, creamy base by puréeing some of the beans. I felt the soup needed a fresh vegetable, so I used Napa cabbage because it cooks very quickly and adds a slightly sweet flavor. Finally, I added fresh herbs and then topped the soup with prosciutto, olive oil, and Parmigiano-Reggiano.

25 MINUTES

Combine the beans and their liquid with the garlic, salt, thyme, basil, and 2 cups of water in a large saucepan and bring to a boil over high heat. Reduce the heat to low and simmer for 5 minutes to meld the flavors. Remove about 1½ cups of the beans, returning any garlic or basil to the saucepan. Use an immersion blender to purée the remaining beans in the pot until smooth. (Alternatively, let the soup cool slightly then transfer it to a blender or food processor and purée, holding the lid down tight so the hot liquid doesn't splatter out.) Stir in the reserved beans and cabbage and thin the soup with water if necessary. Cook the soup over medium heat until the cabbage wilts and is slightly tender, about 5 minutes.

Divide the soup evenly among four large soup plates or bowls, filling them to just below the rim. Drizzle each serving with high-quality olive oil and grate a thin layer of Parmesan cheese over them. Tear one slice of the prosciutto into a few pieces and rumple the pieces onto one bowl of soup; repeat with the remaining prosciutto slices.

4 15-ounce cans creamy **beans** (such as giant white beans, borlotti beans, or cannellini beans), not drained (about 6 cups)

6 large garlic cloves, grated or minced (about 2 tablespoons)

3 teaspoons kosher salt

2 teaspoons fresh thyme leaves

4 large fresh basil leaves

2 cups shredded Napa cabbage (about ¼ head)

High-quality **extra-virgin olive oil**, for drizzling

Parmigiano-Reggiano wedge, for grating

4 thin slices **prosciutto** (about 2 ounces)

Mexican Chicken and Garbanzo Bean Soup with Avocado and Crispy Tortilla Chips

This is a soup that my coauthor, Carolynn, added to the book. It's based on a typical Mexican soup called Tlalpeño soup. This version uses shortcuts such as starting with a cooked chicken and boxed chicken broth, so making it doesn't take half the day, as it does when it's made from scratch. It's topped with ripe avocado and crispy tortilla chips, which get chewy from sitting in the smoky, chipotle-infused broth. I like the rustic look of avocado that is spooned out of the peel rather than sliced or diced.

40 MINUTES

Heat the chicken broth and oregano in a large soup pot over high heat until the broth just begins to boil, about 5 minutes.

Halve the cabbage through the core, and carve out and discard the core. Place the cabbage flat side down and slice it thinly lengthwise.

Add the cabbage and garbanzo beans to the soup and return the soup to a low boil. Stir in the chicken, puréed chipotle, and chopped chipotle pepper, and cook the soup for about 7 minutes, until the cabbage wilts and is slightly tender. Turn off the heat, stir in the juice of one lime, and season with kosher salt and freshly ground black pepper.

Divide the soup evenly among four large soup plates or bowls, filling them to just below the rim. Halve the avocado, remove and discard the pit, and season it with sea salt. Scoop the avocado in spoonfuls onto the soup, scatter a small handful of tortilla chips over each bowl, and serve each with a wedge of lime.

2 1-quart boxes chicken **broth**

½ teaspoon **dried oregano**

1 head green cabbage

1 15-ounce can garbanzo **beans,** rinsed and drained

1 1½-pound **roasted chicken,** meat shredded and skin and bones discarded (3–4 cups)

1 tablespoon puréed **chipotle peppers** in adobo

1 whole **chipotle pepper** in adobo, finely chopped

2 limes (1 for squeezing into the soup, 1 quartered)

Kosher salt and freshly ground black pepper

1 ripe Hass avocado

Sea salt

Corn tortilla chips

Spicy Black Bean Soup Topped with Shrimp and Avocado Ceviche

This simple black bean soup is finished with a little shrimp salad on the top. I call the salad "ceviche" because it's dressed with lime, although since the shrimp are cooked, it isn't technically ceviche. I started the soup with canned black beans and mixed in Mark Miller's Green Chile Salsa, which gives it great flavor without any effort. The salsa contains the same ingredients that you usually sauté to start a soup—onion, garlic, chiles—so it's the perfect way to doctor up the beans. Mexican crema, which I call for to top this soup, has a tangier, more complex flavor than American sour cream and it also has a looser consistency, which makes it nice for drizzling; if you can't find it, sour cream will work just fine.

30 MINUTES

To prepare the ceviche, slice the shrimp in half and place them in a medium bowl. Add the cilantro, lime zest and juice, scallions, kosher salt, and freshly ground black pepper and stir to thoroughly combine. Cut the avocado in half, remove the pit and peel, and dice. Add the avocado to the shrimp salad and toss it gently to combine.

Heat the oil in a large soup pot over medium-high heat with the onions and a pinch of kosher salt and cook for about 4 minutes, stirring occasionally, until the onions are golden brown. Add the garlic and sauté for about 1 1/2 minutes, until the garlic is soft and fragrant, stirring constantly so the garlic doesn't brown. Pour the beans and their liquid into the pan and bring them to a boil over high heat. Reduce the heat and simmer for 5 minutes to meld the flavors. Stir in the salsa, remove the soup from the heat and season with kosher salt and freshly ground black pepper. Use an immersion blender to purée the soup in the pot until it's smooth. (Alternatively, let the soup cool slightly then transfer it to a blender or food processor and purée, holding the lid down tight so the hot liquid doesn't splatter out.)

Divide the soup evenly among four large soup plates or bowls, filling them to just below the rim. Drizzle 1 tablespoon of crema over each serving and spoon the shrimp and avocado salad on top of the crema.

FOR THE CEVICHE

4 ounces cooked and peeled jumbo shrimp (21–25 count), tails removed

1/4 cup chopped fresh cilantro leaves

Grated zest and juice of 1 lime

2 scallions (white parts only), very thinly sliced diagonally

1/2 teaspoon kosher salt

1/4 teaspoon freshly ground black pepper

1 ripe Hass avocado

3 tablespoons **extra-virgin olive oil**

16 small jarred **onions,** coarsely chopped (about 4 ounces or 1 cup)

Kosher salt

4 large garlic cloves, grated or minced (about 1 tablespoon)

4 15-ounce cans black **beans,** not drained (about 6 cups)

1 cup **green chile salsa**

Freshly ground black pepper

1/4 cup **Mexican crema** (or sour cream)

PASTA AND POLENTA

Regardless of the fact that in Italy pasta is traditionally eaten as a first course, here in America pasta is clearly, and always has been, a one-dish meal. When I was cooking for three kids and routinely arrived home exactly at dinnertime, pasta was the thing, in addition to salads, that I relied on most for last-minute meals. It's filling, it's satisfying, and I could always keep boxes and bags of it in the cupboard.

All of the recipes in this chapter are designed so that bringing the water to a boil is the only thing that takes any time. If you're really in a rush, put the water on to boil before you set down your purse (or briefcase), and prepare the rest of the ingredients while the water is coming to a boil and the pasta is cooking.

When I was developing these recipes, I found that they tended to seem less "clever" than some of those in other chapters. I realized that this is because pasta naturally lends itself to this fast, simple style of cooking. Not only does the main ingredient come from a box, but the ingredients commonly used to dress pasta—tomato sauce, canned tomatoes, canned chickpeas, jarred olive tapenade, sun-dried tomatoes, chile flakes, anchovies—are prepared items that you're accustomed to using and that, unless you're a total purist, you're likely to have on hand even without the influence of this book.

Still, I did try to reach beyond those basics for other shortcuts. In so doing, I discovered frozen peas (very tender and tasty); I used saltine crackers to save the step of toasting bread to make breadcrumbs; and I took advantage of the two mushrooms that I like dried, porcini and morels. I was also conscious of choosing pasta shapes that cook in a relatively short amount of time and avoided shapes such as gemelli and fusilli that take a long time to cook.

All of the recipes call for two ounces of dried pasta per person. This may seem like a small portion, but it's actually a typical portion size for pasta when it is not being followed by a meat course in Italy. But that's not why I made my portions this size. I prefer a smallish portion of pasta because I find it very filling. Also, once pasta gets cold on the plate, it really doesn't taste very good—and I don't like leftover pasta. With a Tri-Colore Salad, I think this size makes a nice meal for even a hearty eater. But if you're still not convinced (or if you're one of those people who like cold pasta the next morning for breakfast), any of these recipes can be doubled.

As you'll see in these recipes, I give fairly detailed instructions for cooking the pasta. First, I recommend that the water be salted generously, which means about 2 tablespoons of salt per quart of water, or enough so the water tastes like seawater. You want the salt to penetrate the pasta while it's cooking rather than salting the pasta after it's cooked.

I also recommend that you don't cook any pasta past the al dente stage. Al dente means "to the tooth" in Italian, or "toothsome." You want the pasta to be firm enough that you can feel your teeth biting into it but not too firm or chewy. If it's at all hard or chalky, it's underdone.

The instruction that might not seem so obvious is how to drain the pasta. You don't want to drain it for a long time, and you never want to let it sit in the colander after it's drained; it will become sticky. At home, I have one of those handy pasta cookers with a deep colander inset over the pot, so I can just lift the pasta straight out of the water and immediately dump it wherever I want it. This makes the job much easier and ensures that some of the water from the pasta makes it into the dish. Even if I'm using tongs or draining the pasta in a colander, I make sure to keep the pasta a little wet when I transfer it to the sauce, and I often reserve a cupful of the water the pasta was cooked in to add to the dressed pasta (before it's plated) if it's dry.

When serving pasta, I like to pile and twist long strands of pasta, such as spaghetti and linguine, so it stands up in a high mound. I also like to be able to see the ingredients that are tossed with the pasta. By nipping, tucking, and pulling some of the ingredients out of the mound of pasta, you can see all the different colors and textures and the pasta looks a lot more appetizing.

If, like me, you rely on pasta for throwing together last-minute meals, stocking up for this chapter is a good idea. Pasta really is bomb-shelter food. If you've done your shopping correctly, you might have all the ingredients in the pantry necessary to pull together an entire meal. In addition to the jarred items I mentioned, such as tapenade, pasta sauce, and sun-dried tomatoes, remember that pancetta and bacon will keep a long time in the refrigerator. Throw some sausages and peas in the freezer. And have a bottle of high-quality olive oil on hand for drizzling and a wedge Parmigiano-Reggiano for shaving and grating.

You'll also want to keep a few different shapes of pasta on hand. My favorite brands, both made by artisanal pasta makers in Italy, are Rustichella d'Abruzzo and Latini. The shapes they make, such as trofie and trennette, are really unusual, and the hand-made quality of the pastas adds another dimension to the finished dish.

For the polenta recipes in this chapter (and polenta served as a component in other dishes), I used instant polenta. I'm sure that no self-respecting Italian home cook, or chef in any upscale restaurant, would consider using instant polenta over the traditional kind, which takes as much as an hour to cook and must be stirred constantly at the beginning. They claim that quick-cooking polenta doesn't have the same toothsome texture. For a quick meal, the small difference in texture is worth it to me for the time saved.

Egg Papardelle with Bagna Cauda, Wilted Radicchio, and an Olive Oil–Fried Egg

Bagna cauda, which means "warm bath" in Italian, is a really delicious warm sauce of melted butter, olive oil, garlic, anchovies, and lemon. It's not traditionally served with pasta but the flavors are such an obvious match that it seemed natural to use it in this recipe. I started out thinking I would use a jarred bagna cauda, but after tasting many of them, I found only one (from Ritrivo) that's an okay substitute for the real thing. Since bagna cauda is so easy to make, I decided to give the recipe for it here in case you decide not to use the jarred variety.

30 MINUTES

Bring a large pot of water to a boil over high heat and add a generous amount of kosher salt. Stir in the papardelle, return the water to a boil, and cook the pasta, stirring occasionally to prevent the strands from sticking together, until it's al dente. (Since cooking times vary depending on the thickness of the pasta, refer to the package instructions for the recommended time and taste the pasta for doneness frequently while it cooks.)

While the water is coming to a boil and the pasta is cooking, if you're using jarred bagna cauda, heat it in a large skillet over medium-low heat, stirring occasionally, until it's warmed through.

If you're making the bagna cauda, heat the butter, olive oil, anchovies, and garlic in a large skillet over medium-high heat until the anchovies dissolve and the garlic is soft and fragrant, about 2 minutes, breaking up the anchovies while they cook and stirring constantly so the garlic doesn't brown. Reduce the heat to low and cook the sauce for another 2 minutes to meld the flavors. Turn off the heat, stir in the parsley and lemon zest and juice, and season with kosher salt and freshly ground black pepper.

Heat the olive oil in a large nonstick skillet over high heat for 2 to 3 minutes, until the oil's almost smoking (you will begin to smell the oil at that point). Break one egg into a small bowl and then pour the egg into the skillet. Let it just begin to set around the edges, then break the second egg into the bowl and pour it into the skillet. (By waiting a moment before adding the second egg, the eggs won't set together and will be easy to separate and serve individually.) Cook them for about 1½ minutes, until the edges are golden and crispy and the whites are set but the yolks are still runny. Remove the eggs to a plate and cook the remaining two eggs in the same way.

Use tongs to lift the pasta out of the water and transfer it quickly, while it's still dripping with water, to the skillet with the bagna cauda. Place the skillet

Kosher salt

8 ounces egg papardelle

¾ cup **bagna cauda** (or homemade bagna cauda, recipe follows)

FOR THE BAGNA CAUDA

1 stick (½ cup) unsalted butter

¼ cup **extra-virgin olive oil**

20 **anchovy fillets**, finely chopped (about ¼ cup or 1 2.8-ounce jar)

8 large garlic cloves, grated or minced (about 2 tablespoons)

¼ cup finely chopped fresh Italian parsley leaves

Grated zest and juice of ½ lemon

Kosher salt and freshly ground black pepper

¼ cup **extra-virgin olive oil**

4 large eggs

12 radicchio leaves, torn into large pieces

Parmigiano-Reggiano wedge, for grating

Sea salt

1 heaping tablespoon finely chopped fresh Italian parsley leaves

Freshly ground black pepper

over high heat and add the radicchio. Toss to combine the ingredients and cook for a minute or two, until the radicchio wilts.

Use tongs to lift the pasta out of the skillet and pile it onto four plates, dividing it evenly and twisting it into high mounds. Grate a generous layer of Parmesan cheese over each serving. Sprinkle the eggs with sea salt and place one egg on each serving of pasta. Scatter the parsley over the top and finish each serving with another light grating of Parmesan cheese and freshly ground black pepper.

Sicilian-Style Trennette with Eggplant, Olives, and Ricotta Salata

This pasta is based on Sicily's most famous pasta, pasta alla Norma, which is spaghetti with tomato sauce, eggplant, and ricotta salata. In Sicily, they say that the pasta looks like Mount Etna: the high mound of spaghetti is the mountain, the fried eggplant cubes in the tomato sauce are the lava rocks, and the ricotta salata grated over the top is the snow that caps the mountain almost year-round. Ricotta salata literally translates to "salted ricotta." The cheese is conserved in salt, then aged until it is hard. Its firm texture and pungent, salty flavor make it ideal for grating over pasta. I use whole canned cherry tomatoes in this recipe instead of tomato sauce because I like their look and texture. In Sicily, they wouldn't think of making this dish with any pasta except spaghetti, but I use trennette, a short hollow pasta shape—like penne, only with flat sides—because I think it's easier to eat with the tomatoes and eggplant. If you can't find trennette, penne or pennette ("little penne") will work fine. And if you're a purist, use spaghetti.

30 MINUTES

Bring a large pot of water to a boil over high heat and add a generous amount of kosher salt. Stir in the trennette, return the water to a boil, and cook the pasta, stirring occasionally to prevent it from sticking together, until it's al dente. (Since cooking times vary, refer to the package instructions for the recommended time and taste the pasta for doneness frequently while it cooks.)

While the water is coming to a boil and the pasta is cooking, heat the olive oil, garlic, and a pinch of kosher salt in a medium skillet over medium-high heat until the garlic is soft and fragrant, about 1½ minutes, stirring constantly so the garlic doesn't brown. Turn the heat up to high, add the tomatoes and eggplant and smash the eggplant with a wooden spoon. Cook them just until the ingredients are warmed through, about 3 minutes. Turn off the heat and season with kosher salt and freshly ground black pepper, keeping in mind the olives and ricotta salata will add salt to the dish.

Drain the pasta and transfer it quickly, while it's still dripping with water, to the skillet with the tomatoes and eggplant. Place the skillet over high heat and toss the pasta with the sauce for a minute or two, until the pasta is coated and the sauce is warm.

Spoon the pasta out of the skillet and pile it into high mounds on four plates, dividing it evenly. Sprinkle it with the olives and oregano and using a microplane, grate a generous amount of ricotta salata over each serving.

Kosher salt

8 ounces trennette or pennette

3 tablespoons **extra-virgin olive oil**

4 large garlic cloves, grated or minced (about 1 tablespoon)

1 14-ounce can cherry **San Marzano tomatoes,** drained (about 1½ cups)

7 ounces drained **roasted eggplant** or fried eggplant, cut into 1-inch pieces if large (about 1 cup)

Freshly ground black pepper

28 small pitted **black olives**

1 heaping tablespoon chopped fresh oregano leaves

Wedge of ricotta salata, for grating

Spaghetti with Sardines, Golden Raisins, Fennel, and Crunchy Breadcrumbs

Combining fennel pollen with fresh fennel fronds (the feathery green bits at the end of the stalks) is my way of trying to imitate the inimitable flavor of wild fennel—an essential component of this dish—that's not available in the United States unless you live in Los Angeles, where you can find wild fennel growing alongside our famous freeways. This dish is another classic of Sicily, equally as famous there as pasta alla Norma but not adopted in America as readily. I make it using canned sardines, the thought of which would probably make a Sicilian cringe, but sardines are one of the few canned fish I like. Besides, fresh sardines are nearly impossible to find here. The bread for the breadcrumbs is roughly chopped, not ground into fine crumbs; the texture is important to the dish, so making the breadcrumbs from scratch is essential.

30 MINUTES

Bring a large pot of water to a boil over high heat and add a generous amount of kosher salt. Stir in the spaghetti, return the water to a boil, and cook the pasta, stirring occasionally to prevent the strands from sticking together, until it's al dente. (Since cooking times vary, refer to the package instructions for the recommended time and taste the pasta for doneness frequently while it cooks.)

While the water is coming to a boil and the pasta is cooking, make the breadcrumbs. Stir the chopped toast in a small bowl with the fennel fronds, olive oil, and sea salt.

Mix the verjus and raisins together in a small saucepan and cook them over medium-low heat for about 3 minutes to hydrate and plump the raisins. Turn off the heat and let the raisins sit in the verjus until you're ready to use them.

Drain the sardines of their oil and remove their backbones and tails.

Heat 2 tablespoons of the olive oil with the onions and a pinch of kosher salt in a large skillet over medium-high heat and cook, stirring occasionally, until the onions are golden brown, about 4 minutes. Add the garlic and cook for another 1½ minutes, until the garlic is soft and fragrant, stirring constantly so it doesn't brown. Turn off the heat and stir in the sardines, fennel pollen, chile flakes, and the raisins and verjus; season with kosher salt.

Kosher salt
8 ounces spaghetti

FOR THE CRUNCHY BREADCRUMBS
1–2 thick slices sourdough bread, well toasted and coarsely chopped (about ¾ cup)
¼ cup chopped fennel fronds (from the fronds of 1 bulb)
2 teaspoons **extra-virgin olive oil**
1 teaspoon sea salt

¾ cup **verjus**
½ cup golden raisins
2 3½-ounce cans **sardines** (about 20 sardines)
¼ cup plus 2 tablespoons **extra-virgin olive oil**
12 small jarred **onions,** quartered (about 3 ounces or ¾ cup)
4 large garlic cloves, grated or minced (about 1 tablespoon)
1 heaping tablespoon **fennel pollen**
Pinch of chile flakes
¼ cup chopped fennel fronds (from the fronds of 1 bulb)

Use tongs to lift the pasta out of the water and transfer it quickly, while it's still dripping with water, to the skillet with the sardines. Add the fennel fronds and the remaining ¼ cup olive oil and toss to coat.

Use tongs to lift the pasta out of the skillet and pile it onto four plates, dividing it evenly and twisting it into high mounds. Spoon the sauce left in the pan over each serving and top with the breadcrumbs.

Bucatini with Olives, Sun-Dried Tomatoes, and Basil
Mario Batali • Babbo, New York City

Bucatini is a long, hollow pasta, like very thick spaghetti with a hole running through it. Because it is so hearty, its sauce needs rich ingredients to stand up to it. The basil, sun-dried tomatoes, and black olive tapenade form a flavor-packed, thick sauce that begs to coat the thick, toothsome strands of bucatini. With only five ingredients in this entire recipe, you won't be surprised at how effortless and speedy it is. Cooking the pasta is the only thing that takes any time.

40 MINUTES

Bring a large pot of water to a boil over high heat and add a generous amount of kosher salt. Stir in the bucatini, return the water to a boil, and cook the pasta, stirring occasionally to prevent the strands from sticking together, until it's al dente. (Since cooking times vary, for perfectly cooked pasta, refer to the package instructions for the recommended time and taste the pasta frequently while it cooks.)

Put the tapenade in a large skillet.

Drain the pasta and quickly add it, still dripping with water, to the skillet with the tapenade. Place the skillet over medium heat and cook the pasta, gently stirring to coat the pasta with the tapenade, until it's warmed through, about 1 minute. Turn off the heat, add the basil, parsley, and sun-dried tomatoes and toss to combine.

Use tongs to lift the pasta out of the skillet and pile it onto four plates, dividing it evenly and twisting it into high mounds. Finish each serving with a drizzle of olive oil, a pinch of sea salt, freshly ground black pepper, and Parmesan cheese shavings.

Kosher salt

12 ounces bucatini

3/4 cup black **olive tapenade**

3 cups basil leaves (from about 1 large bunch)

1/2 cup roughly chopped fresh Italian parsley leaves

24 oil-packed **sun-dried tomatoes,** drained and torn into bite-size pieces (heaping 1/2 cup)

High-quality **extra-virgin olive oil,** for drizzling

Sea salt

Freshly ground black pepper

Parmigiano-Reggiano wedge, for shaving

Trofie with Pesto, Pine Nuts, and Sun-Dried Tomatoes

When I first started working on this book, I had a hard time finding a pesto that I liked. I thought, if I can't stand behind store-bought pesto—or black olive tapenade—then I'm in trouble, because pesto and black olive tapenade are two condiments that are commonly called for pre-made and that many people are accustomed to using. So I was relieved when I finally found a pesto I liked. The pasta I use here, trofie, is a small, delicate pasta shaped like tight little hand-twisted ropes. There are a few small Italian producers that make it. If you can't find it and don't want to take the trouble to mail order it, ditalini or pennette or another small, fairly delicate pasta would be the best substitute.

30 MINUTES

Adjust the oven rack to the middle position and preheat the oven to 325°F.

Bring a large pot of water to a boil over high heat and add a generous amount of kosher salt. Stir in the trofie, return the water to a boil, and cook the pasta, stirring occasionally to prevent it from sticking together, until it's al dente. (Since cooking times vary, refer to the package instructions for the recommended time and taste the pasta for doneness frequently while it cooks.)

Spread the pine nuts on a baking sheet and toast them in the oven for 8 to 10 minutes, shaking the pan occasionally for even toasting, until the nuts are lightly browned and fragrant. Remove the nuts from the oven and set them aside to cool slightly.

While the water is coming to a boil and the pasta is cooking, stir the olive oil and pesto together in a bowl big enough to toss the pasta in, season it with kosher salt, and set the bowl aside.

Put the breadcrumbs or saltine crumbs in a small bowl and stir in a few drops of olive oil to just moisten them.

Reserve 1/2 cup of the pasta water, drain the pasta, and transfer it quickly, while it's still dripping with water, to the bowl with the pesto. Toss the pasta with the pesto, adding the reserved pasta water gradually, just until the pesto coats the pasta easily and is not sticky. Add the sun-dried tomatoes, pine nuts, and basil, and toss to combine.

Spoon the pasta out of the bowl and pile it into high mounds on four plates, dividing it evenly. Spoon any sauce or other ingredients left in the bowl over each serving, sprinkle with the breadcrumbs, and grate Parmesan cheese over each serving.

Kosher salt

8 ounces trofie

1/2 cup pine nuts

1/4 cup **extra-virgin olive oil,** plus extra for the breadcrumbs

1/4 cup plus 1 tablespoon **basil pesto**

1/4 cup **breadcrumbs** or 4 **saltine crackers** ground to fine crumbs

8 oil-packed **sun-dried tomatoes,** drained and torn into bite-size pieces (about 1/4 cup)

12 fresh basil leaves

Parmigiano-Reggiano wedge, for grating

Egg Papardelle with Asparagus, Dried Morel Mushrooms, and Fresh Goat Cheese

Dried morels are one of only two kinds of dried mushrooms that I like (the other being porcini), which is why I wanted to use them in this book. Their earthy flavor is the perfect counterpoint to the tangy goat cheese in this dish. The cheese doesn't really melt, but it makes for a thick, creamy sauce.

30 MINUTES

Place the mushrooms in a medium bowl and add enough hot water to cover them. Cover the bowl tightly with plastic wrap and set the mushrooms aside for 10 minutes to soften them. Drain, reserving 1 cup of the water the mushrooms were soaked in. Halve or quarter the mushrooms into small pieces.

Bring a large pot of water to a boil over high heat and add a generous amount of kosher salt. Stir in the papardelle, return the water to a boil, and cook the pasta, stirring occasionally to prevent the strands from sticking together, until it's al dente. (Since cooking times vary, refer to the package instructions for the recommended time and taste the pasta for doneness frequently while it cooks.)

While the water is coming to a boil and the pasta is cooking, remove the tough ends of the asparagus by snapping the stems off one at a time at the natural break. Starting at the tip end, cut the spears diagonally into 1-inch pieces.

Heat the olive oil, garlic, shallots, and a pinch of kosher salt in a large skillet over medium-high heat and cook, stirring constantly to prevent the garlic from browning, until the shallots are soft and the garlic is soft and fragrant, about 1½ minutes. Turn the heat up to high, add the asparagus and another pinch of kosher salt, and cook it for about 2 minutes, until it's just done but still crunchy. Add the morels and the reserved water and simmer until the liquid is reduced by one third.

Use tongs to lift the pasta out of the water and transfer it quickly, while it's still dripping with water, to the skillet with the asparagus and mushrooms. Place the skillet over high heat and stir gently to coat the pasta with the sauce. Crumble the goat cheese over the pasta and fold it in until the cheese is warm and creamy, about 2 minutes.

Use tongs to lift the pasta out of the skillet and pile it onto four plates, dividing it evenly and twisting it into high mounds. Spoon the sauce and vegetables left in the skillet over each serving.

1 ounce dried morel mushrooms (about 1 cup)

Kosher salt

8 ounces egg papardelle

1 pound asparagus spears (preferably pencil asparagus)

3 tablespoons **extra-virgin olive oil**

4 large garlic cloves, grated or minced (about 1 tablespoon)

2 medium shallots, grated or minced (about 1 heaping tablespoon)

6 ounces fresh goat cheese

Orzo with Dried Porcini Mushrooms, Radicchio, and Aged Balsamic Vinegar

Orzo is a tiny pasta the size and shape of a grain of rice. I like it because it has a similar look and feel to risotto, but you don't have to pamper it as it cooks, stirring it constantly for 20 or 25 minutes, as you do with risotto. If you have balsamico "extra vecchio" (the very expensive stuff that's aged fifty years and longer), use just a few drops of that in place of the balsamic vinegar in this recipe.

30 MINUTES

Place the mushrooms in a medium bowl and add enough hot water to cover them. Cover the bowl tightly with plastic wrap and set the mushrooms aside for 10 minutes to soften them. Drain, reserving 1 cup of the water the mushrooms were soaked in.

Bring a large pot of water to a boil over high heat and add a generous amount of kosher salt. Stir in the orzo, return the water to a boil, and cook the pasta, stirring occasionally to prevent it from sticking together, until it's just tender. (Since cooking times vary, refer to the package instructions for the recommended time and taste the pasta for doneness frequently while it cooks.)

While the water is coming to a boil and the pasta is cooking, heat the olive oil, garlic, shallots, and a pinch of kosher salt in a large skillet over medium-high heat and cook, stirring constantly to prevent the garlic from browning, until the shallots are soft and the garlic is soft and fragrant, about 1½ minutes. Turn the heat up to high, stir in the radicchio, mushrooms, and the water the mushrooms were soaked in, and turn off the heat.

Reserve ¼ cup of the pasta water, drain the pasta, and transfer it quickly, while it's still dripping with water, to the skillet with the mushrooms. Place the skillet over high heat, add the pasta water and Parmesan cheese, and stir to combine. Lower the heat and cook for about 30 seconds to thicken the sauce. Add the butter and stir to melt it.

Spoon the pasta out of the skillet and pile it into high mounds on four plates, dividing it evenly. Drizzle high-quality olive oil and the balsamic vinegar and grate a thin layer of Parmesan cheese over each serving; finish with freshly ground black pepper.

1 ounce dried porcini mushrooms (about 2 cups)

Kosher salt

1 cup orzo (about 6½ ounces)

3 tablespoons extra-virgin olive oil

4 large garlic cloves, grated or minced (about 1 tablespoon)

2 medium shallots, grated or minced (about 1 tablespoon)

8 large radicchio leaves, shredded (about 2 cups)

1 cup freshly grated Parmigiano-Reggiano, plus extra for grating over the pasta

½ stick (4 tablespoons) unsalted butter, cut into small pieces

High-quality extra-virgin olive oil, for drizzling

1 tablespoon plus 1 teaspoon aged balsamic vinegar

Freshly ground black pepper

Penne Arrabbiata with Charred Sweet Tomatoes

Arrabbiata is a classic spicy tomato sauce. The best one I tasted was made by Rustichella d'Abruzzo. If you can't find it, any spicy tomato sauce will work in its place. If the sauce you're using is mild, you may want to add more red pepper paste, depending on how spicy you like it. I add sugar to the tomatoes before broiling them; it gives them a hint of sweetness and, more important, it allows them to get nice and charred without being cooked too long.

35 MINUTES

Adjust the oven rack to the highest position and preheat the broiler.

Bring a large pot of water to a boil over high heat and add a generous amount of kosher salt. Stir in the penne, return the water to a boil, and cook the pasta, stirring occasionally to prevent it from sticking together, until it's al dente. (Since cooking times vary depending on the thickness of the pasta, refer to the package instructions for the recommended time and taste the pasta for doneness frequently while it cooks.)

Toss the tomatoes in a medium bowl with 2 tablespoons of the olive oil, sugar, and a generous sprinkling of kosher salt. Scatter them on a baking sheet and place them under the broiler for 5 to 7 minutes, shaking the pan occasionally, until they're charred and burst in places.

Heat the remaining 1/4 cup of olive oil, garlic, red pepper paste, and a pinch of kosher salt in a large skillet over medium-high heat, and sauté until the garlic is soft and fragrant, about 1 1/2 minutes, stirring constantly so the garlic doesn't brown. Reduce the heat to low, add the arrabbiata sauce and cook, stirring occasionally, to warm it through.

Drain the pasta and transfer it quickly, while it's still dripping with water, to the skillet with the sauce, and stir to coat the pasta with the sauce.

Spoon the pasta out of the skillet and pile it into high mounds on four plates, dividing it evenly. Spoon any sauce left in the skillet and the charred tomatoes over the pasta, sprinkle with the parsley, and grate a thin layer of Parmesan cheese over each serving.

Kosher salt

8 ounces penne

28 small, sweet **tomatoes** (scant 1/2 pint), or 14 cherry tomatoes, halved

1/4 cup plus 2 tablespoons **extra-virgin olive oil**

Pinch of sugar

6 large garlic cloves, grated or minced (about 2 tablespoons)

1 tablespoon plus 1 teaspoon **red pepper paste,** or more to taste

1 cup arrabbiata sauce (or any spicy tomato sauce)

1 heaping tablespoon finely chopped fresh Italian parsley leaves

Parmigiano-Reggiano wedge, for grating

Rigatoni with Anchovies, Garbanzo Beans, and Celery
Colman Andrews • Cofounder, *Saveur*

I don't remember when I first tasted anchovies, and I'm sure my parents would have gone woozy at the idea of eating them, but I can't remember when I didn't like them. To me, they are essential. There are very few dishes that they can't add depth and flavor (and, of course, salt) to, even meat and fowl. Anchovy paste is also great to have on hand. (I spread it on toast or on raw celery for a snack.) I could equally use it for this dish, but it isn't, strictly speaking, jarred, canned, bagged, or boxed, so I didn't.

•

I cut this recipe in half so that it was the same size as my pasta recipes. Since I couldn't cut a can of garbanzo beans in half, I threw them all into the pasta. I figured Colman would have done the same thing in my position. (By the way, Colman, tubes are okay!) —Nancy

30 MINUTES

Bring a large pot of water to a boil over high heat and add a generous amount of kosher salt. Stir in the pasta, return the water to a boil, and cook the pasta, stirring occasionally, until it's al dente. (Since cooking times vary depending on the thickness of the pasta, for perfectly cooked pasta, refer to the package instructions for the recommended time and taste the pasta frequently while it cooks.)

While the water is coming to a boil and the pasta is cooking, use a fork to crush the anchovies, with their oil, in a medium bowl. Strain the liquid from the garbanzo beans into the bowl with the anchovies. Set the garbanzo beans aside and stir the liquid and anchovies together to form a thin paste. Stir in the minced celery.

Drain the pasta and, while it's still dripping with water, return it to the pot it was cooked in. Add the anchovy mixture and toss well. Add the garbanzo beans and olive oil, grate about 1 tablespoon of Parmesan cheese into the pot, and season generously with freshly ground black pepper. Toss to combine the ingredients and season with kosher salt.

Spoon the pasta out of the pot and pile it onto four plates, dividing it evenly. Drizzle with the high-quality olive oil, top with a few celery leaves, and serve with grated Parmesan cheese on the side.

Kosher salt

8 ounces rigatoni rigati (or penne rigate)

12 anchovy fillets (including about 1 tablespoon of the packing oil or extra-virgin olive oil)

1 15-ounce can garbanzo beans (1½ cups), not drained

1 small celery stalk, trimmed and minced (about 2 tablespoons), leaves reserved for garnish

2 tablespoons extra-virgin olive oil

Parmigiano-Reggiano wedge, for grating

Freshly ground black pepper

High-quality extra-virgin olive oil, for drizzling

Capellini with Tomato Sauce and Fresh Ricotta

I've often made this dish for my children using common brands of pasta sauce such as Classico. Use whatever pasta sauce you like. However, I do recommend you seek out fresh ricotta cheese, even if it means a special trip to the cheese or specialty food store to get it. You really need to be careful not to overcook capellini—it will turn into something resembling glue or baby food. (It's so thin that this is easy to do.)

25 MINUTES

Bring a large pot of water to a boil over high heat and add a generous amount of kosher salt. Stir in the capellini, return the water to a boil, and cook the pasta, stirring occasionally to prevent the strands from sticking together, until it's al dente. (Since cooking times vary, refer to the package instructions for the recommended time and taste the pasta for doneness frequently while it cooks.)

While the water is coming to a boil, warm the pasta sauce with the olive oil in a medium saucepan over medium heat, stirring occasionally to keep it from scorching. Just before serving, spoon the sauce onto each of four plates, dividing it evenly.

Mix the ricotta with about 1/4 teaspoon of kosher salt and enough olive oil to obtain a loose, spoonable consistency.

Use tongs to lift the pasta out of the water and transfer it directly onto each plate on top of the sauce, dividing it evenly and twisting it into high mounds. Spoon the ricotta on top of each mound of pasta and drizzle it with the high-quality olive oil. Sprinkle the parsley and grate a thin layer of Parmesan cheese over each serving.

Kosher salt

8 ounces capellini

1 26-ounce jar **pasta sauce** (about 2 cups)

1/4 cup **extra-virgin olive oil,** plus extra for thinning the ricotta

1 cup fresh **ricotta**

High-quality **extra-virgin olive oil,** for drizzling

1/4 cup finely chopped fresh Italian parsley leaves

Parmigiano-Reggiano wedge, for grating

Orecchiette with Peas, Prosciutto, and Crème Fraîche

Frozen peas are so tender and sweet that this classic springtime pasta dish isn't compromised by substituting them for fresh-shucked peas. These "little ears" of pasta are the ideal shape for capturing the tiny peas.

35 MINUTES

Bring a large pot of water to a boil over high heat and add a generous amount of kosher salt. Stir in the orecchiette, return the water to a boil, and cook the pasta, stirring occasionally to prevent it from sticking together, until it's al dente. (Since cooking times vary depending on the thickness of the pasta, refer to the package instructions for the recommended time and taste the pasta for doneness frequently while it cooks.)

While the water is coming to a boil and the pasta is cooking, heat the oil, garlic, and a pinch of kosher salt in a large skillet over medium-high heat and sauté until the garlic is soft and fragrant, about 1½ minutes, stirring constantly so the garlic doesn't brown. Reduce the heat to medium and stir in the peas, crème fraîche, and the 1½ teaspoons of kosher salt. Bring the sauce to a simmer and cook, stirring constantly, for about 1 minute, until the sauce is warmed through.

Reserve ⅓ cup of the pasta water, drain the pasta and transfer it quickly, while it's still dripping with water, to the skillet with the sauce. Add the reserved pasta water, stir to coat the pasta with the sauce and cook the pasta and sauce together over high heat for about 2 minutes, until the ingredients are combined.

Spoon the pasta out of the skillet and pile it into high mounds on four plates, dividing it evenly. Spoon the sauce left in the skillet over the pasta. Rumple 3 pieces of prosciutto and lay 3 basil leaves over each serving.

1½ teaspoons kosher salt, plus more for the pasta water

8 ounces orecchiette

3 tablespoons **extra-virgin olive oil**

6 large garlic cloves, grated or minced (about 2 tablespoons)

1 cup frozen **petite peas** (about 4 ounces)

1 cup **crème fraîche**

6 thin slices **prosciutto** (about 3 ounces), torn in half

12 small basil leaves

Pot Sticker and Vegetable Stir-Fry
Tom Douglas • Dahlia Lounge, Seattle

My wife, Jackie, a great home cook, has culinary standards too high to serve this pot sticker stir-fry for dinner. But not me. When it's just our fifteen-year-old daughter, Loretta, and myself, this stir-fry is one of our favorite indulgences. Whenever I go to Costco, I stock up on bags of pot stickers, because they carry my favorite brand, Ling Ling. Loretta loves them so much I sometimes cook them in the morning and pack them in a thermos for her to take to school. I use whatever vegetables I happen to have in the refrigerator, so feel free to substitute for those listed in this recipe what you happen to find in yours. (Note that you want a total of 6 cups of vegetables.) The dipping sauce is pretty salty, so I don't add any salt to the stir-fry. If the dipping sauce you're using contains sesame oil, omit the sesame oil from the stir-fry.

•

Serving these with Nobu Spicy Lemon Dressing was my idea. I had some left over after using it in my recipe for Ling Cod with Sweet Green Peas, Hijiki, and Spicy Lemon Dressing. I tried it with Tom's pot stickers and found they went really nicely together. I chose not to double this recipe to have it serve four, like most of the other recipes in this book do, because I so liked Tom's story of eating this with his daughter. —Nancy

SERVES 2   **40 MINUTES**

Place the pot stickers in a large nonstick skillet with the ginger, 1 tablespoon of the vegetable oil and 1 cup of water. Cover the skillet and bring the water to a boil over high heat. Steam the pot stickers for 3 to 5 minutes, until they're tender, stirring occasionally to prevent them from sticking together. (Cooking times will vary depending on the pot stickers.) Transfer the pot stickers to a plate.

Return the water you cooked the pot stickers in to a boil and boil it down until it has evaporated and only the ginger and starchy residue from the pot stickers remains. Add the mushrooms, scallions, carrot, celery, and bell pepper, reduce the heat to medium-high, cover the skillet, and cook the vegetables for 1 to 2 minutes to soften them. Remove the lid and continue to sauté the vegetables, stirring them or shaking the pan occasionally, until they're caramelized, about 10 to 12 minutes. (If the vegetables are not browning, turn the heat up to high.) Remove the skillet from the heat, add the rice wine vinegar and sesame oil, and toss or stir to combine.

While the vegetables are cooking, heat the remaining tablespoon of vegetable oil in a medium nonstick skillet over high heat for 2 to 3 minutes, until the oil's almost smoking (you will begin to smell the oil at that point). Add half of the pot stickers and cook them for about 5 minutes, stirring them and shaking the pan occasionally for even cooking, until the pot stickers are brown on all sides and slightly crispy in places. Remove the pot stickers to a plate and cook the remaining pot stickers in the oil left in the pan. When they're all done, add all the pot stickers to the skillet with the vegetables and toss to combine.

Divide the pot stickers and vegetables evenly between two plates and scatter the bean sprouts and cilantro leaves over each serving. Pour chile sauce into two ramekins and place one on each plate for dipping.

12 frozen chicken or pork pot stickers (from 1 1-pound bag; preferably Ling Ling)

3 thin slices fresh peeled ginger

2 tablespoons vegetable oil (or canola oil or other neutral-flavored oil)

½ pound shiitake mushrooms, stems removed and caps halved or quartered, depending on their size (about 3 cups)

6 scallions, trimmed and cut into 2-inch pieces (white and green parts)

1 medium carrot, sliced diagonally ⅛ inch thick

1 celery stalk, sliced diagonally ⅛ inch thick

½ red bell pepper, cut into ½-inch-thick strips

2 teaspoons rice wine vinegar

1 teaspoon toasted sesame oil

1 cup mung bean sprouts

¼ cup loosely packed whole fresh cilantro leaves

Thai sweet chile sauce (or Nobu Spicy Lemon Dressing), for dipping

Linguine with Borlotti Beans and Pancetta

Pancetta is so flavorful and salty that even I, a major salt lover, didn't add more salt to this dish. This recipe may seem to call for a lot of arugula, but when the arugula is folded into the hot pasta, it wilts down dramatically and is just enough to add good color and a nice fresh element. If you don't have a skillet large enough to hold the arugula before it wilts, transfer the sauce to a large serving bowl, add the arugula and the hot pasta, and let it sit for about 1 minute so the hot pasta wilts the arugula. Then toss to incorporate the pasta with the sauce.

40 MINUTES

Bring a large pot of water to a boil over high heat and add a generous amount of kosher salt. Stir in the linguine, return the water to a boil, and cook the pasta, stirring occasionally to prevent the strands from sticking together, until it's al dente. (Since cooking times vary, refer to the package instructions for the recommended time and taste the pasta for doneness frequently while it cooks.)

While the water is coming to a boil and the pasta is cooking, slice the pancetta into three 1/4-inch-thick slices and cut each slice crosswise into 1/2-inch pieces.

Heat the olive oil in a large skillet over high heat for 2 to 3 minutes, until the oil's almost smoking (you will begin to smell the oil at that point). Add the pancetta and cook for about 1 1/2 minutes, stirring frequently, until it begins to brown. Reduce the heat to medium and continue to cook the pancetta for about 2 minutes, stirring occasionally, until it's cooked through and evenly browned. Turn the heat up to medium-high, and add the beans, shallot, and garlic and sauté until the shallots are soft and the garlic is soft and fragrant, about 1 1/2 minutes, stirring constantly so the garlic doesn't brown. Add the passato and cook it for about a minute to warm it through. Turn off the heat, add the arugula in handfuls, and fold it into the sauce to wilt the leaves.

Use tongs to lift the pasta out of the water and transfer it quickly, while it's still dripping with water, to the skillet with the sauce. Toss to coat the pasta with the sauce.

Use tongs to lift the pasta out of the skillet and pile it onto four plates, dividing it evenly and twisting it into high mounds. Squeeze a few drops of lemon juice over each serving and top with freshly ground black pepper and a generous grating of Parmesan cheese.

Kosher salt

8 ounces linguine

1 3/4-inch-thick slab **pancetta** (about 4 ounces)

2 tablespoons **extra-virgin olive oil**

1 15-ounce can borlotti **beans** (about 1 1/2 cups), rinsed and drained

1 small shallot, grated or minced (about 1 teaspoon)

1 large garlic clove, grated or minced (about 1 teaspoon)

1 1/2 cups **passato** or roughly chopped **San Marzano tomatoes,** with their juice

12 cups loosely packed arugula leaves

Lemon for squeezing over the pasta

Freshly ground black pepper

Parmigiano-Reggiano wedge, for grating

Spaghettini with Tuna and V8 Sauce
Hiro Sone and Lissa Doumani • Terra, St. Helena, California

The irony of owning a restaurant is that we come home from work exhausted and hungry—and invariably, there's nothing in the fridge. We do have a well-stocked pantry, though. This pasta, made with a can of tuna and a bottle of V8 juice, was the victorious result of late-night desperation. If you want a dish with a bit more zing, use Spicy Hot V8.

•

When my friend Lissa told me about a dish of spaghetti she made with V8 juice, I thought she was crazy. Then I looked at the ingredients list on the V8 can—tomato, carrot, celery, the same ingredients in many Italian tomato sauces—and it made sense. If, as a result of this book, you happen to have jarred or bottled onions around, you can use those in place of the fresh onion in this recipe. —Nancy

30 MINUTES

Bring a large pot of water to a boil over high heat and add a generous amount of kosher salt. Stir in the spaghettini, return the water to a boil, and cook the pasta, stirring occasionally to prevent the strands from sticking together, until it's al dente. (Since cooking times vary, for perfectly cooked pasta, refer to the package instructions for the recommended time and taste the pasta frequently while it cooks.)

While the water is coming to a boil and the pasta is cooking, heat the olive oil and onion together in a large saucepan over medium-high heat and sauté until the onion is just translucent, about 4 minutes. Add the celery, garlic, and chile flakes and cook until the garlic is softened and fragrant, about 1½ minutes, stirring constantly so the garlic doesn't brown. Add the V8 and bring it to a simmer. Stir in the tuna (including the oil it's packed in), capers, and olives and reduce the heat to medium-low, and let the sauce simmer until the pasta is cooked.

Reserve ¼ cup of the pasta water, then use tongs to lift the pasta out of the water and transfer it quickly, while it's still dripping with water, to the skillet with the sauce. Stir in the reserved pasta water and cook the pasta with the sauce over medium-high heat, stirring it to combine, for about 1 minute, so the pasta absorbs the sauce a bit.

Use tongs to lift the pasta out of the skillet and pile it onto four pasta or soup plates, dividing it evenly and twisting it into high mounds. Drizzle with the high-quality olive oil.

Kosher salt

8 ounces spaghettini (or spaghetti)

2 tablespoons extra-virgin olive oil

½ small onion, finely chopped (about ¼ cup)

½ celery stalk, finely chopped (about ¼ cup)

1 large garlic clove, grated or minced (about 1 teaspoon)

Pinch of chile flakes

1 cup V8

6 ounces olive oil–packed tuna, not drained

1 tablespoon capers

3 tablespoons small pitted green olives or black olives, coarsely chopped

High-quality extra-virgin olive oil, for drizzling

Spaghetti with Marinated White Anchovies and Whole Wilted Chives

This very simple, very satisfying dish was inspired by a recipe Matt Molina borrowed from one of Mario Batali's books. I used chile paste in place of chile flakes because I wanted the paste to coat the strands of spaghetti the way pesto and tapenade do. Marinated white anchovies are a totally different product from salted or oil-packed anchovies, which are what people usually think of when they hear the word "anchovy." They're plump, pickled, and not nearly as salty as the canned or jarred variety. You can find them at seafood counters, usually packaged in a little sealed tray, or behind the counter, always refrigerated. Many anchovy haters have been converted when they tasted them, so even if you don't think you like anchovies, I urge you to give this recipe a try. I find the combination of the long anchovies with the long whole chives and long strands of spaghetti visually very appealing.

30 MINUTES

Bring a large pot of water to a boil over high heat and add a generous amount of kosher salt. Stir in the spaghetti, return the water to a boil, and cook the pasta, stirring occasionally to prevent the strands from sticking together, until it's al dente. (Since cooking times vary, refer to the package instructions for the recommended time and taste the pasta for doneness frequently while it cooks.)

While the water is coming to a boil and the pasta is cooking, place the anchovies on a large plate, drizzle them with the olive oil, and sprinkle them with the lemon zest and chile flakes.

Put the breadcrumbs or saltine crumbs in a small bowl and stir in a few drops of olive oil to just moisten them.

Heat the olive oil, red pepper paste, garlic, and a pinch of kosher salt in a large skillet over medium-high heat and sauté until the garlic is soft and fragrant, about 1½ minutes, stirring constantly so the garlic doesn't brown.

Use tongs to lift the pasta out of the water and transfer it quickly, while it's still dripping with water, to the skillet with the red pepper paste. Put the skillet over medium-high heat, add the whole chives, and stir until the chives wilt. Add the anchovies and lemon juice and toss gently to combine.

Use tongs to lift the pasta out of the skillet and pile it onto four plates, dividing it evenly and twisting it into high mounds. Pull a few chives out so you can see the color and sprinkle the breadcrumbs over the top.

Kosher salt
8 ounces spaghetti

FOR THE ANCHOVIES
32 marinated white anchovy fillets
1 tablespoon **extra-virgin olive oil**
Grated zest of 1 lemon
1 teaspoon chile flakes

½ cup **breadcrumbs** or 8 **saltine crackers,** ground to fine crumbs
2 tablespoons **extra-virgin olive oil,** plus extra for the breadcrumbs
1 tablespoon plus 1 teaspoon **red pepper paste**
4 large garlic cloves, grated or minced (about 1 tablespoon)
3 ¾-ounce packages or 2 bunches fresh chives
1 tablespoon fresh lemon juice

Fettuccine with Creamy Black Truffle Sauce
Dana Cowin • Editor in Chief, *Food & Wine*

One day I was scrounging around in the refrigerator for a quick meal to make for a fancy friend who was unexpectedly staying for dinner. I happened to have some truffle paste and mascarpone on hand—leftovers that I'd brought home after a tasting at the magazine (definitely one of the perks of the job)—and I threw together this pasta. I've made it many times since. For a slightly different dish, I often sauté a handful of sliced mushrooms and onions and toss those into the pasta at the end. I recommend either Urbani Black Truffle Paste or La Madia Regale Black Truffle Cream for this recipe.

•

I cut this recipe in half so that it was the same size as all of the other pasta recipes in this book. If you choose to double it, it conveniently uses exactly one 8-ounce container of mascarpone, which is what Dana probably intended! —Nancy

20 MINUTES

Bring a large pot of water to a boil over high heat and add a generous amount of kosher salt. Stir in the fettuccine, return the water to a boil, and cook the pasta, stirring often to prevent the strands from sticking together, until it's al dente. (Since cooking times vary, refer to the package instructions for the recommended time and taste the pasta for doneness frequently while it cooks.)

While the pasta is cooking, whisk the mascarpone with 1/2 cup of hot pasta water in a medium bowl.

Reserving 1/2 cup of the pasta water, drain the fettuccine and quickly return it to the pot you cooked it in. Pour the mascarpone over the pasta, toss gently to combine, and cook the pasta with the sauce over medium-low heat until the sauce becomes thick and creamy. Season with kosher salt and freshly ground black pepper and remove from the heat. Add the chives and truffle paste and toss to combine them with the hot pasta.

Use tongs to lift the pasta out of the pot and pile it onto four plates, dividing it evenly and twisting it into high mounds. Spoon the sauce remaining in the pan over each serving.

Kosher salt

8 ounces fettuccine

4 ounces mascarpone cheese (about 3/8 cup)

Freshly ground black pepper

1 tablespoon chopped fresh chives

1 1/2 teaspoons black truffle paste or black truffle cream

Polenta with Sausage Ragù

Prepackaged sausages are convenient, but when I have the time I like to buy them from a butcher or an Italian grocer.

40 MINUTES

To make the polenta, combine the milk, thyme, garlic, and salt in a large, heavy-bottomed saucepan and bring it to a boil over high heat. Reduce the heat to medium-low and simmer the milk for about 5 minutes to steep the thyme. Remove the thyme sprigs and add the polenta in a slow, thin stream as you stir with a whisk to prevent the polenta from clumping. Bring the polenta to a low boil, reduce the heat to low, and cook it for about 5 minutes, whisking often, until it thickens to a loose, porridge-like consistency. Turn off the heat, stir in the butter, and cover.

Heat the canola oil in a large skillet over high heat for 2 to 3 minutes, until the oil's almost smoking (you will begin to smell the oil at that point). Slash the sausage casings with a knife and squeeze the sausage meat out of the casings and into the skillet; discard the casings. Cook the sausage, stirring occasionally and breaking it into small pieces as it cooks, until it's browned and cooked through, about 8 minutes. Reduce the heat to medium-high, add the garlic and chile flakes, and cook for about 1 minute just to soften the garlic, stirring constantly to prevent it from browning. Stir in the passato, peppers, and tomato paste and cook for 5 to 6 minutes to break down the tomatoes and meld the flavors. Turn off the heat and stir in the oregano and the oil from the peppers.

If the polenta has thickened, place it over medium heat and stir in more milk until it returns to a loose consistency.

Spoon the polenta in mounds on four plates, dividing it evenly, and create an indentation in each mound with the back of a spoon. Spoon the ragù into the indentation and over each serving of polenta. Drizzle with the high-quality olive oil and grate Parmesan cheese over each serving.

FOR THE POLENTA

3 cups whole milk, plus extra as needed

15 fresh thyme sprigs

2 large garlic cloves, grated or minced (about 2 teaspoons)

2 teaspoons kosher salt

½ cup instant **polenta**

½ stick (4 tablespoons) unsalted butter

FOR THE RAGÙ

2 tablespoons canola oil (or other neutral-flavored oil)

4 sweet or spicy Italian pork sausages (preferably flavored with fennel; about ¾ pound)

1 large garlic clove, grated or minced (about 1 teaspoon)

¼ teaspoon chile flakes

¾ cup **passato**

¼ cup chopped roasted **Piquillo peppers** (or any roasted red peppers), plus 2 tablespoons of their oil

1 teaspoon tomato paste

1 tablespoon chopped fresh oregano leaves

High-quality **extra-virgin olive oil,** for drizzling

Parmigiano-Reggiano wedge, for grating

Polenta with Quattro Formaggi and Cheese Condimenti

Don't be intimidated by the long ingredient list for this recipe. The only "cooking" you really have to do is to cook the instant polenta. Each serving is topped with four cheeses, and each cheese is topped with a condiment, so it's really like a cheese course on top of polenta. It's so rich, you may want to serve it with a simple green or Tri-Colore Salad (page 31). If you have individual ovenproof plates, use them for this dish, which goes in the oven for about a minute. Otherwise you can make the dish family style in one or two ovenproof skillets.

45 MINUTES

Adjust the oven rack to the highest position and preheat the broiler.

To make the polenta, combine the milk, thyme, garlic, and salt in a large, heavy-bottomed saucepan and bring it to a boil over high heat. Reduce the heat to medium-low and simmer the milk for about 5 minutes to steep the thyme. Remove the thyme sprigs and add the polenta in a slow, thin stream as you stir with a whisk to prevent the polenta from clumping. Bring the polenta to a low boil, reduce the heat to low, and cook it for about 5 minutes, whisking often, until it thickens to a loose, porridge-like consistency. Turn off the heat, stir in the butter and cover.

Divide the polenta into four large ovenproof soup plates or bowls. Place the Gorgonzola, Taleggio, and truffled cheeses in three of four quadrants over each serving of polenta, reserving one quadrant for the Parmesan. Put the plates under the broiler for about 1 minute, until the cheeses are just melted.

Use a sharp knife or vegetable peeler to cut or shave 24 very thin slices from the wedge of Parmesan cheese and place the slices in the fourth, empty quadrant, dividing them evenly.

Drizzle the Parmesan cheese with high-quality olive oil and top with freshly ground black pepper. Drizzle walnut oil over each serving of Gorgonzola. Drizzle honey and sprinkle a pinch of chile flakes over each serving of Taleggio, and use scissors to snip about 1 teaspoon of chives over each serving of truffled Italian cheese. Drizzle the truffle oil over the fontina, if you're using it.

FOR THE POLENTA

3 cups whole milk, plus extra as needed

15 fresh thyme sprigs

2 large garlic cloves, grated or minced (about 2 teaspoons)

2 teaspoons kosher salt

1/2 cup instant **polenta**

1/2 stick (4 tablespoons) unsalted butter

1/2 ounce sweet Gorgonzola or Roquefort cheese, crumbled (about 2 tablespoons)

1 ounce Taleggio cheese (or another soft, pungent-melting cheese), cut into small pieces (about 1/4 cup)

1 ounce truffled Italian cheese (or fontina), cut into small pieces (about 1/4 cup)

Parmigiano-Reggiano wedge, for shaving

High-quality **extra-virgin olive oil,** for drizzling

Freshly ground black pepper

Walnut oil, for drizzling

Chestnut honey (or buckwheat honey), for drizzling

Chile flakes

20 fresh chives

A few drops of truffle oil (if you are using fontina), for drizzling

EGGS

A lot of people have a hard time conceiving of eating eggs for anything but breakfast. I am not one of those people. I like eggs for dinner. Obviously in order for the recipes in this chapter to be of any use to you, you'll have to get used to the idea, too. It's not uncommon in France, where an omelet is a typical light lunch, or in Italy or Spain, where frittatas and tortillas, respectively, are served by the slice in every bar and café.

The majority of recipes in this chapter are for frittatas. A frittata (which is very much like a Spanish tortilla) is basically an open-faced omelet. I decided to make frittatas for the book because they're so easy. Many people are afraid of making omelets, of folding them over without having them break apart. But a frittata is almost impossible to mess up. First, the eggs are cooked gently then topped with other ingredients, and put in the oven until the eggs are set. Cooking them this way also makes them conducive to serving four people, whereas omelets usually are made individually. The only thing you have to be careful of when making frittatas is to not overcook them. The eggs are already mostly cooked before you put the frittata in the oven, so if you leave it in the oven too long, it will get dry and rubbery—which is many people's mistaken idea of what a frittata is.

Traditionally frittatas contain only one ingredient (besides eggs), such as potatoes or peppers. I added a bigger mix because I thought they needed to have more flavors and textures going on. Also, because I'm recommending that you serve them as a stand-alone meal, they need to feel particularly satisfying. A simple green salad or Tri-Colore Salad (page 31) served alongside any of these makes a nice light supper for four.

Although in these recipes I call for the frittata to be removed from the skillet and onto a plate, if you make them in a nice presentable skillet, such as a cast-iron one, I think they're beautiful served from the pan. Just remember to wrap the handle in a cloth so nobody gets burned.

It's pretty easy to be prepared for this chapter since basically these are dinners made from a dozen eggs. Naturally, the fresher the eggs you use for these recipes, the better. Organic or cage-free eggs bought from a farmers' market are the best. I make my frittatas using clarified butter or ghee (ghee is clarified butter used in Indian cooking) from a jar. This allows me to cook the eggs over high heat without the butter burning, since the milk solids have been removed.

Chorizo, Potato, and Spinach Frittata with Crumbled Fresh Goat Cheese

Spanish chorizo is a spicy hard sausage. It can be difficult to slice as thin as you want for this recipe, so to save yourself that step, buy packaged presliced chorizo or buy the chorizo from a deli where it can be sliced for you on a meat slicer.

30 MINUTES

Adjust the oven rack to the middle position and preheat the oven to 450°F.

Heat the oil in a large ovenproof nonstick skillet over high heat for 2 to 3 minutes, until it's almost smoking (you will begin to smell the oil at that point). Add the chorizo and cook it for about 1 minute, stirring constantly, until it's slightly crisp. Turn off the heat and add the spinach to the pan. Season with a pinch of kosher salt and fold the spinach with the chorizo and oil until it wilts slightly. Remove the spinach and chorizo to a bowl.

Wipe out the skillet and then heat the ghee in it over high heat for about 2 minutes. Add the potatoes and cook them for about 2 minutes, stirring occasionally, until they're warmed through.

While the potatoes are cooking, lightly beat the eggs with the kosher salt and pour them into the skillet over the potatoes. Reduce the heat to medium-high. As the eggs cook, use a heatproof rubber spatula to draw the edges inward, away from the sides of the pan, tilting the pan so the raw egg runs into the space created. Continue cooking in this way for 4 to 5 minutes, until no egg runs off when you tilt the pan but the top layer of the frittata is still runny and wet looking.

Spoon the chorizo and spinach over the eggs in clumps, leaving room to see the egg poking through in spots and a rim of egg around the edge. Scatter the crumbled goat cheese over the spinach and chorizo and bake the frittata until it's just set but not browned, 3 to 4 minutes, depending on how well done you like your eggs.

Run a spatula under the frittata to make sure it's not sticking. Shake the pan slightly to further loosen it, slide it onto a large plate, and season it with freshly ground black pepper.

2 teaspoons canola oil (or other neutral-flavored oil)

1 ounce Spanish **chorizo,** very thinly sliced

2 cups loosely packed baby spinach leaves

2 teaspoons kosher salt, plus extra for seasoning

1 tablespoon plus 1 teaspoon **ghee** or unsalted butter

½ cup canned or jarred **potatoes,** sliced ½ inch thick (about 16 slices)

12 large eggs

2 ounces fresh goat cheese, crumbled (about ¼ cup)

Freshly ground black pepper

Sausage and Piquillo Pepper Frittata with Fresh Mozzarella and Tomato Sauce (on the Side)

I like to serve the tomato sauce on the side with this frittata. I don't pour the sauce on it directly for the same reason I wouldn't serve French fries with the ketchup poured over them: I don't want the eggs to get saturated and soggy. Also, people like to use different amounts on their serving. And, just as important, it doesn't look pretty.

30 MINUTES

Adjust the oven rack to the middle position and preheat the oven to 450°F.

Heat the pasta sauce in a small saucepan over low heat, stirring often to keep it from scorching.

Heat the oil in a large ovenproof nonstick skillet over high heat for 2 to 3 minutes, until the oil's almost smoking (you will begin to smell the oil at that point). Slash the sausage casing with a knife and squeeze the sausage meat out of the casing and into the skillet; discard the casing. Cook the sausage, stirring occasionally and breaking it into small pieces as it cooks, until it's just browned, about 5 minutes. Add the onions and sauté the sausage and onions together for 2 to 3 minutes, until the sausage is cooked through and the onions are golden brown. Transfer the sausage and onions into a bowl and stir in the Piquillo peppers.

Wipe out the pan you cooked the sausages in, then add the ghee and heat it over high heat for about 2 minutes. Lightly beat the eggs with the kosher salt and pour them into the pan. Reduce the heat to medium-high. As the eggs cook, use a heatproof rubber spatula to draw the edges inward, away from the sides of the pan, tilting the pan so the raw egg runs into the space created. Continue cooking in this way for 4 to 5 minutes, until no egg runs off when you tilt the pan, but the top layer of the frittata is still runny and wet looking.

Spoon the sausage and onions over the eggs in clumps, leaving room to see the egg poking through in spots and a rim of egg around the edge. Sprinkle the mozzarella between, not on top of, the sausage mixture, and bake the frittata until it's just set but not browned, 3 to 4 minutes, depending on how well done you like your eggs.

Run a spatula under the frittata to make sure it's not sticking. Shake the pan slightly to further loosen it, slide it onto a large plate, and season it with freshly ground black pepper. Serve the frittata with the tomato sauce on the side.

½ cup **pasta sauce**

2 tablespoons canola oil (or other neutral-flavored oil)

1 sweet or spicy Italian pork sausage (preferably flavored with fennel; about 4 ounces)

4 small jarred **onions,** quartered (about 1 ounce or ¼ cup)

2 roasted **Piquillo peppers,** ripped into small pieces (about 2 tablespoons)

1 tablespoon plus 1 teaspoon **ghee** or unsalted butter

12 large eggs

2 teaspoons kosher salt

2 ounces fresh **mozzarella,** shredded (about ¼ cup)

Freshly ground black pepper

Frittata with Anchovies, Chives, and Shaved Truffle Butter

I use truffle butter in this frittata in two places—first in the skillet to cook the eggs, then shaved over the finished frittata. The shaved truffle butter reminds me of the look of shaved white truffles. D'Artagnan makes a really nice truffle butter, shaped in a tube, but there are other brands that are probably just as delicious.

30 MINUTES

Adjust the oven rack to the middle position and preheat the oven to 450°F.

Melt the truffle butter in a large ovenproof nonstick skillet over medium-high heat and heat it for about 2 minutes, until it's hot but doesn't brown. Lightly beat the eggs with the chives and the kosher salt and pour them into the pan. As the eggs cook, use a heatproof rubber spatula to draw the edges inward, away from the sides of the pan, tilting the pan so the raw egg runs into the space created. Continue cooking in this way for 4 to 5 minutes, until no egg runs off when you tilt the pan, but the top layer of the frittata is still runny and wet looking.

Smear the chopped anchovy over the frittata, using only as much as you like, sprinkle it with the thyme, and bake the frittata until it is just set but not browned, 3 to 4 minutes, depending on how well done you like your eggs.

Run a spatula under the frittata to make sure it's not sticking, shake the pan slightly to further loosen the frittata, and slide it onto a large plate. Use a small, sharp knife to shave truffle butter over the frittata.

2 1/2 ounces frozen truffle butter (about 5 tablespoons), plus extra for shaving on the frittata

12 large eggs

1/2 cup finely chopped fresh chives

1 teaspoon kosher salt

5–8 **anchovy fillets,** finely chopped

1 tablespoon fresh thyme leaves

Olive and Feta Frittata with Fresh Basil

My favorite feta is a French brand, Valbreso. It has an intense flavor without being too salty, and it's creamy, not dry or chalky. I like to use basil whole or, if I really want smaller pieces as in this recipe, I use scissors to cut it. Chopped, it tends to bruise and look black on the edges. Besides, I just don't like it when my basil looks like lawn clippings.

25 MINUTES

Preheat the oven to 450°F and adjust the oven rack to the middle position.

Heat the ghee in a large ovenproof nonstick skillet over high heat for about 2 minutes. Lightly beat the eggs with the kosher salt and pour them into the pan. Reduce the heat to medium-high. As the eggs cook, use a heatproof rubber spatula to draw the edges inward, away from the sides of the pan, tilting the pan so the raw egg runs into the space created. Continue cooking in this way for 4 to 5 minutes, until no egg runs off when you tilt the pan but the top layer of the frittata is still runny and wet looking.

Spoon the olives and feta over the eggs in clumps, leaving room to see the egg poking through in spots and a rim of egg around the edge. Bake the frittata until it's just set but not browned, 3 to 4 minutes, depending on how well done you like your eggs.

Run a spatula under the frittata to make sure it's not sticking. Shake the pan slightly to further loosen it and slide it onto a large plate. Drizzle the frittata with the high-quality olive oil, season it with freshly ground black pepper, and, using scissors, snip the basil into small pieces directly over the top.

1 tablespoon plus 1 teaspoon **ghee** or unsalted butter

12 large eggs

2 teaspoons kosher salt

30 small pitted **black olives**

2 ounces **feta,** crumbled (about ¼ cup)

High-quality **extra-virgin olive oil,** for drizzling

Freshly ground black pepper

4 large fresh basil leaves

Mushroom Frittata with Cantal Cheese and Fresh Thyme

I always resisted the temptation to buy the beautiful jars of mixed marinated mushrooms I saw in Italy because I couldn't imagine that they could possibly taste any better than the horrible, slimy, domestic mushrooms we have here. But after I took the oath for this book—try everything in a jar or can!—I bought them and was pleasantly surprised at how good they tasted. When you're shopping for mushrooms, find a brand that contains a variety. The varying flavors, textures, and shapes make this frittata more interesting. The most important thing in selecting mushrooms for this recipe, though, is that they be marinated in oil, not pickled in vinegar. This frittata is topped with Cantal cheese, a pungent French cow's milk cheese made in a similar way to Cheddar. If you can't find it, substitute Emmenthaler or raclette.

25 MINUTES

Adjust the oven rack to the middle position and preheat the oven to 450°F. Heat the ghee in a large ovenproof nonstick skillet over high heat for about 2 minutes. Lightly beat the eggs with the kosher salt and pour them into the pan. Reduce the heat to medium-high. As the eggs cook, use a heatproof rubber spatula to draw the edges inward, away from the sides of the pan, tilting the pan so the raw egg runs into the space created. Continue cooking in this way for 4 to 5 minutes, until no egg runs off when you tilt the pan but the top layer of the frittata is still runny and wet looking.

Spoon the mushrooms over the eggs in clumps, leaving room to see the egg poking through in spots and a rim of egg around the edge. Sprinkle with the cheese, top with the thyme, and bake the frittata until it's just set but not browned, 3 to 4 minutes, depending on how well done you like your eggs.

Run a spatula under the frittata to make sure it's not sticking. Shake the pan slightly to further loosen it, slide it onto a large plate, and season it with freshly ground black pepper.

1 tablespoon plus 1 teaspoon **ghee** or unsalted butter

12 large eggs

2 teaspoons kosher salt

2 ounces jarred marinated **mushrooms** (about ¼ cup) sliced ¼ inch thick

2 ounces Cantal cheese, shredded (about ½ cup)

2 tablespoons fresh thyme leaves

Freshly ground black pepper

Shrimp and Jalapeño Pepper Frittata with Avocado and Fresh Cilantro

This frittata starts with cooked shrimp. Because you don't recook the shrimp, just bake them directly into the frittata for a few minutes, make sure they're at room temperature before you use them. Otherwise, they may still be cold when you take the frittata out of the oven.

30 MINUTES

Adjust the oven rack to the middle position and preheat the oven to 450°F.

Heat the ghee in a large ovenproof nonstick skillet over high heat for about 2 minutes. Lightly beat the eggs with the kosher salt and pour them into the skillet. Reduce the heat to medium-high. As the eggs cook, use a heatproof rubber spatula to draw the edges inward, away from the sides of the pan, tilting the pan so the raw egg runs into the space created. Continue cooking in this way for 4 to 5 minutes, until no egg runs off when you tilt the pan but the top layer of the frittata is still runny and wet looking.

Randomly arrange the shrimp over the frittata. Sprinkle the jalapeño peppers around the shrimp and bake the frittata until it's just set but not browned, 3 to 4 minutes, depending on how well done you like your eggs.

Run a spatula under the frittata to make sure it's not sticking, shake the pan slightly to further loosen it, and slide it onto a large plate.

Halve the avocado, remove and discard the pit, and season it with sea salt. Scoop the avocado out of the peel in spoonfuls onto the frittata and discard the peel. Sprinkle the cilantro leaves and a few dashes of Tabasco over the frittata and serve it with Tabasco on the table for people to add more if they like.

1 tablespoon plus 1 teaspoon **ghee** or unsalted butter

12 large eggs

2 teaspoons kosher salt

6 ounces cooked jumbo shrimp (21–25 count), peeled and tails removed, at room temperature

2 small **pickled jalapeño peppers,** thinly sliced into rings (seeds intact)

1 ripe Hass avocado

Sea salt

Heaping ¼ cup loosely packed fresh cilantro leaves

Tabasco sauce

Plain Frittata Topped with Prosciutto, Arugula, Shaved Parmesan, and Aged Balsamic Vinegar

This frittata is cooked without adding any extra ingredients to the eggs. The prosciutto and arugula are piled on top at the end, like a salad, and drizzled with aged balsamic vinegar. Italians love the combination of balsamic vinegar and eggs. So do I. I'm conservative with the amount I drizzle over the frittata, because I like to serve the balsamic vinegar at the table for people to season each bite.

20 MINUTES

Adjust the oven rack to the middle position and preheat the oven to 450°F. Heat the ghee in a large ovenproof nonstick skillet over high heat for about 2 minutes. Lightly beat the eggs with the kosher salt and pour them into the pan. Reduce the heat to medium-high. As the eggs cook, use a heatproof rubber spatula to draw the edges inward, away from the sides of the pan, tilting the pan so the raw egg runs into the space created. Continue cooking in this way for 4 to 5 minutes, until no egg runs off when you tilt the pan but the top layer of the frittata is still runny and wet looking.

Bake the frittata until it's just set but not browned, 3 to 4 minutes, depending on how well done you like your eggs.

Run a spatula under the frittata to make sure it's not sticking, shake the pan slightly to further loosen it, and slide it onto a large plate. Drizzle the balsamic vinegar over the frittata and rumple the prosciutto slices over the top so the egg shows between the slices. Pile the arugula in the center of the frittata, leaving a border of egg around the edge. Season the arugula with sea salt and freshly ground black pepper and drizzle it with the high-quality olive oil and a little more balsamic vinegar. Use a small, sharp knife or a vegetable peeler to cut or shave 10 to 14 very thin slices from the wedge of Parmesan and scatter them over the frittata. Serve the frittata with balsamic vinegar on the table for people to drizzle over their slices if they like.

1 tablespoon plus 1 teaspoon **ghee** or unsalted butter

12 large eggs

2 teaspoons kosher salt

1 teaspoon aged **balsamic vinegar,** plus extra for drizzling and for serving on the table

2 ounces thinly sliced **prosciutto**

1½ cups loosely packed arugula leaves

Sea salt and freshly ground black pepper

High-quality **extra-virgin olive oil,** for drizzling

Parmigiano-Reggiano wedge, for shaving

Bacon, Onion, and Gruyère Frittata

Who doesn't like bacon and eggs with melted cheese? The only problem with this combination is that nobody ever eats it except for breakfast. A frittata gives you permission to eat it for dinner, too.

25 MINUTES

Adjust the oven rack to the middle position and preheat the oven to 450°F.

Heat the oil in a large ovenproof nonstick skillet over high heat for about 2 to 3 minutes, until the oil is almost smoking (you will begin to smell the oil at that point). Add the bacon and fry it until it's almost cooked, about 1½ minutes. Add the onion and cook it for about 1 minute, until it's warmed through and the bacon is cooked but still chewy, not browned or crispy. Remove the bacon and onions to a plate.

Wipe out the pan you cooked the bacon in and heat the ghee over high heat for about 2 minutes. Lightly beat the eggs with the kosher salt and pour them into the pan. Reduce the heat to medium-high. As the eggs cook, use a heatproof rubber spatula to draw the edges inward, away from the sides of the pan, tilting the pan so the raw egg runs into the space created. Continue cooking in this way for 4 to 5 minutes, until no egg runs off when you tilt the pan but the top layer of the frittata is still runny and wet looking.

Spoon the bacon and onions over the frittata in clumps, leaving room to see the egg poking through in spots and a rim of egg around the edge. Sprinkle with the cheese, then with the thyme, and bake the frittata until it's just set but not browned, 3 to 4 minutes, depending on how well done you like your eggs.

Run a spatula under the frittata to make sure it's not sticking. Shake the pan slightly to further loosen it, slide it onto a large plate, and season it with freshly ground black pepper.

2 teaspoons canola oil (or other neutral-flavored oil)

4 strips thick-cut applewood-smoked **bacon,** cut into ¼-inch-wide pieces

10 small jarred **onions,** quartered (about 2½ ounces or ⅔ cup)

1 tablespoon plus 1 teaspoon **ghee** or unsalted butter

12 large eggs

2 teaspoons kosher salt

1 ounce Gruyère cheese, shredded (about ¼ cup)

2 tablespoons fresh thyme leaves

Freshly ground black pepper

Skillet Chilaquiles with Fried Eggs
Mary Sue Milliken and Susan Feniger • Border Grill,
Santa Monica, California

Chilaquiles is a dish that makes use of stale tortillas by simmering them in sauce until they're wonderfully crisp and chewy at the same time. It's a standard breakfast item in Mexico. All of the cooks who've worked in our kitchens have their own variation of chilaquiles that they make for staff meals. We've become so fond of chilaquiles that we make them as a special surprise when we're visiting our respective in-laws in the Midwest or friends in Europe. We use bottled salsa (our preference is Amy's Organic Red Salsa) to make the dish especially quick and easy. We urge you to look for organic salsa and chicken broth.

•

Panela cheese is a mild fresh cheese; it's Mexico's version of farmer's cheese or ricotta, either of which can be used as a substitute. You can use pickled jalapeño peppers in place of the fresh if you like. —Nancy

30 MINUTES

Combine the chicken broth and salsa in a large skillet and bring it to a boil over high heat. Reduce the heat to medium-high, add the chips, and gently stir to coat each chip with the sauce. Continue simmering for 1 to 2 minutes. When some of the chips have begun to break up but others are still holding their shape, add the cheese and stir gently to distribute the ingredients and cook for another minute to warm the cheese. Turn off the heat and stir in the onion, cilantro, and jalapeño peppers, and season with kosher salt.

Heat the olive oil in a large nonstick skillet over high heat for 2 to 3 minutes, until the oil's almost smoking (you will begin to smell the oil at that point). Break one egg into a small bowl, and then pour the egg into the skillet. Let it just begin to set around the edges then break the second egg into the bowl and pour it into the skillet. (By waiting a moment before adding the second egg, the eggs won't set together and will be easy to separate and serve individually.) Cook them for about 1½ minutes, until the edges are golden and crispy and the whites are set but the yolks are still runny. Remove the eggs to a plate and cook the remaining two eggs in the same way.

Divide the chilaquiles evenly among four plates and drizzle them with the crema. Halve the avocado, remove and discard the pit, and peel off and discard the skin. Cut the avocado into uneven chunks, sprinkle them with sea salt, and scatter them over the chilaquiles. Place a fried egg atop each serving and sprinkle the eggs with sea salt.

2 cups chicken **broth**

1 cup red salsa

6–8 cups corn tortilla chips

5 ounces panela cheese, roughly diced or broken into ½-inch pieces (about 1 cup)

½ small red onion, finely chopped (about 1 cup)

½ cup chopped fresh cilantro leaves

1 or 2 jalapeño or Serrano peppers, halved, seeded if desired, and minced

Kosher salt

¼ cup **extra-virgin olive oil**

4 large eggs

Mexican crema (or sour cream), for drizzling

1 ripe Hass avocado

Sea salt

Olive Oil–Fried Eggs on Toast with Fresh Mozzarella and Spicy Harissa Sauce

I made a version of this at Jar, a restaurant in Los Angeles where I served a mozzarella menu from the bar on Monday nights. Because this book is about using jarred and prepackaged products, I make the sauce starting with premade harissa, which is a North African spice mixture, instead of making it from scratch. This dish is very rich, but not quite substantial enough for a meal. I recommend you serve it with a simple green salad or Tri-Colore Salad (page 31).

30 MINUTES

Adjust the oven rack to the middle position and preheat the oven to 350°F.

Place the bread slices on a baking sheet, brush the tops with olive oil, and bake for 15 to 20 minutes, until they're lightly toasted and golden brown. (You can also toast the bread in a toaster, but *without* the oil. Then brush the toast with oil after they're done.) Rub the oiled side of the toast with the garlic and set them on each of four plates, garlic side up.

Turn the oven up to broil.

To make the harissa sauce, whisk the olive oil, harissa, red pepper paste, garlic, lemon juice, and kosher salt together in a small bowl. The sauce may appear "broken," but this isn't a problem.

Heat the olive oil in a large nonstick skillet over high heat for 2 to 3 minutes, until the oil's almost smoking (you will begin to smell the oil at that point). Break one egg into a small bowl, and then pour the egg into the skillet. Let it just begin to set around the edges, then break the second egg into the bowl and pour it into the skillet. (By waiting a moment before adding the second egg, the eggs won't set together and will be easy to separate and serve individually.) Cook them for about 1½ minutes, until the edges are golden and crispy and the whites are set but the yolks are still runny. Remove the eggs to a baking pan or dish and cook the remaining two eggs in the same way and add them to the baking pan.

Sprinkle the mozzarella over the eggs and place them under the broiler for about 30 seconds, until the cheese is melted and the very bottom of the yolks are set but the centers are still slightly runny. (The eggs won't have the total runniness of sunny-side-up eggs; they will have more texture than that, but not so much that they are like hard-cooked eggs.)

Remove the pan from the oven and carefully slide the eggs onto the pieces of toast. Sprinkle the eggs with sea salt. Whisk the harissa sauce again and pour it over the eggs, dividing it evenly and making sure not to cover the eggs completely, and scatter the parsley leaves over the tops of the eggs.

4 1-inch-thick slices brioche or large sourdough bread
Extra-virgin olive oil, for brushing the toast
1 large garlic clove

FOR THE HARISSA SAUCE
½ cup **extra-virgin olive oil**
2 teaspoons **harissa**
2 teaspoons **red pepper paste**
1 large garlic clove, grated or minced (about 1 teaspoon)
½ teaspoon fresh lemon juice
¼ teaspoon kosher salt

¼ cup **extra-virgin olive oil**
4 large eggs
6 ounces fresh **mozzarella,** shredded (about 1 cup)
Sea salt
12 fresh Italian parsley leaves

White Asparagus in Brown Butter Topped with a Fried Egg and Capers
Gabrielle Hamilton • Prune, New York City

The first chef I was sure I wanted to ask to contribute a recipe to this book was Gabrielle Hamilton. Just after conceiving of the book, I read an article in *Spain Gourmetour,* an avant-garde food magazine, titled "Top Quality Preserves: When Gourmands Fall for the Can." The article featured Gabrielle as a chef who eats canned foods. I love Gabrielle's restaurant, Prune, in New York's East Village, and I love her sensibility with food—bold, rustic, honest, and humble. At Prune, she serves radishes on Triscuits, and marinated white anchovies with celery and toasted Marcona almonds. So I wasn't surprised to find her, in this article, admitting to eating white asparagus from a jar. She also talked about using them in a dish with brown butter, a recipe that she allowed me to include here. If you have a skillet with a light-colored bottom, I recommend you use it to melt the butter for this recipe. The light skillet allows you to see when the butter has browned and helps prevent burning it. —Nancy

20 MINUTES

Melt the butter in a large skillet over high heat and cook it for about 5 minutes, until it starts to brown and the bubbles subside. Add the asparagus and cook it for about 30 seconds, just long enough to warm it through. Turn off the heat and season the asparagus with kosher salt. Place 6 asparagus spears on each of four plates and pour the butter in a pool over the asparagus, dividing it evenly.

Heat the olive oil in a large nonstick skillet over high heat for 2 to 3 minutes, until the oil's almost smoking (you will begin to smell the oil at that point). Break one egg into a small bowl, and then pour the egg into the skillet. Let it just begin to set around the edges then break the second egg into the bowl and pour it into the skillet. (By waiting a moment before adding the second egg, the eggs won't set together and will be easy to separate and serve individually.) Cook them for about 1½ minutes, until the edges are golden and crispy and the whites are set but the yolks are still runny. Remove the eggs to a plate and cook the remaining two eggs in the same way.

Place 1 egg on top of each serving of asparagus, sprinkle them with sea salt, and scatter the capers over the eggs.

1 stick (½ cup) unsalted butter, cut into ½-inch cubes
24 white asparagus spears (2 11.6-ounce jars)
Kosher salt
¼ cup **extra-virgin olive oil**
4 large eggs
Sea salt
1 heaping tablespoon **capers**

CROSTINI

Crostini, the plural of *crostino,* which loosely translates as "toast" in Italian, are essentially small open-faced sandwiches. When I started this book, I hadn't intended to include them because I felt I'd covered this territory in my *Sandwich Book.* But as I started accumulating products I liked that I'd used in other dishes, I would think: What could I do with the leftovers? Crostini always came to mind.

Not only are crostini the perfect vehicle for the small quantities of products left over from other dishes (not to mention for day-old bread), they're one of the few things with which you can use an item straight out of the jar. Just by layering a few ingredients, the combinations were so delicious, I felt like I had to provide the recipes for them. By the end of a year of recipe testing, I had a full chapter.

I made these crostini on La Brea Bakery's sourdough bâtard, which is a long white loaf similar to a baguette but about twice as wide. I think it's a nice size for crostini, but you can make them any size you want, depending on how you're serving them or what kind of bread you have. Baguette slices are a good size for finger food or party canapés. A large slice of toast from a big round loaf makes a substantially sized open-faced sandwich that, with a Tri-Colore Salad (page 31), works as a perfect light dinner.

Unlike the other recipes in this book, which all make four servings, these recipes, with a couple of exceptions, make one entrée serving. I constructed the recipes this way because I wanted to use small enough amounts so that you could assemble them from leftovers. Also, my thinking was that if you were serving them to guests, better to make just a few of each kind and to make three or five different kinds of crostini so you can offer an assortment. Of course, the quantities used in any of the recipes can be doubled or quadrupled if you like.

When I make crostini, I like them to look very natural and for all the different layers of ingredients to be seen, so as I add another layer I make it a little uneven, not completely smooth and regular, and I make sure not to completely cover whatever is beneath it. I think this kind of "imperfection" is more beautiful and also more appetizing than something that is so precise it looks as if a machine made it. I also never spread to the edges of the bread, so that a bit of crust stays visible.

Crostini with Ventresca, Piquillo Peppers, and Caper Mayonnaise

Ventresca is canned tuna belly marinated in olive oil. It's a delicacy in Spain and Italy. I've been told that it is traditional to use it only with beans, but it's so rich and so much moister and more flavorful than regular tuna, I like to use it whenever the tuna is playing a central role, such as in these crostini.

20 MINUTES

Adjust the oven rack to the middle position and preheat the oven to 350°F.

Place the bread slices on a baking sheet, brush the tops with olive oil, and bake them for 15 to 20 minutes, until they're lightly toasted and golden brown. (You can also toast the bread in a toaster, but *without* the oil. Then brush the toast with oil after they're done.) Rub the oiled side of the crostini with the garlic and set them on your work surface, oiled side up.

Stir the Garlic Mayonnaise and capers together in a small bowl. Spoon about 2 teaspoons of the mayonnaise in an uneven layer on each crostino, dividing it evenly and leaving the edges of the toast visible. Rip the peppers open and lay one pepper on each crostino, lay the tuna on top of the peppers, and sprinkle the crostini with the parsley and a few grains of sea salt.

4 ½-inch-thick slices from a bâtard (or 8 slices from a baguette or 2 slices from a large round rustic white loaf, cut in half)

Extra-virgin olive oil, for brushing the bread

1 garlic clove

3 tablespoons Garlic Mayonnaise (page 33)

2 teaspoons **capers,** chopped

4 roasted **Piquillo peppers**

1 ounce ventresca (see "**Tuna**"; or any olive oil–packed tuna), lightly drained

1 tablespoon finely chopped fresh Italian parsley leaves

Sea salt

Crostini with Salted European-Style Butter, Smoked Sardines, and Pepper Cress

In the midst of trying a bunch of Spanish products for this book, I tasted canned sardines for the first time. I liked them so much I knew I had to think of a way to include them in the book. I tried to think of what Gabrielle Hamilton would do with them. They just seemed like something she would use. So this recipe is dedicated to Gabrielle. I hope she approves. Since butter is a central ingredient in these crostini, I call for a high-fat butter, such as domestic Plugrá or any high-quality European variety. I use regular supermarket varieties of smoked sardines, but I do try to find sardines that say "lightly smoked" so the smoky flavor doesn't overwhelm the flavor of the fish.

20 MINUTES

Adjust the oven rack to the middle position and preheat the oven to 350°F.

Place the bread slices on a baking sheet, brush the tops with olive oil, and bake them for 15 to 20 minutes, until they're lightly toasted and golden brown. (You can also toast the bread in a toaster, but *without* the oil. Then brush the toast with oil after they're done.) Rub the oiled side of the crostini with the garlic and set them on your work surface, oiled side up.

Spread about 2 teaspoons of butter in an uneven layer on each crostino, leaving the edges of the bread visible. Scatter the onion slices over the butter, dividing them evenly, lay 1 sardine on each, and top with the cress and a few grains of sea salt.

4 ½-inch-thick slices from a bâtard (or 8 slices from a baguette or 2 slices from a large round rustic white loaf, cut in half)

Extra-virgin olive oil, for brushing the bread

1 garlic clove

3 tablespoons salted, European-style butter, softened just to a spreadable (not oily) consistency

⅛ small red onion, cut through the core and thinly sliced (about 40 slices)

4 fillets canned smoked sardines, backbones removed

24 stems pepper cress or live watercress

Sea salt

Crostini with Anchovy-Olive Mayonnaise, Hard-Cooked Egg, and Sun-Dried Tomatoes

These crostini are all about the hard-cooked eggs, so you have to get them right. For what a perfect hard-cooked egg should look like, see my note for Arugula with Hard-Cooked Eggs, Artichoke Hearts, Tuna, and Charred Tomatoes (page 16).

20 MINUTES

Adjust the oven rack to the middle position and preheat the oven to 350°F.

Place the bread slices on a baking sheet, brush the tops with olive oil, and bake them for 15 to 20 minutes, until they're lightly toasted and golden brown. (You can also toast the bread in a toaster, but *without* the oil. Then brush the toast with oil after they're done.) Rub the oiled side of the crostini with the garlic and set them on your work surface, oiled side up.

Place the egg in a small saucepan with enough water to cover, salt the water generously, and bring it to a boil over high heat. Reduce the heat to low and simmer the egg for about 5 minutes, until the yolk is bright yellow but slightly wet looking (see page 16 for additional egg information). While the egg is cooking, fill a large bowl with ice water. Use a slotted spoon to remove the egg from the hot water when it's done and immediately plunge it into the ice water to chill. After the egg has cooled, peel and slice it into 8 thin slices with an egg-slicer or cut it into quarters with a large knife.

Spoon about 2 teaspoons of the mayonnaise in an uneven layer on each crostino, leaving the edges of the toast visible. Place the egg on top of the mayonnaise, and sprinkle it with sea salt. Rip the sun-dried tomatoes into small pieces, scatter them over the egg, and top with the arugula leaves.

4 ½-inch-thick slices from a bâtard (or 8 slices from a baguette or 2 slices from a large round rustic white loaf, cut in half)

Extra-virgin olive oil, for brushing the bread

1 garlic clove

1 large egg

Kosher salt

3 tablespoons Anchovy-Olive Mayonnaise (recipe follows)

Sea salt

8 oil-packed **sun-dried tomatoes**

¼ cup loosely packed arugula leaves

Anchovy-Olive Mayonnaise

This is a quick and easy version of anchoïade, a traditional French condiment made of anchovies, garlic, and olive oil. It's delicious dolloped on a steak or seared rare tuna. You could make a simple flavorful light lunch by serving blanched green beans with this mayonnaise drizzled over the top.

¹/₂ CUP   **10 MINUTES**

Stir the mayonnaise, garlic, anchovy fillets, olive oil, olive tapenade, lemon juice, parsley, and kosher salt together in a small bowl. Season with more garlic, lemon juice, or salt to taste.

½ cup **mayonnaise**

3 large garlic cloves, grated or minced (about 1 tablespoon), or more to taste

3 **anchovy fillets,** smashed with the back of a knife

1 tablespoon **extra-virgin olive oil**

2 teaspoons black **olive tapenade**

2 teaspoons fresh lemon juice, or more to taste

2 teaspoons finely chopped fresh Italian parsley leaves

¼ teaspoon kosher salt, or more to taste

Crostini with Chunky Eggplant Spread, Aged Balsamic Vinegar, and Fresh Chives

Dressed up with a drizzle of good balsamic and a few shavings of Parmesan, this crostini makes an elegant little snack. This recipe makes enough eggplant spread for sixteen crostini—it's one of those things that is harder to make in smaller batches—but it keeps well in the refrigerator and it's so delicious, you'll want to make more than one serving anyway.

20 MINUTES

Adjust the oven rack to the middle position and preheat the oven to 350°F.

Place the bread slices on a baking sheet, brush the tops with olive oil, and bake them for 15 to 20 minutes, until they're lightly toasted and golden brown. (You can also toast the bread in a toaster, but *without* the oil. Then brush the toast with oil after they're done.) Rub the oiled side of the crostini with the garlic and set them on your work surface, oiled side up.

To make the eggplant spread, combine the eggplant appetizer, Piquillo peppers, garlic, and lemon-infused olive oil in a medium bowl and stir to mix thoroughly.

Spoon about 2 tablespoons of the eggplant spread in an uneven layer on each crostino, leaving the edges of the toast visible. Sprinkle with sea salt and drizzle balsamic vinegar over the eggplant. Use a sharp knife or a vegetable peeler to cut or shave enough very thin slices from the wedge of Parmesan to scatter a few slices over each of the crostino and use scissors to finely snip about 1/2 teaspoon of chives over each.

4 1/2-inch-thick slices from a bâtard (or 8 slices from a baguette or 2 slices from a large round rustic white loaf, cut in half)

Extra-virgin olive oil, for brushing the bread

1 garlic clove

FOR THE EGGPLANT SPREAD

1/2 cup **eggplant appetizer,** drained

1 1/2 teaspoons finely chopped **Piquillo peppers**

1 small garlic clove, grated or minced (about 1/2 teaspoon)

1 teaspoon **lemon-infused olive oil** (or high-quality **extra-virgin olive oil** combined with a pinch of fresh grated lemon zest)

Sea salt

Aged **balsamic vinegar,** for drizzling

Parmigiano-Reggiano wedge, for shaving

10 fresh chives

Crostini with Prosciutto, Fresh Mozzarella, and Black Olive Tapenade

This is a very classic combination of flavors. How good these crostini will be is totally dependent on the creaminess and deliciousness of the mozzarella you use. Look for fresh mozzarella in your local cheese store or the cheese counter of a specialty food store. Ideally, it will have been made the same day or within the last couple of days.

20 MINUTES

Adjust the oven rack to the middle position and preheat the oven to 350°F.

Place the bread slices on a baking sheet, brush the tops with olive oil, and bake them for 15 to 20 minutes, until they're lightly toasted and golden brown. (You can also toast the bread in a toaster, but *without* the oil. Then brush the toast with oil after they're done.) Rub the oiled side of the crostini with the garlic and set them on your work surface, oiled side up.

If the tapenade is thick and pastelike, put it in a small bowl and stir in a tablespoon or two of olive oil until you obtain a loose, spoonable consistency.

Tear the prosciutto slices in half if necessary so you have four slices and rumple one piece of prosciutto onto each crostino, leaving the edges of the toast visible. Place one mozzarella slice on top of each, and spoon a teaspoon of the tapenade over each slice of mozzarella. Scatter the arugula leaves over the crostini and drizzle with the high-quality extra-virgin olive oil and a few grains of sea salt.

4 ½-inch-thick slices from a bâtard (or 8 slices from a baguette or 2 slices from a large round rustic white loaf, cut in half)

Extra-virgin olive oil, for brushing the bread and for thinning the tapenade if necessary

1 garlic clove

1 heaping tablespoon black **olive tapenade**

2–4 thin slices **prosciutto** (about 2 ounces)

4 ¼-inch-thick slices fresh **mozzarella** (about 1¼ ounces)

¼ cup loosely packed arugula leaves

High-quality **extra-virgin olive oil,** for drizzling

Sea salt

Crostini with Aged Goat Cheese, Walnut Oil, and Fresh Thyme

The walnut oil is the key player in this dish. It's the thing from a jar (or in this case a bottle) that makes this very simple cheese toast into something special. Walnut oil, like all nut oils, can turn rancid quickly, so you'll want to keep it in the refrigerator and always taste it before using it.

20 MINUTES

Adjust the oven rack to the middle position and preheat the oven to 350°F.

Place the bread slices on a baking sheet, brush the tops with olive oil, and bake them for 15 to 20 minutes, until they're lightly toasted and golden brown. (You can also toast the bread in a toaster, but *without* the oil. Then brush the toast with oil after they're done.) Rub the oiled side of the crostini with the garlic and return them to the baking sheets, oiled side up.

Reduce the oven temperature to 325°F.

Spread the walnuts on a baking sheet and toast them in the oven for about 15 minutes, until they're lightly browned and fragrant. Remove the walnuts from the oven, drizzle them with walnut oil, sprinkle them with sea salt, and toss to coat.

Increase the oven temperature to 450°F.

Place one slice of goat cheese atop each crostino and put them back in the oven for 2 to 3 minutes, until the cheese softens and just starts to melt. Sprinkle the crostini with the thyme leaves, place one walnut half on each crostino, and drizzle them with walnut oil.

4 ½-inch-thick slices from a bâtard (or 8 slices from a baguette or 2 slices from a large round rustic white loaf, cut in half)

Extra-virgin olive oil, for brushing the bread

1 garlic clove

4 walnut halves

½ teaspoon **walnut oil,** plus extra for drizzling

Sea salt

4 ounces aged goat cheese, cut into four equal slices about ¼ inch thick

Leaves picked from 4 sprigs of fresh thyme

Crostini with Burrata Cheese, Cherry Tomatoes, and Pesto

Burrata is cream-filled mozzarella cheese. You'll find it at specialty food stores and cheese shops, imported from Italy. A few domestic mozzarella makers are also starting to manufacture burrata. If it's not available where you live, you can use an equal amount of fresh mozzarella or half a cup of fresh ricotta mixed with enough extra-virgin olive oil (and kosher salt to season) to obtain a loose, spoonable consistency.

20 MINUTES

Adjust the oven rack to the middle position and preheat the oven to 350°F.

Place the bread slices on a baking sheet, brush the tops with olive oil, and bake them for 15 to 20 minutes, until they're lightly toasted and golden brown. (You can also toast the bread in a toaster, but *without* the oil. Then brush the toast with oil after they're done.) Rub the oiled side of the crostini with the whole garlic clove and set them on your work surface, oiled side up.

Toss the tomatoes in a small bowl with the olive oil, pesto, and minced garlic, and season them with sea salt.

Place one slice of burrata on each crostino. Scatter the tomatoes over the burrata, dividing them evenly, and drizzle the tomatoes with the pesto remaining in the bowl.

4 ½-inch-thick slices from a bâtard (or 8 slices from a baguette or 2 slices from a large round rustic white loaf, cut in half)

1 tablespoon plus 1 teaspoon high-quality **extra-virgin olive oil** for the tomatoes, plus extra for brushing the bread

2 garlic cloves (1 whole and 1 grated or minced; about ½ teaspoon)

6 cherry **tomatoes,** quartered (or 12 small, sweet tomatoes, cut in half)

2 teaspoons **basil pesto**

Sea salt

4 ¼-inch-thick slices burrata cheese (about 2 ounces; see "**Mozzarella**")

Crostini with Triple-Crème Cheese, Pear Mostarda, and Fresh Chives

These crostini couldn't be simpler: a very rich, creamy cheese topped with the bold, sweet contrasting flavor of mostarda. Mostardas are sweet Italian condiments, similar to chutney, that are used to accent cold meat and cheese. They get their name from the fact that they're traditionally flavored with mustard seed oil. My favorites are those made by Acetaia Leonardi from cherries, figs, strawberries, and, especially, pears. For these crostini, I like to use a triple-crème cheese like Saint André that comes in the shape of a small disk. I cut the disk into little wedge-shaped pieces, which fit perfectly and look really pretty on the crostini.

20 MINUTES

Adjust the oven rack to the middle position and preheat the oven to 350°F.

Place the bread slices on a baking sheet, brush the tops with olive oil, and bake them for 15 to 20 minutes, until they're lightly toasted and golden brown. (You can also toast the bread in a toaster, but *without* the oil. Then brush the toast with oil after they're done.)

Increase the oven temperature to 450°F.

Place one piece of cheese on each crostino and return them to the oven for 2 to 3 minutes, until the cheese is soft and just beginning to melt.

Spoon about 1 teaspoon of mostarda over each slice of cheese and use scissors to snip about ½ teaspoon of chives over each crostini.

4 ½-inch-thick slices from a bâtard (or 8 slices from a baguette or 2 slices from a large round rustic white loaf, cut in half)

Extra-virgin olive oil, for brushing the bread

4 ounces triple-crème cheese (with the rind on), cut into 4 equal-size pieces

1 heaping tablespoon mostarda

10 fresh chives

Crostini with Pea Purée, Prosciutto, and Parmesan

Canned peas have kind of a funky color, but I actually like the way they taste. When they're turned into purée and topped with shaved Parmesan, as they are for these crostini, the color isn't such an issue. Like the Crostini with White Bean Purée, you'll have much more purée than you'll need for four crostini, so you can either quadruple the recipe for the toast, which will use all the purée, or eat the leftover purée with a spoon.

20 MINUTES

Adjust the oven rack to the middle position and preheat the oven to 350°F.

Place the bread slices on a baking sheet, brush the tops with olive oil, and bake them for 15 to 20 minutes, until they're lightly toasted and golden brown. (You can also toast the bread in a toaster, but *without* the oil. Then brush the toast with oil after they're done.) Rub the oiled side of the crostini with the garlic and set them on your work surface, oiled side up.

To make the pea purée, combine the peas, olive oil, garlic, and kosher salt in a large mortar or bowl and mash them together with a pestle or potato masher until they're mostly mashed with some peas left whole.

Tear the prosciutto slices in half if necessary so you have four slices and rumple one piece of prosciutto onto each crostino, leaving the edges of the toast visible. Spoon about 1 tablespoon of the pea purée in an uneven layer over the prosciutto, leaving the edges of the prosciutto exposed. Use a sharp knife or a vegetable peeler to cut or shave enough very thin slices from the wedge of Parmesan to scatter a few slices over each of the crostino and drizzle them with high-quality extra-virgin olive oil.

4 ½-inch-thick slices from a bâtard (or 8 slices from a baguette or 2 slices from a large round rustic white loaf, cut in half)
Extra-virgin olive oil, for brushing the bread
1 garlic clove

FOR THE PEA PURÉE

1 15-ounce can French **petite peas** (about 1½ cups), rinsed and drained
⅔ cup **extra-virgin olive oil**
1 large garlic clove, grated or minced (about 1 teaspoon)
1 teaspoon kosher salt

2–4 thin slices **prosciutto** (depending on their size; about 2 ounces)
Parmigiano-Reggiano wedge, for shaving
High-quality **extra-virgin olive oil,** for drizzling

Crostini with Smoked Trout, Crème Fraîche, and Dill

Smoked fish with crème fraîche and dill is a classic combination. These crostini are like a smoked-fish plate assembled on little toasts. You can find smoked trout at your local fish market or vacuum-packed in specialty food stores.

20 MINUTES

Adjust the oven rack to the middle position and preheat the oven to 350°F.

Crumble the trout into a small bowl in roughly 1½-inch-long pieces. Drizzle with the olive oil and lemon juice, toss, and set it aside to marinate while you prepare the rest of the ingredients.

Place the bread slices on a baking sheet, brush the tops with olive oil, and bake them for 15 to 20 minutes, until they're lightly toasted and golden brown. (You can also toast the bread in a toaster, but *without* the oil. Then brush the toast with oil after they're done.) Rub the oiled side of the crostini with the garlic and set them on your work surface, oiled side up.

Stir the crème fraîche, dill, shallot, and a pinch of kosher salt together in a small bowl.

Spoon a heaping tablespoon of the crème fraîche mixture in an uneven layer on each crostino, leaving the edges of the toast visible. Divide the trout evenly among the crostini and drizzle the marinade left in the bowl over the trout. Top each crostino with three dill sprigs and a few drops of lemon juice.

1 ounce smoked trout

1 teaspoon **extra-virgin olive oil,** plus extra for brushing on the bread

1 teaspoon fresh lemon juice

4 ½-inch-thick slices from a bâtard (or 8 slices from a baguette or 2 slices from a large round rustic white loaf, cut in half)

1 garlic clove

¼ cup **crème fraîche** (or sour cream)

3 tablespoons chopped fresh dill, plus 12 small dill sprigs

1 small shallot, grated or minced (about 1 teaspoon)

Kosher salt

Lemon, for squeezing over the crostini

Crostini with Soft-Scrambled Egg, Black Olive Tapenade, and Caper-Stuffed Anchovies

These toasts are very hearty. While I think one person could eat four of the crostini in this book, I can't imagine anyone wanting more than two of these. Anchovies rolled up with capers and marinated in oil look really pretty on top of the eggs, but if you can't find them, top each crostino with an anchovy fillet stuffed with a caper that you have rolled up yourself.

Adjust the oven rack to the middle position and preheat the oven to 350°F. Place the bread slices on a baking sheet, brush the tops with olive oil, and bake them for 15 to 20 minutes, until they're lightly toasted and golden brown. (You can also toast the bread in a toaster, but *without* the oil. Then brush the toast with oil after they're done.) Rub the oiled side of the crostini with the garlic and set them on your work surface, oiled side up.

If the tapenade is thick and pastelike, put it in a small bowl and stir in a tablespoon or two of olive oil until you obtain a loose, spoonable consistency.

Whisk the eggs with the kosher salt in a small bowl. Melt the butter in a large nonstick skillet over medium heat. When the butter starts to bubble, pour the eggs into the skillet. Using a heatproof rubber spatula, scrape down the sides and bottom of the pan, folding the egg over itself, keeping it continuously moving. Cook for 2 to 3 minutes, until the egg forms large curds but is only very softly scrambled and still wet looking in places.

Pile the scrambled egg on top of the toast, dividing it evenly and leaving the edges of the toast visible. Sprinkle the egg with sea salt, spoon about 1 teaspoon of tapenade on each serving, and top with a caper-stuffed anchovy. Drizzle with the high-quality extra-virgin olive oil and use scissors to snip about 1/4 teaspoon chives over each crostino.

4 1/2-inch-thick slices from a bâtard (or 8 slices from a baguette or 2 slices from a large round rustic white loaf, cut in half)

Extra-virgin olive oil, for brushing the bread and for thinning the tapenade if necessary

1 garlic clove

1 heaping tablespoon black **olive tapenade**

4 large eggs

1/4 teaspoon kosher salt

2 tablespoons unsalted butter

Sea salt

4 caper-stuffed **anchovy fillets** (or 4 anchovy fillets and 4 **capers,** rinsed)

High-quality **extra-virgin olive oil,** for drizzling

5 fresh chives

Crostini with White Bean Purée, Rosemary Olive Oil, and Aged Balsamic Vinegar

I love white bean purée, but I'm also very particular about it. It needs to be slightly chunky, seasoned with plenty of salt, and filled with a pool of olive oil. As long as you do these things, it's going to be delicious. And starting with canned beans, which I'd never done before writing this book, makes the preparation incredibly easy. Unlike the other recipes in this chapter, this recipe makes sixteen crostini, enough to use up all the white bean purée. I've never heard of bottled rosemary-infused olive oil, but my editor, Leyla, says it exists. If you find some and it tastes good, of course you can use it in place of the rosemary olive oil in this recipe.

1/2 CUP   **20 MINUTES**

Adjust the oven rack to the middle position and preheat the oven to 350°F.

To make the rosemary olive oil, combine the olive oil and rosemary in a small saucepan over medium heat and bring to a simmer. Lower the heat and continue to gently simmer the oil until the rosemary begins to sizzle. Turn off the heat and let the rosemary steep in the oil while you prepare the remaining ingredients.

Place the bread slices on a baking sheet, brush the tops with olive oil, and bake them for 15 to 20 minutes, until they're lightly toasted and golden brown. (You can also toast the bread in a toaster, but *without* the oil. Then brush the toast with oil after they're done.) Rub the oiled side of the crostini with the garlic and set them on your work surface, oiled side up.

To make the white bean purée, combine the beans, 2/3 cup of the rosemary-infused olive oil, garlic, and kosher salt together in a large mortar or bowl and mash them with a pestle or potato masher until they're mostly mashed but still slightly chunky.

Place a few arugula leaves on each crostino and spoon 1 heaping table-spoon of the white bean purée in a generous, uneven layer over the arugula, leaving the edges of the toast visible. Use the back of a small spoon to make a crater in each mound of bean purée and spoon about 1/2 teaspoon of the rosemary oil into each crater. Drizzle balsamic vinegar on the bean purée around each crater, and sprinkle the crostini with sea salt.

FOR THE ROSEMARY OLIVE OIL
3/4 cup **extra-virgin olive oil**
1 heaping tablespoon chopped fresh rosemary leaves

16 1/2-inch-thick slices from a bâtard (or 32 slices from a baguette or 8 slices from a large round rustic white loaf, cut in half)
Extra-virgin olive oil, for brushing the bread
1 or 2 garlic cloves

FOR THE WHITE BEAN PURÉE
1 15-ounce can cannellini **beans** or borlotti beans, rinsed and drained
1 small garlic clove, grated or minced (about 1/2 teaspoon)
1 teaspoon kosher salt

1 cup loosely packed arugula leaves
Aged **balsamic vinegar,** for drizzling
Sea salt

Crostini with Fresh Ricotta, Artichoke Hearts, and Currant–Pine Nut Relish

This was probably the most popular item on the mozzarella menu I served at Jar. For this version, I use prepared artichoke hearts, which means the only thing you have to cook is the relish. These crostini are perfect when prepared as below, but they're even prettier topped with a thin shaving of Parmesan. This is no reason to go out and buy a wedge, but if you happen to have one on hand, use it.

20 MINUTES

Adjust the oven rack to the middle position and preheat the oven to 325°F.

To make the relish, spread the pine nuts on a baking sheet and toast them in the oven for 8 to 10 minutes, shaking the pan occasionally for even toasting, until they're lightly browned and fragrant. Remove the nuts from the oven and set them aside to cool slightly.

Combine the balsamic vinegar, currants, onion, garlic, arbol chile, rosemary, and kosher salt together in a small saucepan over high heat and bring to a simmer. Reduce the heat to medium-low and continue simmering the mixture for about 8 minutes, until it forms a thick and syrupy glaze. Stir in the pine nuts and olive oil and simmer for about 30 seconds longer to infuse the flavors.

Increase the oven temperature to 350°F.

Place the bread slices on a baking sheet, brush the tops with olive oil, and bake them for 15 to 20 minutes, until they're lightly toasted and golden brown. (You can also toast the bread in a toaster, but *without* the oil. Then brush the toast with oil after they're done.) Rub the oiled side of the crostini with the garlic and set them on your work surface, oiled side up.

Mix the ricotta in a small bowl with enough olive oil to obtain a loose, spoonable consistency and season with kosher salt to taste.

Spoon about 2 tablespoons of ricotta in an uneven layer on each crostino, leaving the edges of the toast visible. Place 1 artichoke heart on each and fan out the leaves of the artichoke hearts to create a sort of flower. Spoon 1 teaspoon of the currant–pine nut relish over each crostino.

FOR THE CURRANT–PINE NUT RELISH

1/4 cup pine nuts

1/2 cup **balsamic vinegar**

1/2 cup dried currants

1/2 cup finely chopped red onion or shallots

4 large garlic cloves, grated or minced (about 1 tablespoon)

1 dried **arbol chile**

2 fresh rosemary sprigs

1 teaspoon kosher salt, plus extra for seasoning

1/4 cup **extra-virgin olive oil**

4 1/2-inch-thick slices from a bâtard (or 8 slices from a baguette or 2 slices from a large round rustic white loaf, cut in half)

Extra-virgin olive oil, for brushing the bread and for thinning the ricotta

1 garlic clove

1/2 cup fresh **ricotta**

Kosher salt

4 whole marinated **artichoke hearts** (from the deli case or jarred)

TRADITIONAL-STYLE ENTRÉES

When I first conceived of this book, I envisioned egg dishes, salad meals, dressed-up soups, and desserts assembled from good packaged ingredients and premium ice cream. But I didn't imagine a lot of traditional-style entrées. So I was surprised when I started working on the book and these dishes were the first that I wanted to make. And as you can see by the number of recipes in this chapter, once I started, I couldn't stop.

Many of these recipes are the quick versions of tried-and-true meals I've had at Campanile or other restaurants—only this time using ready-made ingredients to make things more manageable. Although I've never done this in past cookbooks—or ever cooked this way—I'm willing to concede that it's the easiest way to re-create the kind of complexity involved in restaurant food, where many components play together to make a dish complete.

In other instances the can or jar came before the dish. After trying canned stuffed grape leaves, for instance, I was so pleasantly surprised by how good they tasted that I invented a dish to use them in: Pomegranate-Glazed Lamb Chops with Stuffed Grape Leaves and Tahini Sauce. The same thing happened with a can of giant white beans in tomato sauce. I tasted them, liked them, and then thought of how I might use them if I'd made them from scratch: Sea Bass with Giant White Beans and Red Pepper Mayonnaise.

To keep cooking times down, I also paid special attention to the cuts of meats I used. I chose only those that didn't require marinating and that cooked in a short time. I stayed away from some of my favorite cuts, like porterhouse steak, which has a bone and needs to be cut thick and therefore takes a long time to cook. Instead, I used filet and skirt steak, both of which can be sliced thin and cook very quickly. The same goes for lamb chops, lamb steak (which does have a bone but doesn't take long to cook), and pork loin—none of which I'd ever cooked much, or at all, before working on this book.

Seafood cooks quickly in general, so the only consideration I took there was to use fillets, which don't require any preparation, such as boning, instead of whole fish. I also avoided any tedious shellfish preparations and instead took advantage of good quality cooked crab and shrimp for the Crab and Shrimp Cakes with Celery Root Rémoulade.

Another item I used in these recipes that I'd never tried before were meat rubs. These are prepared mixes of different herbs and spices that are sold at butcher stores and at the meat counters of specialty food stores. I was amazed to find how pure their ingredient lists were. Those I bought contained the same spices I would use to season the particular meat they were designed to season, and no MSG or anything else that doesn't belong in food. I found the rubs far superior to the bottled marinades I tasted, which contained all kinds of stabilizers and preservatives and tasted synthetic.

In shopping for the recipes in this chapter, I've given you the shortcuts where I can—such as cooked shrimp and crab, bottled onions, canned beans, hassle-free vegetables, and wonderful seasoning condiments such as saba and lemon-infused olive oil. But there are some places where there is no compromise for freshness. Buy the best sushi-grade tuna, the freshest halibut you can find (and if you can't find fresh halibut, use another fresh white-fleshed fish instead), and organic, naturally raised chicken, beef, pork, and lamb. Don't forget that when substituting the fish called for in a recipe you should adjust the cooking time. I found that as long as it's bought from a reliable source, precooked shrimp and crab are often better than when bought raw because they're cooked just after they're caught.

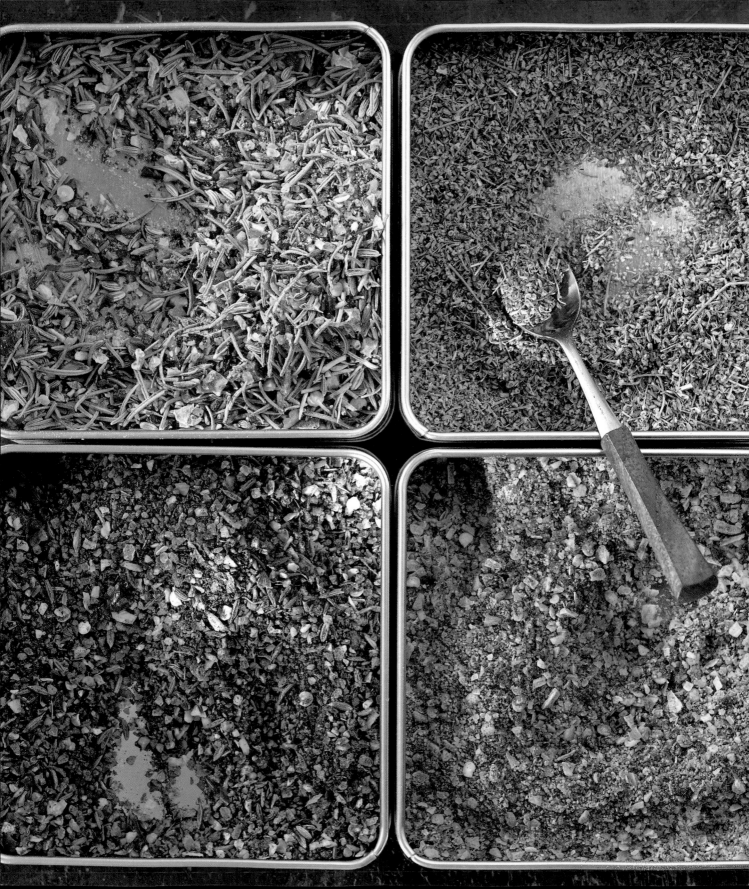

BEEF AND VEAL

Skirt Steak with Mediterranean Herb Butter and Garlicky Broccolini

This is an elevated version of your basic meat and vegetable plate. Broccolini is a hybrid of broccoli rabe and asparagus. It's just as flavorful but doesn't have the bitterness of broccoli rabe. Here, I cook it with jarred whole garlic: the whole cloves are peeled and pickled and have a trace of vinegar flavor that's nice in these greens. This steak is topped with a compound butter, which is butter flavored with the addition of other ingredients. Generally it is made in advance and refrigerated until it's solid. For this book, I just spoon it on soft. Skirt steak comes in very large pieces—at some stores, it's sold rolled up. A single skirt steak can vary in thickness from 1/4 inch to 1 inch at different places on the cut. For this reason, you need to be careful not to overcook it. The cooking times I give here are for 1-inch-thick steaks cooked rare to medium-rare. For medium, cook them for 1 minute longer on each side. When slicing the cooked steak, make sure you're cutting it against the grain. Skirt steak is a really tender cut of meat, but if you cut it with the grain, it can be tough.

30 MINUTES

To make the herb butter, stir the butter, mustard, parsley, tarragon, capers, anchovies, cornichons, garlic, and sea salt together in a small bowl.

To prepare the broccolini, heat 1 tablespoon of the olive oil with the garlic cloves and a pinch of kosher salt in a large skillet over high heat and sauté for about 6 minutes, stirring occasionally, until the garlic is golden. Reduce the heat to medium and add the remaining 2 tablespoons of olive oil, the broccolini, another pinch of salt, and a pinch of chile flakes. Stir to coat the broccolini with the hot oil. Add 3 tablespoons of water, cover the skillet, and cook, stirring occasionally, for about 5 minutes, until the water has evaporated.

Cut the skirt steak into pieces that will fit in the skillet you're using and season both sides of the steaks with kosher salt and freshly ground black pepper.

FOR THE HERB BUTTER

1/2 stick (4 tablespoons) unsalted butter, softened to room temperature but not greasy

2 teaspoons whole-grain **mustard**

2 teaspoons finely chopped fresh Italian parsley leaves

2 teaspoons finely chopped fresh tarragon leaves

2 teaspoons **capers,** rinsed

2 **anchovy fillets,** coarsely chopped

2 **cornichons,** minced

1 small garlic clove, grated or minced (about 1/2 teaspoon)

1/4 teaspoon sea salt

Heat 2 tablespoons of the canola oil in a large skillet over high heat for 2 to 3 minutes, until the oil's almost smoking (you will begin to smell the oil at that point). Add half of the steaks and sear them for 2 minutes (1 minute for very thin steaks), until the surfaces are nicely browned. Turn the steaks and sear for 2 minutes on the other side (1 minute for very thin steaks), until the meat is nicely browned. Transfer the steaks to a plate and repeat, heating the remaining oil and cooking the remaining steaks in the same way.

Place the steaks first-cooked side up and slice them 1/4 inch thick against the grain at an angle. Divide the slices among four plates and drizzle them with the juices from the plate they were resting on. Smear the butter over the center of the steaks in a thick layer so it just begins to melt around the edges but is still visible, and place the broccolini to the side of the steaks.

FOR THE BROCCOLINI

3 tablespoons **extra-virgin olive oil**

20 whole **pickled garlic** cloves, drained (from 1 2 1/4-ounce jar; about 1/3 cup)

Kosher salt

14 ounces broccolini, ends trimmed (about 24 pieces or 2 bunches)

Chile flakes

1 1/2 pounds skirt steak

Kosher salt and freshly ground black pepper

1/4 cup canola oil

Peppered Skirt Steak with Spicy Tomato-Curry Garbanzo Beans and Tangy Greek Yogurt Sauce

There are a lot of good jarred curries out there, but I chose Patak's brand because it's not only delicious but also easy to find—places from specialty shops such as Whole Foods to standard supermarket chains carry it. Regarding how to prepare skirt steak, see my note on page 130.

25 MINUTES

To make the yogurt sauce, stir the yogurt, garlic, lemon juice, and kosher salt together in a small bowl.

Cut the skirt steak into pieces that will fit in the skillet you're using, and season both sides of the steaks with kosher salt and freshly ground black pepper. Heat 2 tablespoons of the canola oil in a large skillet over high heat for 2 to 3 minutes, until the oil's almost smoking (you will begin to smell the oil at that point). Add half of the steaks and sear them for 2 minutes (1 minute for very thin steaks), until the surfaces are nicely browned. Turn the steaks and sear for 2 minutes on the other side (1 minute for very thin steaks), until the meat is nicely browned. Transfer the steaks to a plate and repeat, heating the remaining oil and cooking the remaining steaks in the same way.

Meanwhile, combine the garbanzo beans with the tomato and cardamom sauce in a small saucepan over medium heat, stirring occasionally, to warm them through, about 5 minutes. Turn off the heat and stir in the parsley.

Divide the spinach equally among four plates and sprinkle it with sea salt. Slice the steak at an angle against the grain into 1/4-inch-thick slices. Place the steak slices on top of the spinach, dividing them evenly among the plates, and drizzle them with the juices from the plate they were resting on. Spoon the curried garbanzo beans over the steaks, dollop the yogurt sauce on the garbanzo beans, and sprinkle with parsley.

FOR THE YOGURT SAUCE

1/2 cup strained whole-milk **Greek yogurt**

1 large garlic clove, grated or minced (about 1 teaspoon)

2 tablespoons fresh lemon juice

1 teaspoon kosher salt

1 1/2 pounds skirt steak

Kosher salt and freshly ground black pepper

1/4 cup canola oil (or other neutral-flavored oil)

1 15-ounce can garbanzo **beans,** rinsed and drained (about 1 1/2 cups)

1 10-ounce can **Patak's** Spicy Tomato & Cardamom Sauce (about 1 cup)

1/2 cup finely chopped fresh Italian parsley leaves, plus extra for garnish

4 cups loosely packed baby spinach leaves

Seared Beef Filet with White Beans, Bitter Greens, and Black Olive Tapenade

A version of this dish has been on the Campanile menu since day one. I re-created it for this book using jarred olive tapenade and canned beans—and it's still as delicious as ever.

30 MINUTES

Heat the olive oil in a large skillet over high heat for 2 to 3 minutes, until the oil's almost smoking (you will begin to smell the oil at that point). Add the arugula to the skillet and let it sit for about 30 seconds without stirring. Season it with a pinch or two of kosher salt, add the garlic, and cook, stirring, for another 30 seconds, until some of the leaves are just wilted but some remain bright green. (Some of the leaves may brown slightly, which is fine; it lends a nice flavor to the dish.) Add the beans and 1/2 cup of water. Stir to incorporate, and cook the mixture for about 2 minutes, until it's warmed through.

Season both sides of the steaks with kosher salt and freshly ground black pepper. Heat the canola oil in a large skillet over high heat for 2 to 3 minutes, until the oil's almost smoking (you will begin to smell the oil at that point). Place the steaks in the skillet and sear them on one side for 2 minutes if you want them medium-rare, 4 minutes for medium. Flip the steaks, turn off the heat, and let them sit in the skillet until the skillet goes quiet, about 3 minutes.

If the tapenade is thick and pastelike, put it in a small bowl and stir in a tablespoon or two of olive oil until you obtain a loose, spoonable consistency.

Spoon the beans and greens mixture onto four plates, dividing it evenly. Place the steaks with the first-cooked sides up in the center of each plate and smear the tapenade on the steaks.

1/4 cup **extra-virgin olive oil,** plus more for thinning the tapenade if necessary

5 cups loosely packed arugula leaves (or a mixture of arugula and radicchio)

Kosher salt

2 large garlic cloves, grated or minced (about 2 teaspoons)

1 15-ounce can cannellini **beans** (about 1 1/2 cups), rinsed and drained

4 6-ounce beef filets (about 3/4 inch thick)

Freshly ground black pepper

1/4 cup canola oil (or other neutral-flavored oil)

2 teaspoons black **olive tapenade**

Tagliatta

Tagliatta is a classic Italian dish of sliced steak often topped with arugula and Parmesan. The name comes from the word *tagliare,* which means "to cut" in Italian. I don't call for the meat to be sliced in this version even though that's how the dish got its name. If you have a jar of the "extra vecchio" (super-good and super-expensive) balsamic vinegar, a few drops sprinkled over the Parmesan cheese tastes great. If you serve it on a large slice of toasted rosemary or olive bread, it also makes a delicious open-faced sandwich.

20 MINUTES

To prepare the beef filets, lay them on a flat cutting surface and run a large sharp knife horizontally through the center of each filet lengthwise, stopping just before you cut all the way through. Butterfly the filets open and press down on them gently to flatten them out.

Stir the balsamic vinegar, olive oil, and rosemary together in a baking dish large enough to hold the butterflied filets in a single layer. Place the meat in the marinade, turn it, and rub it with your fingers to coat all sides of the meat with the marinade.

Warm 2 teaspoons of the canola oil in a large nonstick skillet over high heat for 2 to 3 minutes, until the oil's almost smoking (you will begin to smell the oil at that point). Lift two of the steaks out of the marinade and season both sides with kosher salt and freshly ground black pepper. Place the steaks in the skillet to sear for 1½ to 2 minutes, flip them, and sear them on the other side for 10 seconds, just long enough to brown the surface and warm the meat. Transfer the filets to a plate and repeat with the other two filets, heating the remaining teaspoon of canola oil and cooking the remaining two steaks in the same way.

Use a sharp knife or a vegetable peeler to cut or shave 25 to 30 very thin slices from the wedge of Parmesan.

Place one filet first-cooked side up on each of four plates and drizzle the steaks with the juices from the plate they were resting on. Pile a handful of arugula on top of each filet, using only half of the arugula, and season it with sea salt and a few grindings of black pepper. Scatter a few slices of Parmesan cheese over each serving and drizzle the arugula and Parmesan cheese with the high-quality olive oil and a few drops of balsamic vinegar. Repeat, building the second layer of the salad the same as the first.

4 6-ounce beef filets (about 1 inch thick)

⅓ cup aged **balsamic vinegar,** plus extra for drizzling

3 tablespoons **extra-virgin olive oil**

3 tablespoons chopped fresh rosemary leaves

1 tablespoon canola oil (or other neutral-flavored oil)

Kosher salt and freshly ground black pepper

Parmigiano-Reggiano wedge, for shaving

12 cups loosely packed arugula leaves

Sea salt

High-quality **extra-virgin olive oil,** for drizzling

Seared Beef Filet with Horseradish-Spiked Mashed Potatoes and Horseradish Cream

When I first started experimenting with canned potatoes, I was surprised to find so many uses for them; I didn't think I'd find any at all! They turned out to be a good, quick alternative to cooking fresh potatoes, as long as they're marinated, cooked with other spices, or, in this case, mashed with butter, crème fraîche, and horseradish. These mashed potatoes may be lumpy even after you purée them, which is fine. Purée-ing them to a uniform paste is exactly what you don't want to do.

30 MINUTES

To prepare the horseradish cream, stir the grated horseradish, crème fraîche, prepared horseradish, kosher salt, Tabasco, Worcestershire, and freshly ground black pepper together in a small bowl.

To make the mashed potatoes, break the potatoes up into 1-inch pieces. Combine them in a medium saucepan with the cream, butter, garlic, and salt. Put the pan over high heat and bring the potatoes to a boil, stirring often. Reduce the heat and simmer the potatoes for 5 minutes, stirring occasionally. Remove the pan from the heat and use a handheld immersion blender to purée the potatoes for 10 to 15 seconds, until they're mashed but still slightly lumpy (or mash them with a potato masher or purée them in a food mill). Stir in the crème fraîche and cover.

Season both sides of the steaks with kosher salt and freshly ground black pepper. Heat the canola oil in a large skillet over high heat for 2 to 3 minutes, until the oil's almost smoking (you will begin to smell the oil at this point). Place the steaks in the skillet and sear them on one side for 2 minutes if you want them medium-rare, 4 minutes for medium. Flip the steaks, turn off the heat, and let them sit in the skillet until the skillet goes quiet, about 3 minutes.

Spoon the potatoes onto each of four plates, dividing them evenly and smashing them down slightly to create a bed for the steak. Grate about 1 tablespoon of fresh horseradish and use scissors to snip about 1 tablespoon of chives over each serving. Lay the steaks on the potatoes first-cooked side up, dollop 1 tablespoon of the horseradish cream on each steak and serve with the remaining horseradish cream on the side.

FOR THE HORSERADISH CREAM

¼ cup grated peeled fresh horse-radish (from 1 2-inch piece)

2 tablespoons **crème fraîche** (or sour cream)

1 heaping tablespoon **prepared horseradish**

1 teaspoon kosher salt

10 drops **Tabasco** sauce

2 drops Worcestershire sauce

Freshly ground black pepper

FOR THE POTATOES

16 canned or jarred **potatoes** (from 2 12-ounce jars or 2 15-ounce cans)

½ cup cream

2 tablespoons unsalted butter

4 large garlic cloves, grated or minced (about 1 tablespoon)

1 teaspoon kosher salt

2 tablespoons **crème fraîche** (or sour cream)

4 6-ounce beef filets (about ¾ inch thick)

Kosher salt and freshly ground black pepper

¼ cup canola oil (or other neutral-flavored oil)

Peeled fresh horseradish, for grating

30 fresh chives

Seared Beef Filet with Black Beans, Avocado, and Green Chile Salsa

The salsa added to these black beans has all the flavors you need to turn simple canned beans into something worthy of the filet you're putting on top of them.

30 MINUTES

Heat the olive oil, garlic, and a pinch of kosher salt in a medium saucepan over medium-high heat and sauté for about 1½ minutes, until the garlic is soft and fragrant, stirring constantly so the garlic doesn't brown. Turn the heat up to high, add the salsa, and cook for about 2 minutes to warm it through, stirring often to keep the salsa from scorching. Add the black beans, reduce the heat to low, and cook for 3 to 4 minutes to warm the beans through and meld the flavors. Turn off the heat and stir in the cilantro.

Season both sides of each steak with the kosher salt and freshly ground black pepper. Heat the canola oil in a large skillet over high heat for 2 to 3 minutes, until the oil's almost smoking (you will begin to smell the oil at this point). Place the steaks in the skillet and sear them on one side for 2 minutes if you want them medium-rare, 4 minutes for medium. Flip the steaks, turn off the heat, and let them sit in the skillet until the skillet goes quiet, about 3 minutes.

Spoon the black beans onto four plates, dividing them evenly. Place the beef filets first-cooked side up on top of the beans. Halve the avocado, remove the pit, and cut each half crosswise into quarters. (If you're using tiny avocados, cut each avocado in half.) Remove and discard the peel and place one quarter on each filet. Drizzle the avocado with the high-quality olive oil, a few drops of lime juice, sea salt, and freshly ground black pepper. Top with a sprig of cilantro.

¼ cup **extra-virgin olive oil**

2 large garlic cloves, grated or minced (about 2 teaspoons)

2 teaspoons kosher salt, plus extra for seasoning

1 cup **green chile salsa**

1 15-ounce can black **beans,** rinsed and drained (about 1½ cups)

¼ cup chopped fresh cilantro leaves, plus 4 whole sprigs for garnish

4 6-ounce beef filets (about ¾ inch thick)

Freshly ground black pepper

¼ cup canola oil (or other neutral-flavored oil)

1 ripe (or 2 tiny) Hass avocado

High-quality **extra-virgin olive oil,** for drizzling

Lime, for squeezing over the avocado

Sea salt

Chasen's Chili
Suzanne Goin • Lucques, Los Angeles

Every year at Lucques, we have a theme to our New Year's Eve dinner. A few years ago, the theme was Old Hollywood. I researched a lot of menus from various old-school Hollywood restaurants, one of which was Chasen's. Chasen's was a legendary restaurant in Beverly Hills that closed in 1995, equally known for its celebrity clientele as for its chili. I didn't eat at Chasen's when I was little because my dad was a Los Feliz–born anti-westsider, so we never crossed La Cienega except to go to the beach. Still, having grown up in Los Angeles, and especially now, I'd heard about the chili. For our New Year's feast, I jazzed it up a little and made it with pork as well as beef. I usually start with dried pinto beans and a slow-cooked pork shoulder, but I adapted the recipe for Nancy's book. I specify "chili grind" for the beef. If your butcher isn't familiar with this term or they don't sell beef labeled as such at your grocery store, request meat ground coarser than it is for hamburger.

•

Although an hour and ten minutes seems like a long time when you want to get dinner on the table, the actual prep time for making this chili is about 30 minutes. After that, it just needs time to simmer. While it's simmering you may want to toast some thick slices of country bread, sprinkle them with grated Cheddar cheese, and melt them under the broiler. Suzanne serves these toasts on the rim of each bowl of chili.
—Nancy

1 HOUR 10 MINUTES

Combine the beans (including their juice) and the chicken broth in a large saucepan and bring to a low simmer over high heat. Add the tomatoes and return to a low simmer, reduce the heat, and continue to simmer the mixture while you prepare the rest of the chili.

Heat a large skillet over medium-high heat for 2 minutes. Add the olive oil, arbol chile, and rosemary sprig and cook for 1 minute. Add the bell pepper and sauté for about 5 minutes to soften it. Add the onion and thyme and cook, stirring often, until the onion is tender, about 8 minutes. Stir in the parsley and garlic and cook for another minute to soften the garlic, stirring constantly so the garlic doesn't brown. Transfer the pepper-onion mixture to a bowl and remove the rosemary sprig.

Melt the butter in the same skillet over high heat. Add the ground pork and ground beef and cook the meats until they're brown all over, about 8 minutes. Season the meat with kosher salt and freshly ground black pepper and add the pepper-onion mixture. Stir in the chile powder and cumin, and cook for about 10 minutes to meld the flavors. Add this mixture to the simmering beans and simmer the chili, covered, for 20 minutes. Uncover the pot and simmer the chili for another 10 minutes. Season with more kosher salt or freshly ground black pepper if necessary.

Ladle the chili into four large soup plates or bowls, spoon a generous dollop of crème fraîche over each serving, and use scissors to snip the chives into 1-inch pieces over the chili.

2 15-ounce cans pinto **beans** (about 3 cups), not drained

3 cups chicken **broth** (or water)

2 14.5-ounce cans whole **San Marzano tomatoes,** diced (about 2½ cups)

1 tablespoon **extra-virgin olive oil**

1 **arbol chile,** crumbled with your hands

1 fresh rosemary sprig

1 large red bell pepper, diced

1 large yellow onion, diced

1 tablespoon fresh thyme leaves

¼ cup roughly chopped fresh Italian parsley leaves

4 large garlic cloves, grated or minced (about 1 tablespoon)

1 tablespoon unsalted butter

¾ pound ground pork

¾ pound chili grind beef

Kosher salt and freshly ground black pepper

¼ cup chile powder

2 teaspoons ground cumin

½ cup **crème fraîche** (or sour cream)

10 fresh chives

Chopped Sirloin on Toast Topped with a Fried Egg and Green Peppercorn Sauce
Suzanne Tracht • Jar, Los Angeles

Jar is one of my favorite restaurants in Los Angeles and this dish is one of my favorite things to order there. I've always loved the combo of fried eggs and ground steak. I really wanted this recipe in the book and because the green peppercorns come from a jar (or can), they were my excuse to include it. Besides, they're so prominent in the dish—they're what makes the sauce distinctive—that it didn't seem like too much of a stretch. —Nancy

40 MINUTES

To make the sauce, heat the oil with the shallot and garlic in a large, heavy-bottomed saucepan over medium-high heat and sauté for about 1½ minutes, until the shallot is soft and the garlic is soft and fragrant, stirring constantly so the garlic doesn't brown. Add the peppercorns and continue cooking for another minute, stirring frequently and being careful not to let the garlic brown. Season with kosher salt and freshly ground black pepper. Add the flour and stir to mix well. Add the wine and thyme sprigs and stir to combine. Bring the wine to a simmer, reduce the heat, and continue to simmer for 2 minutes. Add the stock, return the heat to high, and bring to a boil. Reduce the heat and simmer the sauce for about 20 minutes, until it's reduced by half. Just before serving, stir in the butter.

Combine the chopped sirloin, one of the eggs, parsley, kosher salt, and freshly ground black pepper together in a large bowl and mix it with your hands just until the ingredients are thoroughly combined. Form the meat into four equally sized thick patties, shaping the patties to fit on the bread slices.

Heat the oil in a large skillet over high heat for 2 to 3 minutes, until the oil's almost smoking (you will begin to smell the oil at that point). Place the patties in the skillet to sear for about 2 minutes per side for rare, 3 minutes per side for medium-rare. Remove the patties from the skillet and place them on a plate while you toast the bread and fry the eggs.

FOR THE SAUCE

2 tablespoons canola oil (or other neutral-flavored oil)

1 small shallot, grated or minced (about 1 teaspoon)

1 large garlic clove, grated or minced (about 1 teaspoon)

4 tablespoons green peppercorns in brine (about 2 ounces), drained

Kosher salt and freshly ground black pepper

2 tablespoons all-purpose flour

1¼ cups red wine, such as Cabernet Sauvignon

2 fresh thyme sprigs (or ¼ teaspoon dried thyme)

2 cups veal **stock** (or beef or chicken **broth**)

½ tablespoon unsalted butter

Toast the bread in a toaster, then brush it on one side with the melted butter.

To fry the eggs, heat the olive oil in a large nonstick skillet over high heat for 2 to 3 minutes, until the oil's almost smoking (you will begin to smell the oil at that point). Break one egg into a small bowl, and then transfer it to the skillet. Let it just begin to set around the edges, then break the second egg into the bowl and pour it into the skillet. (By waiting a moment before adding the second egg, the eggs won't set together and will be easy to separate and serve individually.) Cook them for about 1½ minutes, until the whites are set and the edges are golden and crispy but the yolks are still runny. Remove the eggs to a plate and cook the remaining two eggs in the same way.

Place one piece of toast buttered side up on each of four plates and set the sirloin burgers on top of them. Hold back about 4 teaspoons of the peppercorn sauce for garnishing the egg and pour the remaining sauce over and around the burgers, letting the sauce flow around the toast so the toast can absorb it. Place a fried egg on top of each burger and sprinkle the egg with sea salt and the remaining peppercorn sauce.

1½ pounds chopped sirloin

5 large eggs

1 tablespoon finely chopped fresh Italian parsley leaves

2 teaspoons kosher salt

1 teaspoon freshly ground black pepper

1 tablespoon canola oil (or other neutral-flavored oil)

4 1-inch-thick slices from a large round rustic loaf

1 tablespoon unsalted butter, melted

¼ cup **extra-virgin olive oil**

Sea salt

Veal Involtini with Artichoke Leaf Sauce

Involtini are thin slices of fish or meat—in this case veal—that are stuffed and rolled. Artichoke leaves make a delicate and really pretty sauce.

40 MINUTES

Adjust the oven rack to the middle position and preheat the oven to 500°F. Combine the breadcrumbs, olive oil, arugula, anchovies, and garlic in a food processor.

Lay the veal cutlets out on a flat work surface and season both sides with kosher salt and freshly ground black pepper. Spoon about 2 tablespoons of the breadcrumb mixture onto each cutlet and spread it out in a thin layer. Roll up each cutlet and stick a toothpick through each roll to keep it closed. Line up the rolls in a large baking pan or an ovenproof skillet, making sure they're not touching one another, drizzle with enough olive oil to prevent the veal from drying out, and turn to coat them on all sides. Place the veal in the oven and bake for 10 minutes, until the meat is cooked through.

To prepare the sauce, pull the leaves off the artichoke hearts. (If there are any hearts left, snack on them!)

Heat the olive oil, garlic, and a pinch of kosher salt in a large skillet over medium-high heat and sauté them until the garlic is soft and fragrant, about 1½ minutes, stirring constantly so the garlic doesn't brown. Turn the heat up to high, add the artichoke leaves and the teaspoon of kosher salt, and sauté for 2½ to 3 minutes, stirring constantly, until the leaves start to brown and the water released from the leaves is cooked out.

Scatter the artichoke leaves on four plates, dividing them evenly. Place three veal rolls on each plate, scatter the arugula over them, drizzle them with the high-quality olive oil, and season with sea salt to taste.

2 cups **breadcrumbs** or 30 **saltine crackers,** ground to fine crumbs

⅓ cup **extra-virgin olive oil,** plus extra for drizzling

3 cups loosely packed arugula leaves, plus extra for garnishing

6 **anchovy fillets,** finely chopped

3 large garlic cloves, grated or minced (about 1 tablespoon)

12 2-ounce veal cutlets

Kosher salt and freshly ground black pepper

FOR THE SAUCE

16 whole **artichokes** (in water), rinsed and drained

½ cup **extra-virgin olive oil**

4 large garlic cloves, grated or minced (about 1 tablespoon)

1 teaspoon kosher salt

High-quality **extra-virgin olive oil,** for drizzling

Sea salt

PORK

Italian Sausage with Giant White Beans, Radicchio, and Roasted Onions

If you've made another recipe that called for Garlic Mayonnaise (page 33) and happen to have some left over in the refrigerator, a dollop of it on the plate makes a delicious addition to this hearty, rustic dish.

45 MINUTES

Heat the oil in a large nonstick skillet over medium-high heat for 2 to 3 minutes, until the oil's almost smoking (you will begin to smell the oil at that point). Add the sausages and cook, turning them often for even browning, for about 10 minutes, until they're browned all over but not cooked through. Move the sausages to the side of the skillet to continue to cook while you sear the radicchio. Put a couple of radicchio leaves in the skillet in a single layer and cook them for about 45 seconds on each side, until they're seared and wilted slightly. Remove the leaves to a plate and cook the remaining leaves in the same way, adding a bit more oil to the pan if it's dry. While you sear the radicchio leaves, continue to cook and turn the sausages for another 10 minutes, until they're cooked through, and transfer them to a plate when they're done.

Add a bit more olive oil if necessary to coat the skillet. Add the onions, garlic, and a pinch of kosher salt and sauté for about 1½ minutes, until the onions are soft and the garlic is soft and fragrant, stirring constantly so the garlic doesn't brown. Reduce the heat to medium, add the beans and broth, and simmer them until the liquid is reduced by half, about 5 minutes. Stir in the oregano and season with kosher salt.

Arrange four radicchio leaves in a clover pattern on each of four plates. Spoon the beans over the radicchio, dividing them evenly, and drizzle them with the sauce left in the skillet. Cut the sausages in half at an angle and place the two pieces of each sausage side by side on each plate. Top with a dollop of Garlic Mayonnaise, if you are using it, and drizzle the sausage and beans with the high-quality olive oil.

¼ cup **extra-virgin olive oil,** plus extra as needed

4 sweet or spicy Italian pork sausages (preferably flavored with fennel; about ¾ pound)

16 large whole radicchio leaves

16 small jarred **onions,** quartered (about 4 ounces or 1 cup)

2 large garlic cloves, grated or minced (about 2 teaspoons)

Kosher salt

2 15-ounce cans giant white **beans,** rinsed and drained (about 3 cups)

1 cup vegetable or chicken **broth**

1 heaping tablespoon finely chopped fresh oregano leaves

High-quality **extra-virgin olive oil,** for drizzling

Boneless Pork Chops with Yam Purée and Sautéed Bitter Greens

This is a very autumnal dish and a classic combination, one I've seen at probably every restaurant I've worked in. You may notice that throughout this book, I call for the same types of greens: arugula, baby spinach, radicchio, and endive. That's because they don't require the same kind of prep time as other greens such as chard and kale, which need to be trimmed and washed (sometimes a second and third time) and then, in many cases, blanched before cooking. If you don't mind putting in the effort and want the deeper, more complex flavors of those leafy greens, they would taste great in this dish, accenting the sweetness of the yams. Yam purée is as pure as a canned product can get. The Whole Foods brand of organic yam purée that I bought contained nothing but yams, and since it's a purée, nothing is lost in terms of texture. When you're trying to get dinner on the table quickly, there is no shame in taking advantage of a product like this. If you have a skillet with a light-colored bottom, I recommend you use it to melt the butter for this recipe. The light skillet allows you to see when the butter has browned and helps prevent burning it.

30 MINUTES

2 cups yam purée

1 stick (8 tablespoons) unsalted butter

12 large fresh sage leaves

1 teaspoon kosher salt, plus extra for seasoning

Sea salt

2 teaspoons pork rub (see "**Meat rubs**")

4 5½- to 6-ounce boneless pork chops (about ¾ inch thick)

¼ cup canola oil (or other neutral-flavored oil)

¼ cup **extra-virgin olive oil**

8 cups loosely packed combined Belgian endive, radicchio, and arugula, ripped into roughly 2-inch pieces

1 large garlic clove, grated or minced (about 1 teaspoon)

1 teaspoon aged **balsamic vinegar**

Put the yam purée in a small saucepan and set it aside.

Put the butter with the sage leaves and the kosher salt in a medium skillet over high heat, and cook, swirling the pan, for about 5 minutes, until the bubbles subside and the butter is brown and nutty smelling. Turn off the heat. Remove the sage leaves from the butter, place them on a paper towel to drain, and sprinkle them with sea salt.

Pour the butter over the yam purée. Cover the saucepan and warm the purée over low heat, stirring occasionally, while you prepare the rest of the dish.

Massage the pork rub into both sides of each pork chop, dividing it evenly. Heat the canola oil in a large skillet over high heat for 2 to 3 minutes, until the oil's almost smoking (you will begin to smell the oil at that point). Place the pork chops in the pan and cook them for about 3 minutes, until they're a rich brown color and the rub coating them is browned but not burned. Flip the chops, turn off the heat, and let them sit in the pan until the pan stops sizzling, about 3 minutes. The pork will feel firm to the touch and will no longer be pink in the middle, but will still be moist and juicy. Transfer the chops to a plate while you cook the greens.

Heat the olive oil in the same skillet over high heat for 2 to 3 minutes, until the oil's almost smoking. Add the greens and let them cook without stirring for about 30 seconds. Season them with kosher salt, add the garlic, and stir. Let the greens cook for about 30 seconds longer, until some of the leaves are just wilted. Turn off the heat, drizzle the greens with the balsamic vinegar, and stir to combine.

Spoon the yam purée in mounds on four plates, dividing it evenly, and smash it down slightly with the back of a spoon to form a bed. Pile the greens in the center of the purée so the purée is still showing around the edges. Place the pork chops on the greens, drizzle them with the juices left on the plate they were resting on, and scatter the reserved sage leaves over the top.

Pepper Jelly–Glazed Boneless Pork Chops with Steamed Baby Bok Choy
Sara Foster • Foster's Market, Durham and Chapel Hill, North Carolina

In the South, we use spicy pepper jelly as a condiment on many things, most famously on cream cheese and crackers. I began canning my own seven-pepper jelly because I thought it would taste so much more interesting with the heat and flavor from the various peppers. I normally make this recipe with a pork tenderloin, cooked on the grill. Starting with boneless pork chops makes this recipe even faster. I like to marinate the pork for several hours or even overnight so that it's extra flavorful and moist. For last-minute marinating, I use a tool called an "instant marinator" (the new Flavor Express II). It's a simple, inexpensive gadget that does the job of overnight marinating in minutes.

30 MINUTES

4 6-ounce boneless pork chops (about 3/4 inch thick)

FOR THE MARINADE
1/4 cup Foster's Market Seven Pepper Jelly (or another pepper jelly), plus extra for serving on the side
1/4 cup dry red wine
1 tablespoon red wine **vinegar**
1 tablespoon chopped fresh rosemary leaves
1 large garlic clove, grated or minced (about 1 teaspoon)
1/2 teaspoon chile flakes
Grated zest and juice of 1/2 orange
1/4 teaspoon sea salt
1/4 teaspoon freshly ground black pepper

3 tablespoons **extra-virgin olive oil**
2 large garlic cloves, grated or minced (about 2 teaspoons)
Kosher salt
6 baby bok choy, cored and quartered
Pinch of chile flakes
1/4 cup canola oil (or other neutral-flavored oil)

Rinse the pork chops under cool water, pat them dry with paper towels, and place them in a shallow bowl, baking dish, or large sealable plastic bag.

To make the marinade, whisk together the pepper jelly, wine, vinegar, rosemary, garlic, chile flakes, orange zest and juice, sea salt, and freshly ground black pepper in a small bowl. Pour the marinade over the chops, turn to coat the chops (or seal the bag and shake to coat), and set them aside while you make the bok choy.

Heat the olive oil, garlic, and a pinch of kosher salt in a large skillet over medium-high heat and sauté until the garlic is soft and fragrant, about 1 1/2 minutes, stirring often to prevent it from browning. Turn up the heat, add the bok choy, and cook it for 1 1/2 minutes. Season with kosher salt and sprinkle with the chile flakes and 2 tablespoons water. Cover the pan and steam the bok choy for about 2 minutes, or until it is just tender but still crisp. Turn off the heat and keep the skillet covered while you cook the pork. (Be careful not to overcook the bok choy as it will continue to cook slightly while it rests in the pan.)

Heat the canola oil in a large skillet over high heat for 2 to 3 minutes, until the oil's almost smoking (you can smell the oil at that point). Place the pork chops in the skillet and cook them for about 3 minutes, until they're a rich brown color and the rub coating them is browned but not burned. Flip the chops, turn off the heat, and let them sit in the pan until the pan stops sizzling, about 3 minutes. The pork will feel firm to the touch and will no longer be pink in the middle, but it will still be moist and juicy.

Place one pork chop and one head of bok choy on each of four plates and serve with pepper jelly on the side.

Boneless Pork Chops with Creamy Polenta and Fennel Pollen

Wild fennel is a type of fennel I found that grows wild in the Italian countryside (in Southern California, it grows in empty lots and alongside freeway entrances). I love to cook with it. It has an intense, inimitable flavor. The flavor is earthier and wilder than the fennel you find at the supermarket. Dried fennel pollen is a seasoning I recently discovered; it's the closest I've found to imitating wild fennel's flavor.

35 MINUTES

To make the polenta, combine the milk, thyme, garlic, and salt in a large, heavy-bottomed saucepan and bring it to a boil over high heat. Reduce the heat to medium-low and simmer the milk for about 5 minutes to steep the thyme. Remove the thyme sprigs and add the polenta in a slow, thin stream as you stir with a whisk to prevent the polenta from clumping. Bring the polenta to a low boil, reduce the heat to low, and cook it for about 5 minutes, whisking often, until it thickens to a loose, porridge-like consistency. Turn off the heat, stir in the butter and cover.

Stir the pork rub and fennel pollen together in a small bowl. Massage the mixture into both sides of each pork chop, dividing it evenly. Heat the canola oil in a large skillet over high heat for 2 to 3 minutes, until the oil's almost smoking (you will begin to smell the oil at that point). Place the pork chops in the skillet and cook them for about 3 minutes, until they're a rich brown color and the rub coating them is browned but not burned. Flip the chops, turn off the heat, and let them sit in the pan until the pan stops sizzling, about 3 minutes. The pork will feel firm to the touch and will no longer be pink in the middle, but it will still be moist and juicy. Transfer the chops to a plate while you cook the arugula.

Add the arugula to the pan you cooked the pork in, season it with kosher salt, and cook it over medium-high heat for about 30 seconds, stirring constantly, until it's just wilted.

If the polenta has thickened too much as it cooled, place it over medium heat and stir in more milk until it returns to a loose consistency.

Spoon the polenta in mounds on four plates, dividing it evenly, and smash it down slightly with the back of a spoon to form a bed. Lay the sautéed arugula over and around the polenta and place the pork chops on top of the arugula.

FOR THE POLENTA

3 cups whole milk, plus extra as needed

15 fresh thyme sprigs

2 large garlic cloves, grated or minced (about 2 teaspoons)

2 teaspoons kosher salt

1/2 cup instant polenta

1/2 stick (4 tablespoons) unsalted butter

2 teaspoons pork rub (see "**Meat rubs**")

1/2 teaspoon **fennel pollen**

4 6-ounce boneless pork chops (about 3/4 inch thick)

1/4 cup canola oil (or other neutral-flavored oil)

4 cups loosely packed arugula leaves

Kosher salt

Boneless Pork Chops with Radicchio Slaw

The pork chops in this dish are covered with a slaw that features contrasting flavors—bitter radicchio, sweet balsamic, and salty capers. It's a delicious combination and really quick and easy to put together. The slaw is heavily dressed, but the extra vinaigrette makes a nice "sauce" with the pork.

30 MINUTES

Massage the pork rub into both sides of each pork chop, dividing it evenly. Heat the canola oil in a large skillet over high heat for 2 to 3 minutes, until the oil's almost smoking (you will begin to smell the oil at that point). Place the pork chops in the pan and cook them for about 3 minutes, until they're a rich brown color and the rub coating them is browned but not burned. Flip the chops, turn off the heat, and let them sit in the pan until the pan stops sizzling, about 3 minutes. The pork will feel firm to the touch and will no longer be pink in the middle, but it will still be moist and juicy. Leave the chops in the pan until you're ready to serve them.

Stir the olive oil, vinegar, capers, shallots, rosemary, and lemon juice together in a medium bowl and season with kosher salt and freshly ground black pepper. Add the radicchio and toss to coat it with the dressing.

Place one pork chop on each of four plates and top each with the radicchio slaw, dividing it evenly, and drizzle the remaining vinaigrette over the radicchio.

2 teaspoons pork rub (see "**Meat rubs**")

4 6-ounce boneless pork chops (about 3/4 inch thick)

1/4 cup canola oil (or other neutral flavored oil)

3/4 cup **extra-virgin olive oil**

1/4 cup aged **balsamic vinegar**

1/4 cup **capers,** rinsed and chopped

2 medium shallots, grated or minced (about 1 heaping tablespoon)

1/2 teaspoon chopped fresh rosemary leaves

1/2 teaspoon fresh lemon juice

Kosher salt and freshly ground black pepper

1 small head radicchio, shredded 1/4 inch thick (about 4 cups)

LAMB

Seared Lamb Chops with Ratatouille

Ratatouille is a Provençal "stew" of summer's bounty—tomatoes, peppers, sweet onions, and eggplant—that gets its character from long cooking. This ratatouille, made with already cooked, jarred ingredients, is a delicious shortcut. If you like ratatouille, double the recipe so you'll have some to serve the next day with seared halibut or sea bass.

30 MINUTES

To make the ratatouille, heat the olive oil in a large skillet over high heat for 2 to 3 minutes, until the oil's almost smoking (you will begin to smell the oil at that point). Add the zucchini and sauté until it begins to soften, about 2 minutes. Add the onions, garlic, chile flakes, and a pinch of kosher salt and sauté until the onions are soft and the garlic is soft and fragrant, about 1½ minutes, stirring constantly so the garlic doesn't brown. Add the tomatoes and peppers, reduce the heat to low, and simmer for about 3 minutes, until the juices released from the tomatoes begin to thicken. Add the eggplant, olives, and basil, cook for about 1½ minutes, to warm the eggplant, and season with kosher salt.

Massage the lamb rub into both sides of each lamb chop, dividing it evenly.

Heat 2 tablespoons of the canola oil in a large skillet over high heat for 2 to 3 minutes, until the oil's almost smoking (you will begin to smell the oil at that point). Add half of the lamb chops, reduce the heat to medium-high, and cook them for 2 minutes. Turn the chops over and cook them for another 30 seconds if you want them rare or 1 minute for medium-rare. Transfer the lamb chops to a plate and repeat, heating the remaining 2 tablespoons of canola oil and cooking the other lamb chops in the same way.

Spoon the ratatouille onto four plates, dividing it evenly, and place the lamb chops four to a plate on top of the ratatouille, fanning them out. Drizzle the chops with the juices from the plate they were resting on and sprinkle the small basil leaves over them.

FOR THE RATATOUILLE

2 tablespoons **extra-virgin olive oil**

1 small zucchini, cut in half lengthwise and sliced into thin half-moons

10 small jarred **onions,** quartered (about 2½ ounces or ⅔ cup)

4 large garlic cloves, grated or minced (about 1 tablespoon)

¼ teaspoon chile flakes

Kosher salt

1 14.5-ounce can **San Marzano tomatoes,** drained and roughly chopped

4 roasted **Piquillo peppers,** ripped in half

½ cup **eggplant appetizer,** drained

32 small pitted **black olives**

10 basil leaves

3 tablespoons lamb rub (see "**Meat rubs**")

16 bone-in lamb chops (about 2 pounds)

¼ cup canola oil (or other neutral-flavored oil)

12 small basil leaves for garnish

Seared Lamb Chops with Preserved Lemon, Artichoke Hearts, and Fresh Mint

Mint and artichokes is a combination that makes me think of spring. Preserved lemons, traditional to Moroccan cuisine, are whole lemons preserved in salt water. Treating the lemons in this way breaks down the rind, which is the part of the preserved lemon that is used, not the pulp.

20 MINUTES

Massage the lamb rub into both sides of each lamb chop, dividing it evenly.

Heat 2 tablespoons of the canola oil in a large skillet over high heat for 2 to 3 minutes, until the oil's almost smoking (you will begin to smell the oil at that point). Add half of the lamb chops, reduce the heat to medium-high, and cook them for 2 minutes. Turn the chops over and cook them for 30 seconds if you want them rare or 1 minute for medium-rare. Transfer the chops to a plate and repeat, heating the remaining 2 tablespoons of canola oil and cooking the remaining lamb chops in the same way.

Drain all but 1 teaspoon of the oil from the pan you cooked the lamb in. Add the garlic and swirl the pan off the heat for about 1½ minutes to soften the garlic slightly from the heat of the oil. Turn the heat to high, add the wine, and simmer for about 2½ minutes, until the wine is almost completely evaporated. Add the vegetable broth, artichoke hearts, and preserved lemon, stir, and simmer until the sauce is reduced by a third, about 2 minutes; season with kosher salt.

Spoon the artichokes and sauce onto four plates, dividing them evenly. Place the lamb chops four to a plate on top of the sauce, fanning them out, and drizzle them with juices from the plate they were resting on. Squeeze a few drops of lemon juice over each chop, crumble the feta over them, drizzle them with the high-quality olive oil, and top with the mint.

3 tablespoons lamb rub (see "**Meat rubs**")

16 bone-in lamb chops (about 2 pounds)

¼ cup canola oil (or other neutral-flavored oil)

3 large garlic cloves, grated or minced (about 1 tablespoon)

½ cup dry white wine

½ cup vegetable **broth**

4 whole marinated **artichoke hearts,** quartered (from the deli case or 2 6½-ounce jars)

¼ **preserved lemon,** pulp discarded and skin finely chopped (about 2 teaspoons)

Kosher salt

Lemon for squeezing over the lamb

2 ounces **feta**

High-quality **extra-virgin olive oil,** for drizzling

2 teaspoons finely chopped fresh mint leaves

Pomegranate-Glazed Lamb Chops with Stuffed Grape Leaves and Tahini Sauce

Pomegranate molasses, which is used to coat these lamb chops, is pomegranate juice that has been reduced to a thick, dark, sweet syrup. It's available at Middle Eastern markets and specialty food stores.

The combination of pomegranate with lamb is a classic in Middle Eastern cooking. I normally don't care for sweet flavors with meat, but lamb is an exception because a little sweetness offsets the meat's slightly gamy flavor. To keep with the Middle Eastern theme, I serve the lamb with stuffed grape leaves and tahini sauce (although the yogurt sauce that accompanies the Spicy Lamb Sausage Patties, page 161, is equally delicious). Stuffed grape leaves was one of two canned items that I was completely shocked to find how good they were. (The other was giant white beans in tomato sauce.) Because the stuffed grape leaves are so hearty, I serve this dish with three lamb chops per person instead of four, as I do in the other lamb chop recipes.

20 MINUTES

To make the tahini sauce, stir the tahini, lemon juice, garlic, kosher salt, and 3 tablespoons of hot water (or enough to make a smooth, loose sauce) together in a small bowl.

Combine the pomegranate molasses, olive oil, and shallots together in a medium bowl.

Season both sides of the lamb chops with kosher salt and freshly ground black pepper and dip them one at a time into the pomegranate mixture, being sure to coat all sides.

Heat 2 tablespoons of the canola oil in a large skillet over medium-high heat for 2 to 3 minutes, until the oil's almost smoking (you will begin to smell the oil at that point). Add half of the lamb chops and cook them for 2 minutes. Turn the chops over and cook them for another 30 seconds if you want them rare or 1 minute for medium-rare. Transfer the lamb chops to a plate and repeat, heating the remaining 2 tablespoons of canola oil and cooking the remaining lamb chops in the same way.

Place three grape leaves on each plate with two side by side and one on top perpendicular to the others and spoon the tahini sauce over them, dividing it evenly. Place the lamb chops three to a plate in front of the grape leaves, fanning them out, and drizzle them with the juices from the plate they were resting on.

FOR THE TAHINI SAUCE

¼ cup **tahini,** well-stirred

2 teaspoons fresh lemon juice

1 large garlic clove, grated or minced (about 1 teaspoon)

1 teaspoon kosher salt

¼ cup pomegranate molasses

¼ cup **extra-virgin olive oil**

2 medium shallots, grated or minced (about 1 heaping tablespoon)

12 bone-in lamb chops (about 1½ pounds)

Kosher salt and freshly ground black pepper

¼ cup canola oil (or other neutral-flavored oil)

12 rice-stuffed grape leaves (from a deli case or 1 13-ounce can), at room temperature

Lamb Chops with Arugula, Shaved Parmesan, and Saba

Made with fresh arugula and shaved Parmesan, this dish is like the lamb version of Tagliatta (page 134). Saba is grape must from Sardinia. Its taste is similar to aged balsamic vinegar and is used in the same way.

20 MINUTES

To make the marinade, stir the olive oil, saba, balsamic vinegar, and rosemary together in a small bowl and season with kosher salt and freshly ground black pepper.

Massage the lamb rub into both sides of each lamb chop, dividing it evenly. Heat 2 tablespoons of the canola oil in a large skillet over high heat for 2 to 3 minutes, until the oil's almost smoking (you will begin to smell the oil at that point). Add half of the lamb chops, reduce the heat to medium-high, and cook them for 2 minutes. Turn the chops over and cook them for 30 seconds if you want them rare or 1 minute for medium-rare. Transfer the lamb chops to a plate and repeat, heating the remaining 2 tablespoons of canola oil and cooking the remaining lamb chops in the same way.

When all the chops are cooked, return them and the juices collected on the plate they were resting on to the skillet (don't worry if they don't all fit in one layer). Pour the marinade over the chops and turn to coat them on all sides with the marinade.

Use a sharp knife or a vegetable peeler to cut or shave 15 to 20 very thin slices from the wedge of Parmesan.

Mound the arugula onto four plates, dividing it evenly. Sprinkle the arugula with sea salt and scatter the Parmesan shavings on top. Place the lamb chops four to a plate on top of the arugula, fanning them out. Drizzle about 1 tablespoon of the marinade left in the skillet over each serving and squeeze a few drops of lemon juice over each chop.

FOR THE SABA MARINADE

2 tablespoons **extra-virgin olive oil**

2 tablespoons **saba**

2 teaspoons **balsamic vinegar**

1 teaspoon chopped fresh rosemary leaves

Kosher salt and freshly ground black pepper

3 tablespoons lamb rub (see "**Meat rubs**")

16 bone-in lamb chops (about 2 pounds)

¼ cup canola oil (or other neutral-flavored oil)

Parmigiano-Reggiano wedge, for shaving

12 cups loosely packed arugula leaves

Sea salt

Lemon, for squeezing over the lamb

Seared Lamb Chops with Creamy Polenta and Balsamic Onion and Sun-Dried Tomato Glaze

I don't use sun-dried tomatoes very often. When I do use them, I prefer those packed in olive oil or the semi-dried variety that are sold in sealed packages. In either case, I make sure to select those that are red and plump. The flavor of the ones that are brown and shriveled is too concentrated.

40 MINUTES

To make the polenta, combine the milk, thyme, garlic, and salt in a large, heavy-bottomed saucepan and bring it to a boil over high heat. Reduce the heat to medium-low and simmer the milk for about 5 minutes to steep the thyme. Remove the thyme sprigs and add the polenta in a slow, thin stream as you stir with a whisk to prevent the polenta from clumping. Bring the polenta to a low boil, reduce the heat to low, and cook it for about 5 minutes, whisking often, until it thickens to a loose, porridge-like consistency. Turn off the heat, stir in the butter, and cover.

Place the onions and their juice in a small saucepan and cook over medium-high heat for about 10 minutes, until the sauce is reduced by half and forms a thick glaze. Stir in the sun-dried tomatoes and turn off the heat.

Massage the lamb rub into both sides of each lamb chop, dividing it evenly. Warm 2 tablespoons of the canola oil in a large skillet over high heat for 2 to 3 minutes, until the oil's almost smoking (you will begin to smell the oil at that point). Add half of the lamb chops, reduce the heat to medium-high, and cook for 2 minutes. Turn the chops and cook 30 seconds more for rare or 1 minute for medium-rare. Transfer the lamb chops to a plate and repeat, heating the remaining 2 tablespoons of canola oil and cooking the remaining chops in the same way.

If the polenta has thickened, place it over medium heat and stir in more milk until it returns to a loose consistency.

Spoon the polenta in mounds on four plates, dividing it evenly, and smash it down with the back of a spoon to form a bed. Place one whole basil leaf on the side of each mound of polenta and spoon the onion and sun-dried tomatoes over the polenta, reserving the liquid in the pan. Place the lamb chops, four to a plate, on top of the polenta, fanning them out. Drizzle the chops with the juices from the plate they were resting on, and spoon the remaining glaze over them. Drizzle high-quality olive oil around and over each serving and top with the remaining basil leaves.

FOR THE POLENTA

3 cups whole milk, plus extra as needed

15 fresh thyme sprigs

2 large garlic cloves, grated or minced (about 2 teaspoons)

2 teaspoons kosher salt

1/2 cup instant **polenta**

1/2 stick (4 tablespoons) unsalted butter

10 small balsamic-roasted jarred **onions** (including 1/2 cup of their juice or 10 jarred onions and 1/2 cup **balsamic vinegar**)

8 large oil-packed **sun-dried tomatoes** or semi-dried tomatoes, drained and torn in half (about 1/4 cup)

3 tablespoons lamb rub (see "**Meat rubs**")

16 bone-in lamb chops (about 2 pounds)

1/4 cup canola oil (or other neutral-flavored oil)

High-quality **extra-virgin olive oil,** for drizzling

12 small basil leaves

Lamb Steaks with Anchovies, Black Olives, and Lemon Zest Sauce

I'd never heard of lamb steaks until I went to the grocery store recently looking for quick-cooking cuts of meat. They're cut from the leg and have a small bone in the center. I love lamb leg, but it takes a long time to cook so I was pleased to discover the steaks. Not only do they cook very quickly, they're really convenient to work with—one steak makes a nice single portion.

25 MINUTES

Massage the lamb rub into both sides of each of the lamb steaks, dividing it evenly. Heat 2 tablespoons of the canola oil in a large skillet over high heat for 2 to 3 minutes, until the oil's almost smoking (you will begin to smell the oil at that point). Place two of the lamb steaks in the pan and cook them for 2 minutes. Reduce the heat to medium-low and cook the steaks for another 2 minutes. Turn the steaks and cook them again on the first side for 2 more minutes, then turn again and cook for a final 2 to 4 minutes if you want them medium-rare. Cook them for 1 more minute for medium. Transfer the lamb steaks to a plate and repeat, heating the remaining 2 tablespoons of canola oil and cooking the remaining steaks in the same way.

Heat the olive oil, butter, anchovies, and garlic together in a small saucepan over low heat and cook them for about 4 minutes, smashing the anchovies with a wooden spoon to break them up, until the mixture starts to bubble. Turn off the heat and stir in the olives, parsley, and lemon zest.

Mound the spinach onto four plates, dividing it evenly. Place the lamb steaks on top of the spinach and drizzle them with the juices from the plate they were resting on. Spoon the sauce over the meat and squeeze lemon juice over each lamb steak.

2 tablespoons plus 2 teaspoons lamb rub (see "**Meat rubs**")

4 6- to 7-ounce boneless lamb steaks, 1–1½ inches thick

¼ cup canola oil (or other neutral-flavored oil)

¼ cup **extra-virgin olive oil**

2 tablespoons unsalted butter

8 **anchovy fillets**

4 large garlic cloves, grated or minced (about 1 tablespoon)

32 small pitted **black olives**

1 heaping tablespoon finely chopped fresh Italian parsley leaves

Grated zest of 1 lemon

8 cups loosely packed baby spinach leaves

Lemon, for squeezing over the lamb

Spicy Lamb Sausage Patties with Chunky Red Pepper Spread and Tangy Greek Yogurt Sauce

These patties are really flavorful. They're made with a combination of pungent spices and also served with chunky red pepper spread. The spread has chopped roasted peppers in it, which is what I wanted since I'm not mixing it with anything, just spooning it straight from the jar onto the sausage patties. I borrowed the spice mixture I use to season the lamb patties from Paula Wolfert's Slow Mediterranean Kitchen. *I give you the recipe for the spice blend here but my editor, Leyla, who's Turkish, pointed out that there's a ready-made spice blend you can buy called köfte baharatı. I've never used it, but she swears by it. It's available at Middle Eastern food stores and from online sources.*

25 MINUTES

To make the yogurt sauce, stir the yogurt, garlic, lemon juice, and kosher salt together in a small bowl.

To make the spice mixture, combine the paprika, allspice, cinnamon, coriander, cloves, cumin, and kosher salt together in a small bowl.

Slash the sausage casings with a knife and squeeze the sausage meat out of the casings and into a medium bowl; discard the casings. Add the spice mixture and use your hands to mix it in thoroughly. Form the meat into 8 equally sized ½-inch-thick patties.

Heat the oil in a large skillet over high heat for 2 to 3 minutes, until the oil's almost smoking (you will begin to smell the oil at that point). Place the lamb patties in the pan and cook them for about 3 minutes, until they're browned on one side. Turn the patties over, reduce the heat to medium, and cook them for another 3 minutes, until the second side is browned and the patties are cooked through.

While the lamb patties are cooking, warm the pitas by placing them, one at a time, directly on the burner of a gas or electric stove over medium-high heat for about 1 minute, turning them several times to prevent them from burning, until they're warmed through. Cut each pita into quarters.

Spoon 1 tablespoon of the chunky red pepper spread onto the center of each of four plates, using the back of the spoon to swirl the sauce into a larger circle. Place two patties on top of the spread and drop 1 tablespoon of the yogurt sauce on the side of each serving. Place two pita quarters on each plate and serve the patties with extra red pepper spread and the remaining yogurt sauce on the side.

FOR THE YOGURT SAUCE

½ cup strained whole-milk **Greek yogurt**

1 large garlic clove, grated or minced (about 1 teaspoon)

2 tablespoons fresh lemon juice

1 teaspoon kosher salt

FOR THE SPICE MIXTURE

2 teaspoons smoked Spanish **paprika**

1 teaspoon ground allspice

½ teaspoon ground cinnamon

½ teaspoon ground coriander

½ teaspoon ground cloves

½ teaspoon ground cumin

½ teaspoon kosher salt

1½ pounds lamb sausage

2 tablespoons canola oil (or other neutral-flavored oil)

2 pita breads

4 tablespoons **chunky red pepper spread,** plus extra for serving on the side

Lamb Meatballs with Spicy Garbanzo Beans

This is a quick and easy version of a very popular appetizer that we served at Campanile for years. I like to make the garbanzo beans with the meatballs still in the pan, pushed to the side after they've been cooked. This way, the meatballs soak up the flavor of the gravy the garbanzo beans are cooking in. The paprika and pepper pastes that I use to season the garbanzo beans came from Jons Marketplace, a grocery store in L.A. that carries many imported products from around the world and Jons was a real source of inspiration for me in conceiving many of the recipes in the book. If you can't get to Jons, look for ethnic markets where you live, or look at the sources section in the back of this book.

25 MINUTES

To make the meatballs, in a large bowl, combine the lamb, eggs, parsley, thyme, garlic, salt, paprika, and chile flakes and mix the ingredients with your hands just until they are thoroughly combined. Divide the mixture into halves, then quarters, and so on, until you have 16 pieces. Roll each piece between your palms to form the meatballs.

Heat the oil in a large skillet over high heat for 2 to 3 minutes, until it's almost smoking (you will begin to smell the oil at that point). Add the meatballs and cook them for 4 to 5 minutes, turning them occasionally, until they're browned all over. Push the meatballs to one side of the pan and reduce the heat to medium-low.

Put the garbanzo beans, vegetable broth, paprika paste, and red pepper paste in the empty side of the skillet and stir to combine. Simmer the garbanzo beans until the sauce is reduced by half, to the consistency of thin gravy. Turn off the heat and stir the meatballs and garbanzo beans together to coat the meatballs with the gravy.

Mound the spinach onto four plates, dividing it evenly. Spoon the garbanzo beans and sauce over the spinach, reserving about 1/4 cup of the sauce, and place the meatballs, four to a plate, on top of the garbanzo beans. Spoon the reserved sauce over the meatballs. Put a tablespoon of yogurt on each serving of meatballs, sprinkle them with the reserved parsley and season them with sea salt.

FOR THE MEATBALLS

2 pounds ground lamb

2 large eggs, lightly beaten

1/4 cup finely chopped fresh Italian parsley leaves, plus extra for garnish

2 tablespoons chopped fresh thyme leaves

3 large garlic cloves, finely chopped or grated (about 1 teaspoon)

1 heaping tablespoon kosher salt

2 teaspoons smoked Spanish **paprika**

1/4 teaspoon chile flakes

3 tablespoons canola oil (or other neutral-flavored oil)

FOR THE GARBANZO BEANS

1 15-ounce can garbanzo **beans** (about 1 1/2 cups), rinsed and drained

1 1/2 cups vegetable **broth**

1 tablespoon plus 1 teaspoon **paprika paste**

1 tablespoon plus 1 teaspoon **red pepper paste**

2 cups loosely packed baby spinach leaves

1/4 cup strained whole-milk **Greek yogurt**

Sea salt

CHICKEN

Sautéed Herbed Chicken Breasts on Pepper Cress

Demi-glace, which is stock that has been reduced until it's very rich and flavorful, used to be reserved for chefs, who could afford the time and ingredients it took to make it. Today there are a few really good frozen ones available. Using demi-glace in this dish is the perfect example of how taking advantage of one prepared ingredient turns something very simple, a perfectly prepared chicken breast, into a dish with as much flavor as something you might get in a restaurant.

40 MINUTES

Rub canola oil on both sides of the chicken breasts and place each breast in a separate sandwich-size plastic bag. Use a mallet or heavy skillet to pound each chicken breast until it's about 1/2 inch thick and has roughly doubled in size. Remove the chicken from the bags and massage the poultry rub into both sides of each breast, dividing it evenly.

Heat 1/4 cup of the canola oil in a large skillet over medium-high heat for 2 to 3 minutes, until the oil's almost smoking (you will begin to smell the oil at that point). Place two of the chicken breasts in the skillet and cook them for 2 minutes. Flip the chicken and cook for 2 minutes more. Transfer the chicken breasts to a plate, wipe out the pan and repeat, heating the remaining 1/4 cup of canola oil and cooking the other two chicken breasts in the same way.

Add the shallot, garlic, and a pinch of kosher salt to the oil remaining in the pan and sauté for about 1 1/2 minutes, until the shallot is soft and the garlic is soft and fragrant, stirring constantly so the garlic doesn't brown. Turn the heat up to high, add the wine, and simmer for about 3 minutes, until it's reduced by two thirds. Add the demi-glace and bring it to a boil. Turn off the heat and stir in the butter until it melts completely and the sauce does not appear separated. Stir in the lemon juice and season with kosher salt and freshly ground black pepper.

Divide the cress evenly among four plates and sprinkle with sea salt.

Place the chicken breasts first-cooked side up on the cress. Drizzle them with the juices from the plate they were resting on, then drizzle the pan sauce over them.

1/2 cup canola oil (or other neutral-flavored oil), plus extra for coating the chicken breasts

4 6-ounce skinless, boneless chicken breasts

3 tablespoons poultry rub (see "**Meat rubs**")

1 medium shallot, grated or minced (about 2 teaspoons)

2 large garlic cloves, grated or minced (about 2 teaspoons)

Kosher salt

1/2 cup dry white wine

1 cup frozen chicken **demi-glace**

1/2 stick (4 tablespoons) unsalted butter, cut into pieces

2 teaspoons fresh lemon juice

Freshly ground black pepper

8 cups loosely packed pepper cress (or watercress, trimmed of tough ends, or baby spinach or baby arugula leaves)

Sea salt

Seared Chicken Breasts with Asparagus, Garlic Mayonnaise, and Green Olive Sauce

I like to use pencil asparagus instead of the bigger spears whenever I can find them. They have so much more flavor. For this dish, the asparagus spears are cooked over very high heat so the outsides are nice and caramelized—"color is flavor" is what we say in the kitchen—while the insides stay crisp and firm.

40 MINUTES

Stir the olive oil, olive paté, and sliced olives together in a small bowl.

Rub canola oil on both sides of the chicken breasts and place each breast in a separate sandwich-size plastic bag. Use a mallet or heavy skillet to pound each chicken breast until it's about 1/2 inch thick and has roughly doubled in size. Remove the chicken from the bags and season both sides of each breast with kosher salt and freshly ground black pepper.

Heat 1/4 cup of the canola oil in a large skillet over medium-high heat for 2 to 3 minutes, until the oil's almost smoking (you will begin to smell the oil at that point). Place two of the chicken breasts in the skillet and cook them for 2 minutes. Flip the chicken and cook for 2 minutes more. Transfer the chicken breasts to a plate, wipe out the pan and repeat, heating 1/4 cup of the remaining canola oil and cooking the other two chicken breasts in the same way.

To remove the tough ends of the asparagus, snap the stems off one at a time at the natural break. Heat 2 tablespoons of the remaining canola oil in a large nonstick skillet over high heat for 2 to 3 minutes, until the oil's almost smoking. Add half the asparagus, season it with kosher salt, and cook it for about 3 minutes (for pencil asparagus; 6 minutes for thicker spears), until it's browned on all sides but still slightly firm to the touch. Remove the asparagus from the pan. Add the remaining 2 tablespoons of canola oil, heat, and cook the rest of the asparagus in the same way.

Divide the asparagus evenly among four plates. Place the chicken breasts first-cooked side up on the asparagus and drizzle them with the juices from the plate they were resting on. Dollop a tablespoon of Garlic Mayonnaise over each chicken breast and spoon the olive mixture over the mayonnaise.

1 tablespoon plus 1 teaspoon **extra-virgin olive oil**

1 heaping tablespoon green olive paté (see "**Olive tapenade**")

20 medium anchovy-stuffed **green olives,** thinly sliced

3/4 cup canola oil (or other neutral flavored oil), plus extra for coating the chicken breasts

4 6-ounce skinless, boneless chicken breasts

Kosher salt and freshly ground black pepper

1 pound asparagus spears (preferably pencil asparagus)

Garlic Mayonnaise (page 33)

Potato and Chicken Boulanger

This recipe is based on a French dish, potatoes boulanger, or "baker's potatoes," so named because supposedly it was what went into the baker's oven after the bread had been baked and the oven was still hot. The addition of the chicken breasts makes this version into a meal. I call for you to use poultry rub, but it really is optional. The dish has enough flavor without it.

40 MINUTES

Rub canola oil on both sides of the chicken breasts and place each breast in a separate sandwich-size plastic bag. Use a mallet or heavy skillet to pound each chicken breast until it's about ½ inch thick and has roughly doubled in size. Remove the chicken from the bags and massage the poultry rub into both sides of each breast, dividing it evenly.

Heat ¼ cup of the canola oil in a large skillet over medium-high heat for 2 to 3 minutes, until the oil's almost smoking (you will begin to smell the oil at that point). Place two of the chicken breasts in the skillet and cook them for 2 minutes. Flip the chicken and cook for 2 minutes more. Transfer the chicken breasts to a plate, wipe out the pan, and repeat, heating the remaining ¼ cup canola oil and cooking the other two chicken breasts in the same way.

Meanwhile, cook the bacon in a large skillet over medium heat for 5 to 7 minutes, stirring often until it is done but still chewy, not browned or crispy. Remove the bacon from the skillet and place it on paper towels to drain, reserving the fat in the skillet. Add the onions to the pan and cook them over medium heat for about 1½ minutes, breaking up the layers while they cook, until they just begin to brown. Add the potato slices and garlic and sauté them for about 1½ minutes more, until the garlic is soft and fragrant and the potatoes are warmed through, stirring constantly so the garlic doesn't brown. Season with kosher salt and freshly ground black pepper. Reduce the heat to low, add the demi-glace to the pan, bring the sauce to a simmer, and simmer until it's thickened, about 6 minutes. Remove the sauce from the heat and stir in the bacon and thyme.

Spoon the potatoes with the sauce onto four plates, dividing them evenly. Place the chicken first-cooked side up on top of the potatoes and drizzle it with the juices from the plate it was resting on.

½ cup canola oil (or other neutral-flavored oil), plus extra for rubbing on the chicken breasts

4 6-ounce skinless, boneless chicken breasts

3 tablespoons poultry rub (see "**Meat rubs**"), optional

8 strips thick-cut applewood-smoked **bacon,** cut diagonally into 1-inch pieces

8 small jarred **onions,** quartered (about 2 ounces or ½ cup)

8 ounces canned or jarred **potatoes** (from 1 14-ounce can), sliced (about 2 cups)

4 large garlic cloves, grated or minced (about 1 tablespoon)

Kosher salt and freshly ground black pepper

1 cup canned or frozen chicken **demi-glace**

¼ cup fresh thyme leaves

Prosciutto-Wrapped Chicken with Sage Pesto

This is basically a quick version of saltimbocca, the classic Italian dish of veal rolls, but made with chicken in place of veal. The name means "jump in the mouth," referring to the surprise of flavors the rolls contain. This recipe is one of the few in this book that calls for a very specific ingredient. The ingredient is sage pesto, and as far as I know, Rustichella d'Abruzzo, imported by Manacaretti, is the only brand that makes it. If you can't find it, arugula or artichoke pesto would be a good alternative.

25 MINUTES

Rub canola oil on both sides of the chicken breasts and place each breast in a separate sandwich-size plastic bag. Use a mallet or heavy skillet to pound each chicken breast until it's about 1/2 inch thick and has roughly doubled in size.

Press 3 sage leaves onto the skinned (smooth) side of each chicken breast. Wrap one slice prosciutto around each chicken breast, leaving about 1 1/2 inches exposed on both ends of the breast. Season with kosher salt and freshly ground black pepper on both sides. Repeat with the remaining prosciutto and chicken.

Heat 1/4 cup of the canola oil in a large skillet over high heat for 2 to 3 minutes, until the oil's almost smoking (you will begin to smell the oil at that point). Place two of the chicken breasts in the skillet, sage side down, and sear them for 2 minutes. Flip the chicken and cook for 2 minutes more. Transfer the chicken breasts to a plate, wipe out the pan and repeat, heating the remaining 1/4 cup of canola oil and cooking the other two chicken breasts in the same way.

Heap the greens onto four plates, dividing them evenly, and sprinkle them with sea salt. Lay the chicken breasts first-cooked side up on top of the greens. Pour the juices from the plate the chicken was resting on into the pan. Add the sage pesto to the pan and warm it over medium-high heat, stirring constantly, until it bubbles. Add the vegetable broth and cook until the sauce is reduced by a third and thickens slightly. Pour the sauce over the chicken breasts and drizzle with the lemon-infused olive oil.

1/2 cup canola oil (or other neutral-flavored oil), plus extra for coating the chicken breasts

4 6-ounce skinless, boneless chicken breasts

12 large fresh sage leaves

4 large slices **prosciutto,** not too thinly sliced (about 3 ounces)

Kosher salt and freshly ground black pepper

8 cups loosely packed mixed baby greens

Sea salt

1/3 cup Rustichella d'Abruzzo Sage Pesto

1/2 cup vegetable **broth**

Lemon-infused olive oil (or high-quality **extra-virgin olive oil** combined with a pinch of fresh grated lemon zest), for drizzling

Mole Poblano Chicken Casserole with Black Beans and Queso Fresco
Jimmy Shaw • Lotería! Grill, Los Angeles

At Lotería! Grill, we make our mole poblano from scratch. This is a very time-consuming task and not very practical to do at home. At outdoor *mercados* and modern grocery stores throughout Mexico, you can purchase a wide range of wonderful moles in paste form or, more practical still, jarred. Every home cook in Mexico has her way of "fixing" these pastes, adding broth and any number of "secret ingredients" to make the mole her own. In the case of Doña María Mole, a popular jarred brand, ask one hundred cooks how to prepare it and you will get as many secret recipes. My dear friend Yareli Arizmendi, of *Like Water for Chocolate* fame (she translated the screenplay from Spanish and played the role of Rosaura in the movie), adds star anise and cinnamon sticks. Since I like sweeter moles, my "fix" includes a bit of plantain, Mexican chocolate, and freshly toasted sesame seeds. This lasagne-style casserole is so rich that all you need is a nice green side salad to make a grand meal. *¡Buen provecho!*

•

I halved this recipe so it would serve four, like all the other recipes in the book. The result is that you use only half of the jar of mole so you can either double the casserole to serve eight, or reserve the mole for another use. It takes a half hour to bake but I wanted to include it anyway because it's so different from anything else in the book—and so delicious. Once you get it in the oven you can go do your laundry or something while it bakes. —Nancy

55 MINUTES

Adjust the oven rack to the middle position and preheat the oven to 300°F.

Heat the vegetable oil in a large skillet over high heat for 2 to 3 minutes, until the oil's almost smoking (you will begin to smell the oil at that point). Place one tortilla in the oil to fry for about 5 seconds, until it's golden brown. Place it on paper towels to drain while you fry the remaining tortillas in the same way, adding more oil to the skillet if necessary and heating it before adding another tortilla. When all the tortillas have been fried, stack them and cut them in half.

To make the mole, toast the sesame seeds in a large skillet over medium heat for about 3 minutes, shaking the pan often to prevent them from burning, until they're light golden and fragrant.

In a large pot, combine the mole with the chicken broth and bring to a light boil over high heat. Reduce the heat to a simmer. Stir in half of the sesame seeds and the chocolate and return the mole to a light boil, stirring constantly. Simmer for 15 minutes, stirring often to keep it from scorching.

Spoon just enough mole to cover the bottom of an 8-by-8-inch baking pan. Cover the mole with a layer of overlapping tortilla halves, using six of the halves, with the flat sides facing the edges of the pan. Cover the tortillas with a thin layer of mole (about 1/3 cup). Scatter a third of the shredded chicken over the mole, top with a third of the jack cheese, a third of the onion, and a third of the black beans. Cover with mole, then more tortillas topped with more mole as before. Repeat the layering two more times, ending with a layer of tortillas slathered with mole. Scatter the queso fresco over the top of the casserole. Drizzle it with the crema, sprinkle with the remaining sesame seeds and onion, and season with the kosher salt.

Cover the pan with foil and bake the casserole for 20 minutes. Uncover the pan and bake for another 10 minutes, until the cheese is melted and the casserole is heated through.

1/4 cup vegetable or corn oil, plus extra as needed

12 corn tortillas

FOR THE MOLE

1 teaspoon sesame seeds

1/2 8-ounce jar Doña María Mole (about 1/2 cup)

3 cups chicken broth

1 wedge of Mexican chocolate (such as Ibarra)

1/2 roasted chicken (about 3/4 pound), meat shredded and skin and bones discarded (1 1/2–2 cups)

4 ounces Monterey Jack cheese, shredded (about 1 cup)

1/4 small white onion, finely chopped or sliced into thin rings, plus extra to top the casserole

1 15-ounce can black beans, rinsed and drained (about 1 1/2 cups)

2 ounces queso fresco, crumbled

1/4 cup Mexican crema (or sour cream)

Kosher salt

Tandoori Chicken with Couscous, Cucumbers, Mint, and Green Masala Yogurt

Tandoori is an East Indian style of cooking in a cylindrical, clay tandoor oven, but in this country it's come to refer to the spice mixture that gives "tandoori chicken" its distinctive bright-red color. Green masala is an Indian curry paste made from fresh mint and cilantro. The yogurt sauce made with it in this recipe is so delicious that it's nice to have some in the refrigerator to spoon over grilled meats and to spread on sandwiches. (It will keep for up to a week.) If you have a mandoline, use it to slice the cucumbers. If not, I suggest you go out and buy one of the inexpensive Japanese mandolines, such as a Benriner, that are available now. They're so handy, you'll be happy you did. In the meantime, use a large knife to slice the cucumbers as thin as you can.

1 HOUR

Put the couscous in a large mixing bowl. Stir 1 teaspoon of the kosher salt into the boiling water and pour it over the couscous. Seal the bowl tightly with plastic wrap and set it aside until the couscous has absorbed all the water, about 5 minutes. Remove the plastic wrap and break up the couscous with your fingers.

Combine the cucumbers, parsley, mint, and garlic in a medium bowl. Drizzle with the olive oil and lemon juice and toss to combine. Add the tomatoes and toss again gently.

Rub canola oil on both sides of the chicken breasts and place each breast in a separate sandwich-size plastic bag. Use a mallet or heavy skillet to pound each chicken breast until it's about ½ inch thick and has roughly doubled in size. Remove the chicken from the bags and rub the tandoori paste into both sides of each breast.

Heat ¼ cup of the canola oil in a large skillet over medium-high heat for 2 to 3 minutes, until the oil's almost smoking (you will begin to smell the oil at that point). Place two of the chicken breasts in the skillet and sear them for 2 minutes. Flip the chicken and cook for 2 minutes more. Transfer the chicken breasts to a plate, wipe out the pan, and repeat, heating the remaining ¼ cup of canola oil and cooking the other two chicken breasts in the same way.

While the chicken is cooking, mix the yogurt and masala paste together in a small bowl.

Season the tomato-cucumber mixture with the remaining 2 teaspoons of

FOR THE COUSCOUS

1 cup couscous

3 teaspoons kosher salt

1 cup boiling water

2 small cucumbers (such as Persian or Japanese, or 1 thin hothouse cucumber; if a larger cucumber is your only option, cut it in half and scrape out the seeds), sliced 1/16 inch thick (about 1 cup)

1 cup finely chopped fresh Italian parsley leaves

¼ cup finely chopped fresh mint leaves

1 large garlic clove, grated or minced (about 1 teaspoon)

1 cup **extra-virgin olive oil**

½ cup fresh lemon juice

32 small, sweet **tomatoes** (about ½ pint), cut in half, or 16 cherry tomatoes, quartered

½ cup canola (or other neutral-flavored oil), plus extra for rubbing on the chicken breasts

4 6-ounce skinless, boneless chicken breasts

1 heaping tablespoon **tandoori paste**

FOR THE GREEN MASALA YOGURT

½ cup strained whole-milk **Greek yogurt**

4 teaspoons **green masala paste**

kosher salt and toss to combine. Add it to the bowl with the couscous and toss again gently to combine.

Spoon the couscous onto four plates, dividing it evenly. Place the chicken breasts first-cooked side up on top of the couscous and drizzle them with the juices from the plate they were resting on. Top with a spoonful of the masala yogurt and serve with the remaining masala yogurt on the side.

Chicken Tonnato

The classic version of this dish is veal tonnato: thin slices of roasted veal served cold with a tuna and mayonnaise sauce over it. It sounds strange, I know, but it's a delicious combination. Lately, maybe because people have issues about veal or because it's expensive, I've seen a lot of chefs using different meats in place of the veal. My friend Jonathan Waxman serves pork tonnato at his New York restaurant, Barbuto. And Gino Angelini, one of my favorite chefs in Los Angeles, serves one made with chicken at La Terza, one of his two restaurants. Gino's version is really unusual in that the chicken is shredded and tossed with the sauce rather than the sauce being drizzled over thin slices of meat. I thought it was such a brilliant idea that I copied it. This recipe is basically a direct rip-off of Gino's, so thank you, Gino! Taste the oil the tuna you're using is preserved in. If you like the way it tastes, use it in place of the extra-virgin olive oil in this recipe.

25 MINUTES

Place two radicchio leaves on each of four plates and sprinkle them with sea salt.

Put the Garlic Mayonnaise in a large bowl. Crumble the tuna into the bowl, add the olive oil and one third of the capers, and mix it all together with a fork, breaking up the tuna as you stir. Season with kosher salt. Add the chicken and the lemon juice and stir until the chicken is completely coated with the sauce.

Scoop the tonnato onto the radicchio leaves, dividing it evenly. Sprinkle the remaining capers and, using a microplane, grate a touch of lemon zest over each serving.

8 large radicchio leaves

Sea salt

1¼ cups Garlic Mayonnaise (page 33)

18 ounces olive oil–packed tuna, lightly drained

3 tablespoons extra-virgin olive oil (or the oil the tuna was packed in)

¼ cup capers, rinsed and chopped

Kosher salt

1 1½-pound roasted chicken, meat shredded and skin and bones discarded (3–4 cups)

2 teaspoons fresh lemon juice, or more to taste

Lemon, for grating

Chicken with Potato-Lentil Curry, Green Masala Yogurt, and Fresh Cilantro

This recipe couldn't be easier to make. It gets its flavor from the two curry sauces that it's made with. The yogurt sauce and fresh herbs that top it really brighten up the dish.

20 MINUTES

To make the green masala yogurt, mix the yogurt and masala paste together in a small bowl.

Put the potato curry, lentils, olive oil, and a generous pinch of kosher salt in a large skillet over medium heat and cook for about 5 minutes, stirring occasionally, until the mixture is warmed through.

Spoon the lentil curry onto four plates, dividing it evenly. Pile the shredded chicken on top of the lentils. Spoon the green masala yogurt over the chicken, and sprinkle with the cilantro and mint.

FOR THE GREEN MASALA YOGURT

1/2 cup strained whole-milk **Greek yogurt**

4 teaspoons **green masala paste**

1 1/4 cups **Patak's** Spicy Bombay Potato Curry

1 15-ounce can **lentils** or 1 19-ounce can lentil soup, rinsed and drained (about 1 1/2 cups)

3 tablespoons **extra-virgin olive oil**

Kosher salt

1 1 1/2-pound **roasted chicken,** meat shredded and skin and bones discarded (3–4 cups)

1 tablespoon fresh cilantro leaves, julienned

1 tablespoon fresh mint leaves, julienned

Ginger-Soy Poached Chicken with Soba Noodles, Japanese Eggplant, and Haricots Verts
Charlie Trotter • Charlie Trotter's, Chicago

The kick of ginger blended with the headiness of the hijiki seaweed makes a delicious sauce for poaching chicken breasts in. Mirin is a sweet sake, or rice wine, used in Japanese cooking; it's available at specialty and health food stores.

•

Charlie serves this dish on a bed of black rice. The rice took too long for my purposes for this book, so instead I used soba noodles, which is a Japanese pasta made of buckwheat and wheat flours. If you have the time, by all means try it with the black rice as Charlie suggests. To make fresh ginger juice, finely grate fresh gingerroot, then push the gratings through a fine strainer with the back of a spoon. —Nancy

30 MINUTES

1 tablespoon grapeseed oil (or canola oil or other neutral-flavored oil), plus extra for coating the chicken breasts and for tossing the soba noodles

4 6-ounce skinless, boneless chicken breasts

Kosher salt and freshly ground black pepper

2$\frac{1}{4}$ cups Charlie Trotter's Ginger-Soy-Hijiki Sauce

4 ounces soba noodles

4 small Japanese eggplants (about 12 ounces), sliced diagonally $\frac{1}{2}$ inch thick

2 cups haricots verts (about 5 ounces)

1$\frac{1}{2}$ tablespoons soy sauce

2 teaspoons mirin (or sake or Shaoxing wine)

1$\frac{1}{2}$ teaspoons coarsely chopped fresh Italian parsley leaves

1 teaspoon coarsely chopped fresh cilantro leaves, plus 6 whole cilantro leaves, sliced into a chiffonade

1 teaspoon fresh ginger juice

Adjust the oven rack to the middle position and preheat the oven to 400°F. Rub grapeseed oil on both sides of the chicken breasts and place each breast in a separate sandwich-size plastic bag. Use a mallet or heavy skillet to pound each chicken breast until it's about $\frac{1}{2}$ inch thick and has roughly doubled in size. Remove the chicken breasts from the bags and season both sides of each breast with kosher salt and freshly ground black pepper.

Place the chicken breasts in a large ovenproof skillet and pour the ginger-soy-hijiki sauce over the chicken to completely cover it, adding a bit of water to the skillet if there is not enough sauce to cover the chicken. Place the skillet over high heat until the sauce comes to a simmer, about 3 minutes. Transfer the skillet to the oven and bake the chicken breasts for about 5 minutes, turning them over halfway through the cooking time, until they're cooked through. Remove the skillet from the oven. Lift the chicken out of the poaching liquid and place them on a plate to rest. Season the poaching liquid with kosher salt and freshly ground black pepper.

Bring a large pot of water to a boil over high heat and add a generous amount of kosher salt. Stir in the soba noodles and cook, stirring occasionally, for 4 to 5 minutes, until they're al dente. (Since cooking times vary depending on the thickness of the noodles, for perfectly cooked noodles refer to the package instructions for the recommended time and taste the noodles frequently while they cook.) Drain the noodles in a colander and toss them with a little bit of grapeseed oil to keep them from sticking together.

Heat the tablespoon of grapeseed oil in a large nonstick skillet over high heat for 2 to 3 minutes, until the oil's almost smoking (you will begin to smell the oil at that point). Add the eggplant slices and cook them until they're golden brown and caramelized on both sides, about 1½ minutes per side. Reduce the heat to medium, add the haricots verts, and sauté them with the eggplant for about 4 minutes, until they're just tender. Turn off the heat and stir in the soy sauce, mirin, parsley, chopped cilantro, and ginger juice.

Mound the soba noodles in the center of four plates and lay the vegetables over the noodles, dividing them evenly. Thinly slice each chicken breast and fan the pieces out on top of the vegetables. Drizzle 1 to 2 tablespoons of the poaching liquid over and around each chicken breast, discarding the rest of the liquid or reserving it for another use. Sprinkle each serving with the chiffonade of cilantro and freshly ground black pepper.

Pulled Barbecue Chicken with Cole Slaw on Garlic Sourdough Toast

When it comes to barbecue sauce, people's tastes really vary. I like Stubb's Bar-B-Q Sauce, a tomato-based, Texas-style variety, but you should use whichever sauce you like best, whether it's sweet or spicy, tomato- or vinegar-based. I love cole slaw with a barbecue sandwich. Sauerkraut was a perfect solution for making a fast slaw with no chopping.

30 MINUTES

Adjust the oven rack to the middle position and preheat the oven to 350°F.

Place the bread slices on a baking sheet, brush the tops with olive oil, and bake for 15 to 20 minutes, until they're lightly toasted and golden brown. (You can also toast the bread in a toaster, but *without* the oil. Then brush the toast with oil after they're done.) Rub the oiled side of the toast with the garlic.

Heat the olive oil, onions, garlic, and a pinch of kosher salt in a medium saucepan over medium-high heat and sauté for about 1½ minutes, until the onions are soft and the garlic is soft and fragrant, stirring constantly so the garlic doesn't brown. Add the chicken, barbecue sauce, cayenne pepper, and cumin, and stir to combine. Bring the sauce to a boil, reduce the heat to low, and simmer the chicken in the sauce for 5 minutes, stirring occasionally to keep it from scorching.

Meanwhile, to make the cole slaw, combine the sauerkraut, crème fraîche, mayonnaise, mustard, vinegar, lemon juice, and garlic in a medium bowl. Season with the kosher salt and freshly ground black pepper and toss thoroughly to mix.

Place one piece of toast oiled side up on each of four plates. Mound the coleslaw on top of the toasts with the edges of the toast visible and pile the chicken on top of the cole slaw.

4 ½-inch-thick slices from a large round sourdough loaf

1 tablespoon **extra-virgin olive oil,** plus extra for brushing the bread

1 garlic clove

5 small jarred **onions,** quartered (about 1½ ounces or ⅓ cup)

2 large garlic cloves, grated or minced (about 2 teaspoons)

Kosher salt

1 1½-pound **roasted chicken,** meat shredded and skin and bones discarded (3–4 cups)

1 cup barbecue sauce

½ teaspoon cayenne pepper

½ teaspoon ground cumin

FOR THE COLE SLAW

2 cups **sauerkraut,** rinsed and drained

¼ cup **crème fraîche** (or sour cream)

3 tablespoons **mayonnaise**

2 teaspoons Dijon **mustard**

1 teaspoon apple cider **vinegar**

1 teaspoon fresh lemon juice

1 small garlic clove, grated or minced (about ½ teaspoon)

½ teaspoon kosher salt

Freshly ground black pepper

Lentils with Balsamic-Marinated Chicken and an Olive Oil–Fried Egg

I stole the idea for this dish from Gino Angelini's restaurant La Terza, where they serve it on the lunch menu. The only thing I do differently— besides starting with canned lentils, which is a major change—is tossing the shredded chicken with balsamic vinegar and pine nuts, which really brings out the flavor of the chicken.

25 MINUTES

Adjust the oven rack to the middle position and preheat the oven to 325°F.

Toss the chicken in a medium bowl with the balsamic vinegar, olive oil, lemon juice, and a pinch of kosher salt, and set it aside to marinate.

Spread the pine nuts on a baking sheet and toast them in the oven for 8 to 10 minutes, shaking the pan occasionally for even toasting, until the nuts are lightly browned and fragrant. Remove the nuts from the oven and set them aside to cool to room temperature. Add them to the bowl with the chicken and toss to combine.

To make the lentils, combine the lentils, olive oil, garlic, and a pinch of kosher salt together in a small bowl, and stir to mix thoroughly.

Heat the olive oil in a large nonstick skillet over high heat for 2 to 3 minutes, until the oil's almost smoking (you will begin to smell the oil at that point). Break one egg into a small bowl, and then pour the egg into the skillet. Let it just begin to set around the edges then break the second egg into the bowl and pour it into the skillet. (By waiting a moment before adding the second egg, the eggs won't set together and will be easy to separate and serve individually.) Cook them for about 1½ minutes, until the edges are golden and crispy and the whites are set but the yolks are still runny. Remove the eggs to a plate and cook the remaining two eggs in the same way.

Spoon the lentils into mounds on each of four plates and top each mound with the chicken, dividing it evenly. Place one egg on top of each serving and sprinkle them with sea salt and freshly ground black pepper. Scatter the parsley leaves over the eggs and lentils.

½ **roasted chicken** (about ¾ pound), meat shredded and skin and bones discarded (1½–2 cups)

3 tablespoons aged **balsamic vinegar**

1 tablespoon plus 1 teaspoon **extra-virgin olive oil**

1 teaspoon fresh lemon juice

Kosher salt

¼ cup pine nuts

FOR THE LENTILS

2 15-ounce cans **lentils** or 2 19-ounce cans lentil soup, rinsed and drained (about 3 cups)

3 tablespoons **extra-virgin olive oil**

1 small garlic clove, grated or minced (about ½ teaspoon)

Kosher salt

¼ cup **extra-virgin olive oil**

4 large eggs

Sea salt

Freshly ground black pepper

¼ cup loosely packed fresh Italian parsley leaves

SEAFOOD

Crab and Shrimp Cakes with Celery Root Rémoulade

Crabmeat is one of those delicacies that's all about the season, the freshness, and the fact that it isn't always available. But for something like crab cakes, which have so many other ingredients mixed in with the crab, you not only don't need to go to the trouble of steaming fresh crab and taking the meat out of the shell, you wouldn't really want to use good fresh crabmeat for that purpose (at least I wouldn't). The seafood counter at most supermarkets carry cooked lump crabmeat. The brand I choose to use is called Blue Star. The flavor is good, and the chunks are big enough to give a nice texture to the cakes. Devonshire cream is an English brand of double cream, which has double the butterfat of heavy cream. It needs to be at room temperature; refrigerated, it's so thick you can't even pour it. Hot cherry peppers are round red peppers that have just the amount of heat, flavor, and crunch I like.

30 MINUTES

To make the crab cakes, combine the crabmeat, shrimp, breadcrumbs, Devonshire cream, chives, lemon juice, cherry peppers, cayenne, and kosher salt and mix thoroughly to combine. Form the crab mixture into 8 equally sized patties about 3 inches wide and ½ to ¾ inch thick and press them together firmly to prevent them from breaking apart while they're cooking. Set them aside while you prepare the rémoulade.

FOR THE CRAB AND SHRIMP CAKES

8 ounces cooked crabmeat

8 ounces cooked bay shrimp

¾ cup **breadcrumbs** or 12 **saltine crackers,** ground to fine crumbs

1 5.6-ounce jar Devonshire cream (1 cup plus 2 tablespoons), at room temperature

3 tablespoons finely chopped fresh chives

1 tablespoon plus 1 teaspoon fresh lemon juice

Heaping ½ teaspoon finely chopped jarred hot cherry peppers

Heaping ½ teaspoon cayenne pepper

½ teaspoon kosher salt

To make the rémoulade, stir the mayonnaise, crème fraîche, mustard, tarragon, chives, chervil, capers, vinegar, lemon juice, garlic, cornichons, and kosher salt together in a medium bowl. Add the celery root and gently stir to coat it with the rémoulade.

Pour the flour on a plate and dredge the cakes in the flour to coat them on both sides.

Heat 1/4 cup of the oil in a large skillet over high heat for 2 to 3 minutes, until the oil's almost smoking (you will begin to smell the oil at that point). Place half of the cakes in the skillet and cook them for about 1 1/2 minutes, until they're golden brown. Turn the cakes over carefully so they don't break, reduce the heat to medium, and cook them for 1 minute on the second side. Transfer the cakes to paper towels to drain. Turn the heat up to high, heat the remaining 1/4 cup oil, and cook the remaining cakes in the same way.

Scatter the greens on each of four plates, dividing them evenly, and sprinkle them with sea salt. Place two crab and shrimp cakes first-cooked side up on each plate on top of the greens and squeeze a few drops of lemon juice and spoon a dollop of the rémoulade on each cake. Sprinkle the chives over the rémoulade. Serve the remaining rémoulade on the side.

FOR THE RÉMOULADE

3 tablespoons **mayonnaise**

1/4 cup **crème fraîche**

2 teaspoons Dijon **mustard**

2 teaspoons finely chopped fresh tarragon leaves

2 teaspoons finely chopped fresh chives, plus extra for garnish

2 teaspoons finely chopped fresh chervil leaves

1 teaspoon **capers,** chopped

1 teaspoon apple cider **vinegar**

1 teaspoon fresh lemon juice

1 small garlic clove, grated or minced (about 1/2 teaspoon)

4 **cornichons,** thinly sliced

1/2 teaspoon kosher salt

1 cup jarred shredded **celery root** (from 1 12.5-ounce jar) or **mixed salad,** drained and patted dry with paper towels

1/2 cup flour, for dredging the cakes

1/2 cup canola oil (or other neutral-flavored oil)

8 cups loosely packed mixed baby greens

Sea salt

Lemon, for squeezing over the crab cakes

Salmon and Ritz Cracker Cakes with Chipotle Mayonnaise

This is a version of the salmon patties Carolynn's mother made for her when she was a little kid, using whole smoked salmon fillet instead of canned salmon. The Ritz cracker crumbs give them a nice flavor. The crackers have a lot of salt in them, so I didn't add more. I like these cakes best coated in panko, but as an alternative you can grind up more Ritz crackers and coat the cakes with those instead.

30 MINUTES

Divide the radish sprouts evenly among four plates and season them with sea salt. Leaving the root ends attached, remove the leaves from the radishes, keeping one pretty leaf intact on each radish, and set them aside.

Crumble the salmon into a medium bowl. Add the mayonnaise, cracker crumbs, dill, and chives and mix to thoroughly combine. Form the mixture into 8 equally sized patties about 3 inches wide and 1/2 to 3/4 inch thick and press them together firmly to prevent them from falling apart while they're cooking. Pour the panko on a plate and press the salmon cakes into the panko to coat them on all sides.

To cook the salmon cakes, heat 1/4 cup of the oil in a large skillet over high heat for 2 to 3 minutes, until the oil's almost smoking (you will begin to smell the oil at that point). Place half of the salmon cakes in the skillet and cook them for about 1 1/2 minutes, until they're golden brown. Turn the cakes over carefully so they don't break, reduce the heat to medium, and cook them for 1 minute on the second side. Transfer the cakes to paper towels to drain. Turn the heat up to high, heat the remaining 1/4 cup of oil, and cook the remaining salmon cakes in the same way.

Place two salmon cakes on each plate on top of the radish sprouts and nestle three radishes on each plate next to the cakes. Squeeze a few drops of lemon juice and spoon a dollop of the Chipotle Mayonnaise on each salmon cake.

2 cups radish sprouts (or 4 cups loosely packed mixed baby greens)

Sea salt

12 French breakfast radishes or other small radishes (about 1 bunch)

16 ounces **smoked salmon fillet** (in a thick chunk, not sliced)

1 cup **mayonnaise**

24 Ritz crackers, ground to fine crumbs

1/4 cup finely chopped fresh dill

1 heaping tablespoon finely chopped fresh chives

1/2 cup **panko**

1/2 cup canola oil (or other neutral-flavored oil)

Lemon, for squeezing over the salmon cakes

Chipotle Mayonnaise (page 35)

Sautéed Halibut with Salsify and Scallions

Salsify is one of those "exotic" vegetables you don't see very often. I was introduced to it while waitressing at a French café in college. It's a root vegetable that looks similar to a long, white carrot but is less sweet and much earthier tasting than a carrot. It's often braised and it's always fully cooked; it never comes to the table al dente the way that asparagus or broccoli might. I was happy to find that canned salsify had a very similar texture and taste to braised fresh salsify. I chose to serve it here because the white-on-white pairing of the mild white fish with the white vegetable looks spare and elegant—and tastes delicious.

20 MINUTES

Rinse the halibut fillets under cool water, pat them dry with paper towels, and season both sides with kosher salt and freshly ground black pepper.

Heat the oil in a large nonstick skillet over high heat for 2 to 3 minutes, until the oil's almost smoking (you will begin to smell the oil at that point). Place the halibut fillets in the skillet skinned (rounded) side down and sear them for 2 minutes, until the cooked sides are golden brown. Carefully turn the fillets and cook them for 1 minute, until the second sides are golden and the fish is opaque and flakes easily when pierced with a sharp knife but is still moist. Transfer the halibut to a plate.

Place the skillet over medium-high heat, add the butter, and cook it for about 1 minute, until it melts and starts to bubble and brown. Add the salsify and cook it for about 30 seconds, just long enough to warm it through. Turn off the heat and stir in the scallions and lemon juice.

Stack the salsify into piles in the center of four plates, dividing it evenly. Place the halibut fillets with the first-cooked side up on top of the salsify, drizzle them with the juices from the plate they were resting on, and use scissors to snip about 1 teaspoon of chives over each fillet.

4 6-ounce halibut fillets (1–1½ inches thick; or any mild-flavored, nonoily white fish, such as bass, branzino, grouper, or snapper), skinned and deboned

Kosher salt and freshly ground black pepper

3 tablespoons canola oil (or other neutral-flavored oil)

1 stick (½ cup) unsalted butter

1 8-ounce can salsify (about 30 pieces), drained and patted dry with paper towels

8 scallions, very thinly sliced diagonally (white and halfway up the green parts)

1 teaspoon fresh lemon juice

20 fresh chives

Pan-Seared Halibut with Salsify, Shiitake Mushrooms, and Caper-Raisin Vinaigrette
Tom Colicchio • Craft, New York City

When I saw this vinaigrette recipe in the *New York Times,* I knew I had to include it in this book. It's one of those things for which you're likely to have all the ingredients (except the fish, of course) already on hand in your pantry. I used canned salsify, which I discovered during the process of working on this book, in place of Tom's braised fresh salsify. —Nancy

30 MINUTES

To make the vinaigrette, combine the verjus, capers, raisins, and olive oil in a small saucepan over high heat and bring it to a low boil. Reduce the heat and simmer for 5 minutes. Reduce the heat again to medium-low and let the capers and raisins steep in the verjus for 5 minutes to meld the flavors. Transfer the mixture to a blender and purée it until it's very smooth. Season the vinaigrette with kosher salt and freshly ground black pepper.

Heat the olive oil in a large skillet over high heat for 2 to 3 minutes, until the oil's almost smoking (you will begin to smell the oil at that point). Add the mushrooms and a pinch of kosher salt and sauté them for about 5 minutes, stirring occasionally, until they brown slightly. Add the salsify and cook, stirring constantly, to heat it through, about 1 minute. Add the butter and stir until it melts. Turn off the heat and season the vegetables with more kosher salt.

Rinse the halibut fillets, pat them dry with paper towels, and season both sides with kosher salt and freshly ground black pepper.

Heat the canola oil in a large nonstick skillet over high heat for 2 to 3 minutes, until the oil's almost smoking (you will begin to smell the oil at that point). Place the fillets in the skillet skinned (rounded) side down and sear them for 2 minutes, until the cooked sides are golden brown. Carefully turn the fillets and cook them for 1 minute, until the second sides are golden and the fish is opaque and flakes easily when pierced with a sharp knife but is still moist.

While the fish is cooking, spoon the sauce in a circular pattern, like a doughnut with a hole in the center, onto four plates, dividing it evenly. Place the salsify in the center of the sauce and put the halibut fillets with the first-cooked side up on top of the salsify. Squeeze a few drops of lemon juice over each fillet, spoon the mushrooms over them, and garnish each serving with a sprig of thyme.

FOR THE VINAIGRETTE
½ cup **verjus**
¼ cup **capers**
¼ cup golden raisins
½ teaspoon **extra-virgin olive oil**
Kosher salt and freshly ground black pepper

1 tablespoon **extra-virgin olive oil**
16 baby shiitake mushrooms (about 8 ounces), stems removed
Kosher salt
1 8-ounce can **salsify** (about 30 pieces), drained and patted dry with a paper towel
1 tablespoon unsalted butter
4 6-ounce halibut fillets (1–1½ inches thick; or any mild-flavored, nonoily white fish, such as bass, branzino, grouper, or snapper), skinned and deboned
Freshly ground black pepper
3 tablespoons canola oil (or other neutral-flavored oil)
Lemon, for squeezing over the fish
4 fresh thyme sprigs

Mustard-Crusted Halibut with Paprika Potatoes and Fresh Parsley Leaves

Potatoes with paprika was the first dish I ever cooked. I was nine years old and showing off, and I decided to make my lifelong friend Margy Rochlin and myself something to eat. I opened up a can of Hunt's potatoes and sautéed them with butter (well, okay, it was margarine!) and *way* too much paprika. We thought the potatoes were so delicious; all these years later, Margy still talks about them. The *sale erbe,* or "herb salt," I use in this recipe contains rosemary, sage, garlic, and freshly ground black pepper and is a really nice product to season meat and fish with. There are many brands that make *sale erbe,* so it isn't hard to find, but if you can't find it, use a good quality fish rub instead.

25 MINUTES

Adjust the oven rack to the middle position and preheat the oven to 450°F. Stir the Dijon mustard, dry mustard, and 1 tablespoon of water together in a small bowl.

Rinse the halibut fillets under cool water, pat them dry with paper towels, and season both sides with the herb salt, dividing it evenly.

Heat the canola oil in a large nonstick skillet (ovenproof if possible) over high heat for 2 to 3 minutes, until the oil's almost smoking (you will begin to smell the oil at that point). Place the fish fillets skinned (rounded) side down in the skillet and sear them for about 2 minutes, until the cooked sides are golden brown. Turn off the heat and carefully turn the fillets. Smear the mustard sauce over the cooked sides of the fish, dividing it evenly, and sprinkle the breadcrumbs over the mustard. If you are not using an ovenproof skillet, transfer the fillets to a baking sheet. Place the fish in the oven to bake for 4 to 6 minutes, until the mustard sauce is set, the breadcrumbs are golden brown, and the fish is cooked through but still moist.

While the fish is baking, melt the butter in a large skillet or saucepan over medium-high heat for about 1 minute, until it starts to bubble and brown. Add the potatoes, sprinkle them with the paprika, and stir. Sauté the potatoes, shaking the pan occasionally, for 6 to 8 minutes, until they're browned. Turn off the heat, season them with kosher salt, add the parsley leaves, and toss to combine.

Place the halibut fillets breadcrumb side up on four plates and squeeze a few drops of lemon juice over each fillet. Surround each fillet with potatoes, dividing them evenly.

1/4 cup Dijon **mustard**

2 tablespoons dry mustard, such as Coleman's

4 6-ounce halibut fillets (1–1 1/2 inches thick; or any mild-flavored, nonoily white fish, such as bass, branzino, grouper, or snapper), skinned and deboned

1 tablespoon plus 1 teaspoon *sale erbe*

1/4 cup canola oil (or other neutral-flavored oil)

1/4 cup **breadcrumbs** or **panko**

2 tablespoons unsalted butter

2 cups canned or jarred **potatoes** (from 1 12-ounce jar or 1 14 1/2-ounce can), broken into 1-inch pieces if large

2 teaspoons smoked Spanish **paprika**

Kosher salt

1/2 cup loosely packed fresh Italian parsley leaves

Lemon, for squeezing over the fish

Fillet of Sole with Preserved Lemon Butter Sauce

The intense flavor of the preserved lemon used in this dish adds a layer of complexity to what is otherwise a pretty typical lemon-butter sauce.

35 MINUTES

Mound the spinach onto four plates, dividing it evenly, and sprinkle it with sea salt.

Rinse the preserved lemon under cool water and scoop out and discard the pulp. Cut the peel into 1/8-inch strips and set aside.

Rinse the sole fillets under cool water, pat them dry with paper towels, and season both sides with kosher salt and freshly ground black pepper.

Heat 2 tablespoons of the canola oil in a large nonstick skillet over high heat for 2 to 3 minutes, until the oil's almost smoking (you will begin to smell the oil at that point). Put two of the fish fillets skinned (rounded) side down in the skillet, place a flat lid or a heatproof plate smaller than the diameter of the pan directly on the fish to keep it pressed down, and cook for about 1 minute. Remove the lid or plate, reduce the heat to medium, and continue to cook the fish for 1 to 2 minutes, until the cooked sides are golden brown. Carefully turn the fillets over, turn off the heat, and cook them from the residual heat of the pan, uncovered, for 1 to 2 minutes more, until the second sides are golden and the fish flakes easily when pierced by a sharp knife but is still moist. Transfer the fillets to a plate, wipe out the pan, and repeat, heating the remaining 2 tablespoons of canola oil and cooking the other two fish fillets in the same way.

To make the sauce, reduce the heat to medium-high. Add the shallots, garlic, and a pinch of kosher salt to the skillet and oil you cooked the fish in and sauté for about 1 1/2 minutes, until the shallots are soft and the garlic is soft and fragrant, stirring constantly so the garlic doesn't brown. Add the preserved lemon and wine and cook for about 1 minute, until the liquids are reduced and the pan is almost dry. Turn the heat up to high, add the fish stock, and bring it to a boil. Reduce the heat to medium-high and add the butter piece by piece, whisking constantly as you do so to emulsify the sauce. Turn off the heat and stir in the chives, capers, and a few drops of lemon juice.

Place the sole fillets first-cooked side up on top of the spinach, drizzle them with the juices from the plate they were resting on, and pour the sauce over them.

8 cups loosely packed baby
  spinach leaves

Sea salt

Half of a **preserved lemon**

4 6-ounce sole fillets (1–1 1/2 inches
  thick; or any mild-flavored,
  nonoily white fish, such as
  branzino, grouper, halibut, or
  snapper), skinned and
  deboned

Kosher salt and freshly ground
  black pepper

1/4 cup canola oil (or other
  neutral-flavored oil)

2 medium shallots, grated or
  minced (about 1 heaping
  tablespoon)

2 large garlic cloves, grated or
  minced (about 2 teaspoons)

2 tablespoons dry white wine

1/2 cup fish **stock**

1/2 stick (1/4 cup) unsalted butter,
  cut into small pieces

1/4 cup finely chopped fresh
  chives

1/4 cup **capers,** chopped

Lemon, for squeezing into
  the sauce

Fillet of Sole with Warm Farro and Tomato Salad and Tangy Greek Yogurt Sauce

This yogurt sauce is the perfect example of a quick, flavorful sauce (or condiment) that makes a very simple dish special. You can use this yogurt sauce with steak, lamb, chicken, or any fish, as I have throughout this book.

30 MINUTES

To make the yogurt sauce, stir the yogurt, garlic, lemon juice, and kosher salt together in a small bowl.

To make the farro, heat the olive oil in a large skillet over high heat for 2 to 3 minutes, until the oil's almost smoking (you will begin to smell the oil at that point). Add the tomatoes and cook them for 4 to 5 minutes, until they're soft and the skins are shriveled. Turn the heat off, stir in the shallots, garlic, and a pinch of kosher salt and sauté them in the residual heat for about 1½ minutes, until the garlic is soft and fragrant. Stir in the farro, parsley, vinegar, and lemon juice. Season with additional kosher salt and freshly ground black pepper and lemon juice to taste.

Rinse the sole fillets under cool water, pat them dry with paper towels, and season both sides with kosher salt and freshly ground black pepper.

Heat 2 tablespoons of the canola oil in a large nonstick skillet over high heat for 2 to 3 minutes, until the oil's almost smoking (you will begin to smell the oil at that point). Put two of the fish fillets skinned (rounded) side down in the skillet, place a flat lid or a heatproof plate smaller than the diameter of the pan directly on the fish to keep it pressed down (this prevents the fish from curling), and cook for about 1 minute. Remove the lid or plate, reduce the heat to medium, and continue to cook the fish for 1 to 2 minutes, until the cooked sides are golden brown. Carefully turn the fillets over, turn off the heat, and cook them from the residual heat of the pan, uncovered, for 1 to 2 minutes more, until the second sides are golden and the fish flakes easily when pierced by a sharp knife but is still moist. Transfer the fillets to a plate, wipe out the pan, and repeat, heating the remaining 2 tablespoons of canola oil and cooking the other two fish fillets in the same way.

Spoon the farro salad onto four plates, dividing it evenly. Place the sole fillets first-cooked side up on top of the farro and drizzle them with the juices from the plate they were resting on. Spoon the yogurt sauce over the fish and top with the whole parsley leaves.

FOR THE YOGURT SAUCE

½ cup strained whole-milk **Greek yogurt**

1 large garlic clove, grated or minced (about 1 teaspoon)

2 tablespoons fresh lemon juice

1 teaspoon kosher salt

FOR THE FARRO

¼ cup **extra-virgin olive oil**

48 small, sweet **tomatoes** (scant pint), cut in half, or 24 cherry tomatoes, quartered

2 medium shallots, grated or minced (about 1 heaping tablespoon)

2 large garlic cloves, grated or minced (about 2 teaspoons)

Kosher salt

¾ cup jarred cooked **farro**

1 cup loosely packed fresh Italian parsley leaves

1 tablespoon champagne **vinegar**

Juice of ½ lemon, or more for seasoning

Freshly ground black pepper

4 6-ounce sole fillets (1–1½ inches thick; or any mild-flavored, nonoily white fish, such as branzino, grouper, halibut, or snapper), skinned and deboned

Kosher salt and freshly ground black pepper

¼ cup canola oil (or other neutral-flavored oil)

Fresh Italian parsley leaves, for garnish

Seared Rare Tuna with Mashed Flageolet Beans and Radicchio

I love the way the flavors and textures of fish and soft, creamy beans work together in a dish. The combination is more common in Europe than it is here, where many people are surprised to find the two together. Topping the beans with oil, aged balsamic vinegar, lemon, and freshly ground black pepper just before serving them really livens up the flavor of the finished dish.

35 MINUTES

To make the beans, heat ¼ cup of the olive oil with the garlic over medium-high heat and cook for about 1½ minutes, until the garlic is soft and fragrant, stirring constantly so the garlic doesn't brown. Turn the heat up to high, add the beans, rosemary, kosher salt, and ¼ cup water, and bring it to a boil. Reduce the heat to low and simmer the beans for 2 minutes, until they're tender enough to smash easily with a fork. Transfer the beans and their cooking liquid to a large mortar or bowl. Add the remaining 2 tablespoons of olive oil and the balsamic vinegar, and mash with a pestle or a potato masher until the beans are mashed but still slightly chunky. Add a few drops of warm water if necessary to obtain a creamy, spoonable consistency.

Rinse the tuna steaks under cool water, pat them dry with paper towels, and season both sides with kosher salt and freshly ground black pepper.

Heat the canola oil in a large heavy-bottomed skillet over high heat for 2 to 3 minutes, until the oil's almost smoking (you will begin to smell the oil at that point). Place the tuna steaks in the pan and sear them for 1 minute on each side if you want them rare, 1½ minutes per side for medium-rare. Transfer the tuna to a plate to rest.

If the skillet is dry, add enough canola oil to coat it and heat it over high heat. Put 4 of the radicchio leaves in the skillet in a single layer and cook them for about 45 seconds on each side, until they're seared and wilted slightly. Remove the leaves from the skillet and place two leaves on each of two plates. Add a bit more oil to the pan if it's dry, cook the remaining leaves in the same way.

Spoon the mashed beans onto the radicchio, dividing them evenly and smashing them down slightly to create a bed. Drizzle each serving of beans with the high-quality olive oil, balsamic vinegar, and freshly ground black pepper. Place the tuna steaks first-seared side up on top of the beans, drizzle them with the juices from the plate they were resting on, and squeeze a few drops of lemon juice over them.

FOR THE BEANS

¼ cup plus 2 tablespoons **extra-virgin olive oil**

2 large garlic cloves, grated or minced (about 2 teaspoons)

1 15-ounce can flageolet **beans,** rinsed and drained (about 1½ cups)

2 teaspoons chopped fresh rosemary leaves

2 teaspoons kosher salt

2 teaspoons aged **balsamic vinegar**

4 6-ounce sushi-grade tuna steaks (1–1½ inches thick)

Kosher salt and freshly ground black pepper

¼ cup canola oil (or other neutral-flavored oil), plus extra for searing the radicchio if necessary

8 large whole radicchio leaves

High-quality **extra-virgin olive oil,** for drizzling

Aged **balsamic vinegar,** for drizzling

Lemon, for squeezing over the fish

Seared Rare Tuna with Marinated Shell Beans and Heirloom Tomatoes

I call for a mix of shell beans in this recipe because their different sizes, shapes, colors, and flavors make an interesting ragù. In creating such a selection, you're going to have some beans left over. If you're wondering what to do with them, I suggest you use them to make the Tuna and White Bean Salad (page 21). A dollop of Garlic Mayonnaise (page 33) is the perfect finish for this dish, but I made it optional because you may not want to take the time to make it—and the dish is still delicious without it. Use the heirloom tomatoes only in the summer. When they're not in season, substitute small, sweet tomatoes (see "Tomatoes"), cut in half.

20 MINUTES

Place two tomato slices on each of four plates, drizzle them with a generous amount of the high-quality olive oil, sprinkle them with sea salt, and set them aside to marinate.

To make the beans, combine the beans, pesto, olive oil, and scallions in a medium bowl, toss gently to coat, and season them with kosher salt and freshly ground black pepper.

Rinse the tuna steaks under cool water, pat them dry with paper towels, and season both sides with kosher salt and freshly ground black pepper.

Heat the canola oil in a large heavy-bottomed skillet over high heat for 2 to 3 minutes, until the oil's almost smoking (you will begin to smell the oil at that point). Place the tuna steaks in the pan and sear them for 1 minute on each side if you want them rare, 1½ minutes per side for medium-rare.

Place the tuna steaks with the first-seared side up on the tomato slices and squeeze a few drops of lemon juice over them. Spoon the beans over the tuna steaks, dividing them evenly, put a dollop of Garlic Mayonnaise on top of each serving of beans (if you are using it), and use scissors to snip about ½ teaspoon of chives directly over each tuna steak.

2 large heirloom tomatoes, each cut into 4 thick slices

High-quality **extra-virgin olive oil,** for drizzling

Sea salt

FOR THE MARINATED SHELL BEANS

2 cups mixed canned **beans** (including any combination of cannellini beans, garbanzo beans, flageolet beans, borlotti beans, lima beans, or giant white beans), rinsed and drained

3 tablespoons **basil pesto**

3 tablespoons **extra-virgin olive oil**

2 scallions, very thinly sliced diagonally (white and halfway up the green parts)

Kosher salt and freshly ground black pepper

4 6-ounce sushi-grade tuna steaks (1–1½ inches thick)

Kosher salt and freshly ground black pepper

¼ cup canola oil (or other neutral-flavored oil)

Lemon, for squeezing over the fish

Garlic Mayonnaise (optional; page 33)

10 fresh chives

Seared Rare Tuna with Lima Bean Purée and Harissa

I don't think I've ever met a vegetable with a worse reputation than lima beans. I once told a friend to close his eyes and take a taste of lima bean purée I'd made similar to the one here. He thought it was delicious, but when I told him what it was, he spit it out and refused to eat another bite. "I hate lima beans!" he said. Well, I happen to love them. Here I start with frozen or canned (both are remarkably good). They're stewed in olive oil until they have a rich flavor and buttery texture. You'll have some of the olive oil left, which you can use to dress a salad or to drizzle over fish. The spicy harissa adds a nice counterpoint to the rich tuna and beans.

25 MINUTES

To make the purée, combine the lima beans and olive oil in a small saucepan over medium-high heat and cook for 5 minutes to infuse the beans with the olive oil. Turn off the heat and drain the beans, reserving both the beans and the oil.

In a large bowl, stir together the parsley, mint, cilantro, harissa, 1 teaspoon of the lemon juice, vinegar, half of the garlic, 1/2 teaspoon of the kosher salt, and 1/4 cup plus 2 tablespoons of the olive oil the lima beans were cooked in. Add 1 cup of the lima beans, stir to combine, and set them aside to marinate.

Transfer the remaining beans to a large mortar or bowl and mash with a pestle or potato masher until they're mashed but still slightly chunky. Add 1/2 cup of the reserved olive oil (save the rest for another use), the remaining teaspoon of kosher salt, the other half of the garlic, and the remaining table-spoon of lemon juice and stir to combine.

Scatter 1 cup of greens on each of four plates and season with sea salt. Spoon the lima bean purée onto the center of each plate and use the back of a small spoon to make a crater in each mound of purée. Leaving some of the oil in the bowl, spoon the whole beans into the indentation.

Rinse the tuna steaks under cool water, pat them dry with paper towels, and season both sides with kosher salt and freshly ground black pepper.

Heat the canola oil in a large heavy-bottomed skillet over high heat for 2 to 3 minutes, until the oil's almost smoking (you will begin to smell the oil at that point). Place the tuna steaks in the pan and sear them for 1 minute on each side if you want them rare, 1 1/2 minutes per side for medium-rare.

Place the tuna steaks with the first-seared side up on top of the beans and squeeze a few drops of fresh lemon juice over each steak.

FOR THE LIMA BEAN PURÉE

3 cups frozen lima beans, thawed, or 2 15-ounce cans lima beans, rinsed and drained

1 1/2 cups extra-virgin olive oil

3 tablespoons finely chopped fresh Italian parsley leaves

3 tablespoons finely chopped fresh mint leaves

3 tablespoons finely chopped fresh cilantro leaves

2 tablespoons harissa

1 tablespoon plus 1 teaspoon fresh lemon juice

1 teaspoon red wine vinegar

1 large garlic clove, grated or minced (about 1 teaspoon)

1 1/2 teaspoons kosher salt

4 cups loosely packed mixed baby greens

Sea salt

FOR THE TUNA

4 6-ounce sushi-grade tuna steaks (1–1 1/2 inches thick)

Kosher salt and freshly ground black pepper

1/4 cup canola oil (or other neutral-flavored oil)

Lemon, for squeezing over the fish

Seared Rare Tuna with Fregola Sarda, Puttanesca Sauce, and Caper Relish

Puttanesca, a spicy tomato sauce with black olives, capers, anchovies, and chile flakes, gets its name from the Italian word *puttana,* which means "whore," supposedly because the aroma of the sauce cooking was appealing to men who frequented houses of ill repute. When buying jarred puttanesca sauce, look for one that has either tuna or anchovies in it (some grocery store brands don't have any fish in them at all). Rustichella d'Abruzzo is my preferred brand. If you can't find it or any jarred puttanesca you like, substitute your favorite spicy tomato sauce. The relish is made with both capers and caperberries: capers are the buds of a Mediterranean bush and caperberries are the actual fruits of the same bush. Fregola sarda is a kind of semolina pasta traditional to Sardinia. *Fregola* means "crumbs," for the small size and shape of the pasta, which looks like big, pearly couscous. If you can't find it, substitute Israeli couscous.

30 MINUTES

To make the relish, stir the caperberries, olive oil, parsley, onion, capers, and garlic together in a small bowl.

To make the puttanesca sauce, heat the olive oil with the garlic in a medium skillet over medium-high heat and sauté for about 1½ minutes, until the garlic is soft and fragrant, stirring constantly so the garlic doesn't brown. Stir in the chile flakes, and cook for about 30 seconds, then stir in the puttanesca sauce, season with kosher salt, and cook for about 3 minutes more, just long enough to warm the sauce through. Turn off the heat and stir in the parsley.

To cook the pasta, bring a large pot of water to a boil over high heat and add a generous amount of kosher salt. Stir in the fregola sarda and cook, stirring occasionally to prevent the pasta from sticking together, until it's al dente. (Since cooking times vary depending on the thickness of the pasta, for perfectly cooked pasta, refer to the package instructions for the recommended time and taste the pasta frequently while it cooks.) Reserve a few tablespoons of the pasta water, then drain the pasta and transfer it quickly to the skillet with the puttanesca. Stir in the reserved water if the sauce is too thick, and bring it to a boil over high heat, stirring to coat the pasta with the sauce.

While the water is coming to a boil and the pasta is cooking, rinse the tuna steaks under cool water, pat them dry with paper towels, and season both sides with kosher salt and freshly ground black pepper.

FOR THE CAPER RELISH

½ cup **caperberries,** thinly sliced
¼ cup **extra-virgin olive oil**
¼ cup finely chopped fresh Italian parsley leaves
½ small red onion, finely chopped
2 tablespoons **capers,** chopped
1 large garlic clove, grated or minced (about 1 teaspoon)

FOR THE PUTTANESCA SAUCE

3 tablespoons **extra-virgin olive oil**
4 large garlic cloves, grated or minced (about 1 tablespoon)
Pinch of chile flakes
¾ cup jarred puttanesca sauce (or any spicy tomato sauce)
Kosher salt
¼ cup finely chopped fresh Italian parsley leaves

Kosher salt
4 ounces fregola sarda
4 6-ounce sushi-grade tuna steaks (1–1½ inches thick)
Freshly ground black pepper
¼ cup canola oil (or other neutral-flavored oil)
Lemon, for squeezing over the fish

Heat the canola oil in a large heavy-bottomed skillet over high heat for 2 to 3 minutes, until the oil's almost smoking (you will begin to smell the oil at that point). Place the tuna steaks in the pan and sear them for 1 minute on each side if you want them rare, 1½ minutes per side for medium-rare.

Spoon the pasta out of the skillet onto four plates, dividing it evenly. Place the tuna steaks first-seared sides up on top of the pasta, squeeze a few drops of lemon juice over each steak, and top with a spoonful of the caper relish.

Seared Rare Tuna with Tomato-Olive Salsa

The key to shopping for this recipe is to get a chunky olive tapenade, not the more common kind, which is completely puréed. It's sometimes called olive bruschetta. The one I found made by Aiello contains olives, olive oil, peppers, capers, garlic, vinegar, salt, and spices. Look for one with an equally "pure" ingredient list.

20 MINUTES

To make the salsa, stir the tomatoes, olive tapenade, parsley, and garlic together in a small bowl and set aside.

Rinse the tuna steaks under cool water, pat them dry with paper towels, and season both sides with kosher salt and freshly ground black pepper.

Heat the canola oil in a large heavy-bottomed skillet over high heat for 2 to 3 minutes, until the oil's almost smoking (you will begin to smell the oil at that point). Place the tuna steaks in the pan and sear them for 1 minute on each side if you want them rare, $1\frac{1}{2}$ minutes per side for medium-rare.

Pile the arugula in the center of each of four plates, dividing it evenly, and sprinkle with sea salt. Place the tuna steaks first-seared side up on top of the arugula. Squeeze a few drops of lemon juice over each steak, drizzle with a little of the high-quality olive oil, and spoon the salsa on top.

FOR THE TOMATO-OLIVE SALSA

32 small, sweet **tomatoes** (about $\frac{1}{2}$ pint), cut in half, or 16 cherry tomatoes, quartered

$\frac{1}{2}$ cup chunky **olive tapenade**

1 heaping tablespoon finely chopped fresh Italian parsley leaves

1 large garlic clove, finely chopped or grated (about 1 teaspoon)

4 6-ounce sushi-grade tuna steaks (1–$1\frac{1}{2}$ inches thick)

Kosher salt and freshly ground black pepper

$\frac{1}{4}$ cup canola oil (or other neutral-flavored oil)

8 cups loosely packed arugula leaves

Sea salt

Lemon, for squeezing over the fish

High-quality **extra-virgin olive oil**, for drizzling

Ling Cod with Sweet Green Peas, Hijiki, and Spicy Lemon Dressing

Hijiki, a stringy brown seaweed used in Japanese cooking, is not something I normally cook with—or eat. I don't even think I knew what it was until Matt Molina convinced me to try it with this fish. He thought it would work well in combination with the Asian-inspired dressing on the fish, and he was right. I loved them together. I recommend a very specific product, Nobu Spicy Lemon Dressing, as the sauce for this fish, but if you find another lemony dressing you think would work well here, by all means use it.

25 MINUTES

Place the hijiki in a medium bowl and pour the hot water over it. Set it aside to soak for about 10 minutes, until it's tender and plump. Drain the hijiki in a colander, rinse thoroughly, then return it to the bowl. Add the lemon dressing and garlic and stir to combine. Season with kosher salt and set aside to marinate.

Rinse the cod fillets under cool water, pat them dry with paper towels, and season both sides with kosher salt and freshly ground black pepper.

Heat the canola oil in a large nonstick skillet over high heat for 2 to 3 minutes, until the oil's almost smoking (you will begin to smell the oil at that point). Put the cod fillets skin side down in the skillet. Place a flat lid or plate smaller than the diameter of the pan on the fish and press down on it gently for about 1 minute. (This helps render a crispy skin.) Remove the lid or plate, reduce the heat to medium, and cook the fillets for about 3 more minutes, until the skin sides are golden brown and crispy. Slide a thin spatula under the fillets to release any sticking spots and gently turn them over. Cook the fish on the second side for about 3 minutes, until it's opaque and flakes easily when pierced with a sharp knife but is still moist.

Meanwhile, place the peas in a small saucepan over medium-low heat and cook them for 3 to 4 minutes, just enough to warm them through. (Do not cook the peas until they darken and discolor.)

Spoon the peas onto four plates, dividing them evenly. Place the cod skin side up on top of the peas, pile the hijiki on top of the cod, and drizzle any remaining dressing over the hijiki.

1/4 cup dried **hijiki**
2 cups very hot water
1/4 cup Nobu Spicy Lemon Dressing
1 large garlic clove, grated or minced (about 1 teaspoon)
Kosher salt
4 6-ounce ling cod fillets (1–1 1/2 inches thick; or Atlantic cod, black cod, or snapper), with skin on
Freshly ground black pepper
1/4 cup canola oil (or other neutral-flavored oil)
1 cup frozen **petite peas,** thawed

Cod with Malaysian Chile Sauce and Basil Oil
Jean-Georges Vongerichten • Spice Market,
New York City

Kuala Lumpur is one of my favorite spots for street food. On one of my trips there I had this chile sauce with a piece of local, just-caught fish. When I returned to the States, I came up with this recipe to try to capture my memory of that sauce. Shaoxing wine is a Chinese brown rice wine similar in taste to dry sherry, which can be used as a substitute. Guilin Chili Sauce is a sweet and spicy Hong Kong chile sauce. You can find it or a similar sauce in Asian grocery stores.

•

Pea sprouts are long, thin sprouts generally found in plastic containers in the produce section of grocery stores. They were my addition. You may find you don't want to add any sugar or salt to the sauce. Taste it first and add a pinch of either according to your taste. —Nancy

30 MINUTES

To make the basil oil, stir the grapeseed oil and basil paste together in a small bowl.

To make the chile sauce, heat the grapeseed oil, ginger, and garlic together in a large skillet over medium-high heat for about 1½ minutes, until the garlic is soft and the ginger is soft and lightly browned, stirring constantly to prevent them from burning. Add the scallion whites and stir to mix. Pour out the oil and discard it, leaving the garlic, ginger, and scallions in the skillet. Add the Shaoxing wine, Guilin Chili Sauce, soy sauce, rice wine vinegar, and sugar. Bring to a simmer over medium-high heat, reduce the heat to medium, and cook the sauce for about 2½ minutes, until it has reduced to a jamlike consistency. Turn off the heat, stir in the scallion greens, season with kosher salt, and set aside to cool to room temperature.

Rinse the fish fillets under cool water, pat them dry with paper towels, and season both sides with kosher salt and freshly ground black pepper.

Heat the grapeseed oil in a large nonstick skillet over high heat for 2 to 3 minutes, until the oil's almost smoking (you will begin to smell the oil at that point). Put the cod fillets skin side down in the skillet. Place a flat lid or plate smaller than the diameter of the pan on the fish and press down on it gently for about 1 minute. (This helps render a crispy skin.) Remove the lid or plate, reduce the heat to medium, and cook the fillets for about 3 more minutes, until the skin sides are golden brown and crispy. Slide a thin spatula under the fillets to release any sticking spots and gently turn them over. Cook the fish on

FOR THE BASIL OIL
¼ cup grapeseed oil (or canola oil or other neutral-flavored oil)
1 tablespoon **basil paste**

FOR THE CHILE SAUCE
¼ cup grapeseed oil (or canola oil or other neutral-flavored oil)
¼ cup grated peeled fresh ginger (from 1 4-inch piece)
8 large garlic cloves, grated or minced (about 2 tablespoons)
8 scallions, very thinly sliced diagonally (white and green parts separated)
¼ cup Shaoxing wine (or dry sherry)
2 tablespoons Guilin Chili Sauce
2 tablespoons light soy sauce
2 tablespoons rice wine vinegar
Pinch of sugar
Kosher salt

4 6-ounce ling cod fillets (1–1½ inches thick), with skin on
Kosher salt and freshly ground black pepper
¼ cup grapeseed oil (or canola oil or other neutral-flavored oil)
4 small handfuls of **pea sprouts** (or radish sprouts, about 3 ounces)

the second side for about 3 minutes, until it's opaque and flakes easily when pierced with a sharp knife but is still moist.

Mound the pea sprouts onto four plates, dividing them evenly. Place the cod fillets skin side up on top of the sprouts, spoon the chile sauce over the fish, and drizzle with the basil oil.

Sicilian Swordfish with Tomato Sauce and Fresh Mint

This recipe uses the classic Sicilian combination of pine nuts and currants and also a favorite Sicilian fish, swordfish. You can use tuna steaks instead of swordfish if you prefer.

30 MINUTES

Adjust the oven rack to the middle position and preheat the oven to 325°F.

Spread the pine nuts on a baking sheet and toast them in the oven for 8 to 10 minutes, shaking the pan occasionally for even toasting, until the nuts are lightly browned and fragrant. Remove the nuts from the oven and set them aside to cool slightly.

Increase the oven temperature to 500°F.

To make the tomato sauce, combine the pasta sauce, olives, capers, pine nuts, currants, garlic, anchovies, and chile flakes together in a large ovenproof skillet and cook the sauce over medium-high heat for about 5 minutes, stirring occasionally, just to warm it through.

Rinse the swordfish steaks under cool water, pat them dry with paper towels, and season both sides with kosher salt and freshly ground black pepper.

Place the swordfish in the skillet on top of the tomato sauce, drizzle a teaspoon of the olive oil over each steak, and place the skillet in the oven for 6 to 8 minutes, until the fish is opaque and flakes apart easily when pierced with a sharp knife but is still moist.

Lift the swordfish steaks out of the sauce and place them on four plates. Stir the sauce to incorporate the juice contracted from the fish, and spoon it over the fish. Squeeze a few drops of lemon juice over each steak and sprinkle with the mint.

FOR THE TOMATO SAUCE

3 tablespoons pine nuts

1 26-ounce jar **pasta sauce** (about 2 cups)

32 small pitted **black olives**

3 tablespoons **capers**

3 tablespoons dried currants

2 large garlic cloves, grated or minced (about 2 teaspoons)

4 **anchovy fillets,** chopped

Pinch of chile flakes

4 6-ounce swordfish steaks (about 1 inch thick; or tuna steaks)

Kosher salt and freshly ground black pepper

1 tablespoon plus 1 teaspoon **extra-virgin olive oil**

Lemon, for squeezing over the fish

1 heaping tablespoon finely chopped fresh mint leaves

Sea Bass with Spicy Giant White Beans and Salami

I've always been a stickler for properly cooked beans, beans that are cooked all the way through, so they're creamy, not mealy or chalky, and never al dente. I have to say that after tasting canned and jarred beans, I think they're cooked better than 90 percent of the beans I have at restaurants.

25 MINUTES

Rinse the sea bass fillets under cool water, pat them dry with paper towels, and season both sides with kosher salt and freshly ground black pepper.

Heat 2 tablespoons of the canola oil in a large nonstick skillet over high heat for 2 to 3 minutes, until the oil's almost smoking (you will begin to smell the oil at that point). Put two of the fish fillets skin side down in the skillet. Place a flat lid or plate smaller than the diameter of the pan on the fish and press down on it gently for about 1 minute. (This helps render a crispy skin.) Remove the lid or plate, reduce the heat to medium, and cook the fillets for about 3 more minutes, until the skin is golden brown and crispy. Slide a thin spatula under the fillets to release any sticking spots and gently turn them over. Cook the fish on the second side for about 3 minutes, until the fish is opaque and flakes easily when pierced with a sharp knife but is still moist. Transfer the fillets to a plate, wipe out the pan, and repeat, heating the remaining 2 tablespoons of canola oil and cooking the other two fish fillets in the same way.

Add the salami slices to the skillet and the oil you cooked the fish in and fry them over medium-high heat until they're crisp on both sides, about 1 minute per side. Add the garlic and sauté for about 1½ minutes, until it is soft and fragrant, stirring constantly so it doesn't brown. Add the beans, red pepper paste, and ¾ cup water and continue to cook over high heat, stirring, until the beans are warmed through. Turn off the heat and stir in the parsley.

Divide the beans and salami evenly among four plates. Place the fish fillets skin side up on top of the beans and drizzle them with the juices from the plate. Drizzle lemon-infused olive oil over the fillets and sprinkle them with sea salt.

4 6-ounce sea bass fillets (about 1½ inches thick; or any mild flavored, nonoily white fish, such as branzino, grouper, halibut, snapper, or another bass), with skin on

Kosher salt and freshly ground black pepper

¼ cup canola oil (or other neutral-flavored oil)

24 ¼-inch-thick slices Italian hard salami (about 5 ounces)

1 large garlic clove, finely chopped or grated (about 1 teaspoon)

2 15-ounce cans giant white beans, rinsed and drained (about 3 cups)

¼ cup red pepper paste

¼ cup finely chopped fresh Italian parsley leaves

Lemon-infused olive oil (or high-quality extra-virgin olive oil combined with a pinch of fresh grated lemon zest), for drizzling

Sea salt

Sea Bass with Giant White Beans and Red Pepper Mayonnaise

The beans are served hot in this dish, so don't worry if the first two fish fillets you cook fall to room temperature. The beans will heat them up and the dish will be delicious. Besides, I don't think food needs to come to the table piping hot. It's not a restaurant. And even in restaurants, I prefer my food be served to me at room temperature than to have it kept warm and then come to the table discolored, wilted, or dried out. Aged sherry vinegar, like aged balsamic vinegar, is in another category altogether from vinegar that isn't aged. It adds a nice, slightly sweet accent to salads and seafood dishes such as this one. Baked giant white beans in tomato sauce is a very specific product, but I found more than one brand I liked. My favorite is Palirria baked giant beans, which I found at an import store in Los Angeles, Jons Marketplace. It's also available from many online food sources.

30 MINUTES

Combine the beans, olive oil, and ¼ cup water in a large saucepan over low heat, and cook for 5 to 7 minutes, stirring occasionally, until the beans are warmed through. Turn off the heat.

Rinse the fish fillets under cool water, pat them dry with paper towels, and season both sides with kosher salt and freshly ground black pepper.

Heat 2 tablespoons of the canola oil in a large nonstick skillet over high heat for 2 to 3 minutes, until the oil's almost smoking (you will begin to smell the oil at that point). Put two of the fish fillets skin side down in the skillet. Place a flat lid or plate smaller than the diameter of the pan on the fish and press down on it gently for about 1 minute. (This helps render a crispy skin.) Remove the lid or plate, reduce the heat to medium, and cook the fish for about 3 more minutes, until the skin is golden brown and crispy. Slide a thin spatula under the fillets to release any sticking spots and gently turn them over. Cook the fish on the second side for about 3 minutes, until it's opaque and flakes easily when pierced with a sharp knife but is still moist. Transfer the fillets to a plate, wipe out the pan, and repeat, heating the remaining 2 tablespoons of canola oil and cooking the other two fish fillets in the same way.

Warm the beans over medium heat if necessary, stir in all but 2 teaspoons of the parsley, and season with a few drops of the sherry vinegar.

Spoon the beans onto four plates, dividing them evenly. Place the fish fillets skin side up on top of the beans and drizzle them with the juices from the plate they were resting on. Spoon a dollop of Red Pepper Mayonnaise over each fillet and sprinkle with chopped parsley.

2 10-ounce cans baked giant white **beans** in tomato sauce (about 1½ cups)

2 tablespoons **extra-virgin olive oil**

4 6-ounce sea bass fillets (about 1½ inches thick; or any mild-flavored, nonoily white fish, such as branzino, grouper, halibut, snapper, or another bass), with skin on

Kosher salt and freshly ground black pepper

¼ cup canola oil (or other neutral-flavored oil)

¼ cup finely chopped fresh Italian parsley leaves

Aged **sherry vinegar,** for drizzling

Red Pepper Mayonnaise (recipe follows)

Red Pepper Mayonnaise

This mayonnaise is based on rouille, a French condiment made of spicy red peppers, garlic, olive oil, saffron, and breadcrumbs or potato. This is my shortcut, using prepared mayonnaise as a base.

1/2 CUP   10 MINUTES

Stir the mayonnaise, red pepper paste, olive oil, garlic, lemon juice, and kosher salt together in a small bowl and season with more lemon juice, garlic, or salt to taste.

1/2 cup **mayonnaise**

1 heaping tablespoon **red pepper paste**

1 tablespoon **extra-virgin olive oil**

3 large garlic cloves, grated or minced (about 1 tablespoon), or more to taste

2 teaspoons fresh lemon juice, or more to taste

1/4 teaspoon kosher salt, or more to taste

Seared Salmon with Lentils and Salsa Rustica

Salsa rustica is an interesting mix of hard-cooked eggs, almonds, basil, and mint. You don't see it very often and I don't know why that is because it's delicious and very easy to make. I like to use thick salmon fillets in this dish, so I cook them on all four sides.

30 MINUTES

Adjust the oven rack to the middle position and preheat the oven to 325°F.

Spread the almonds on a baking sheet and toast them in the oven, shaking the pan occasionally for even toasting, for 15 to 20 minutes, until they're lightly browned and fragrant. Remove the almonds from the oven, drizzle them with olive oil, sprinkle them with kosher salt, and toss to coat. Set the almonds aside to cool slightly, and then coarsely chop them.

To hard-cook the eggs, place them in a medium saucepan with enough water to cover, salt the water generously, and bring it to a boil over high heat. Reduce the heat to low and simmer the eggs for about 5 to 8 minutes until the yolks are cooked but bright yellow (I sometimes put an extra "tester" in the pot). While they're cooking, fill a large bowl with ice water. When the eggs are done, drain and immediately plunge them into the ice water to chill. (This prevents the eggs from cooking any further before they are peeled.) When the eggs are cool, peel them and separate the whites and yolks.

To make the salsa rustica, coarsely chop the egg whites and egg yolks separately and place both in a medium bowl. Add the almonds, olive oil, mint, and basil paste and toss gently to combine. Season with kosher salt if necessary.

To make the lentils, heat ½ cup of the olive oil with the garlic and a pinch of kosher salt in a medium saucepan over medium-high heat and sauté for about 1½ minutes, until the garlic is soft and fragrant, stirring constantly so the garlic doesn't brown. Add the lentils and cook them for about 3 minutes, stirring occasionally, until they're warmed through. Remove the pan from the heat and season the lentils with kosher salt.

FOR THE SALSA RUSTICA

¼ cup whole almonds, with their skins on

3 tablespoons **extra-virgin olive oil,** plus more to toss with the almonds

Kosher salt

2 large eggs

3 tablespoons finely chopped fresh mint leaves

1 heaping tablespoon **basil paste**

FOR THE LENTILS

1 cup **extra-virgin olive oil**

2 large garlic cloves, grated or minced (about 2 teaspoons)

Kosher salt

2 15-ounce cans **lentils** or 2 19-ounce cans lentil soup, rinsed and drained (about 3 cups)

Rinse the salmon fillets under cool water, pat them dry with paper towels, and season both sides with kosher salt and freshly ground black pepper.

Heat the canola oil in a large, nonstick skillet over high heat for 2 to 3 minutes, until the oil's almost smoking (you will begin to smell the oil at that point). Put the salmon fillets in the pan, skin side down. Place a flat lid or plate smaller than the diameter of the pan on top of the fish and press down on it gently for about 4 minutes. (This helps to render a crispy skin.) Remove the lid or plate and reduce the heat to medium. Slide a thin spatula under the salmon fillets to release any sticking spots and gently turn them on their sides; cook for 1 minute on each of the two sides. Turn and cook the salmon on the fourth side for 1 minute. Turn off the heat and let the salmon cook from the residual heat of the pan for 1 minute more.

Spoon the lentils onto four plates, dividing them evenly, and place the salmon skin side up on top of the lentils. Squeeze a few drops of lemon juice and sprinkle sea salt over each fillet and spoon the salsa rustica on top.

4 6-ounce king salmon fillets
(about 1½ inches thick;
preferably wild king salmon),
with skin on, or 4 6-ounce sushi-
grade tuna steaks
(1½ inches thick)
Kosher salt and freshly ground
black pepper
¼ cup canola oil (or other
neutral-flavored oil)
Lemon, for squeezing over the fish
Sea salt

Seared Salmon with Lentils, Bacon, and Pickled Red Cabbage

Salmon and lentils are a classic combination. Starting with lentil soup is a great shortcut to cooking lentils. The soup has just enough seasoning and the lentils are surprisingly firm. The pickled cabbage offsets the richness of the other ingredients. As in the Seared Salmon with Lentils and Salsa Rustica recipe, the salmon fillets used in this dish are so thick I cook them on all four sides.

30 MINUTES

Cook the bacon in a large skillet over medium heat for 8 to 10 minutes, stirring often, until it is done but still chewy, not browned or crispy. Remove the bacon pieces from the skillet and place them on paper towels to drain. Pour off the bacon grease but don't wipe the skillet clean.

Add the garlic to the skillet and sauté it over medium-high heat for about 1½ minutes, until it is soft and fragrant, stirring constantly so it doesn't brown. Add the bacon, lentils, lentil broth, cabbage, balsamic vinegar, olive oil, and capers, season with kosher salt, and cook the mixture over medium heat, stirring occasionally, for about 5 minutes, until it's warmed through.

Rinse the salmon fillets under cool water, pat them dry with paper towels, and season both sides with kosher salt and freshly ground black pepper.

Heat the canola oil in a large, nonstick skillet over high heat for 2 to 3 minutes, until the oil's almost smoking (you will begin to smell the oil at that point). Put the salmon fillets in the pan, skin side down. Place a flat lid or plate smaller than the diameter of the pan on top of the fish and press down on it gently for about 4 minutes. (This helps to render a crispy skin.) Remove the lid or plate and reduce the heat to medium. Slide a thin spatula under the salmon fillets to release any sticking spots and gently turn them on their sides; cook for 1 minute on each of the two sides. Turn and cook the salmon on the fourth side for 1 minute. Turn off the heat and let the salmon cook from the residual heat of the pan for 1 minute more.

Spoon the lentils onto four plates, dividing them evenly, and place the salmon skin side up on top of the lentils. Squeeze a few drops of lemon juice over each fillet, drizzle them with the high-quality olive oil, and sprinkle them with sea salt.

FOR THE LENTILS

8 strips thick-cut applewood-smoked **bacon,** cut diagonally into 1-inch pieces

1 large garlic clove, grated or minced (about 1 teaspoon)

1 19-ounce can **lentil** soup, drained, ½ cup of the broth reserved, or 1½ cups lentils

1 cup **pickled red cabbage** (from 1 12-ounce jar; preferably not finely chopped), drained

1 tablespoon plus 1 teaspoon aged **balsamic vinegar**

1 tablespoon plus 1 teaspoon **extra-virgin olive oil**

1 heaping tablespoon **capers,** chopped

Kosher salt

FOR THE SALMON

4 6-ounce king salmon fillets (about 1½ inches thick; preferably wild king salmon), with skin on

Kosher salt and freshly ground black pepper

½ cup canola oil (or other neutral-flavored oil)

Lemon, for squeezing over the salmon

High-quality **extra-virgin olive oil,** for drizzling

Sea salt

Seared Scallops with Sweet Corn, Edamame, and Brown Butter

Edamame are fresh soybeans; they have a slightly sweet flavor and a nice, firm texture. You may have encountered them already at Japanese restaurants, where they're served steamed and salted as an appetizer. Shelled edamame are pretty easy to find in the frozen food section of most supermarkets. If you don't like or can't find edamame, substitute an equal amount of lima beans instead. Scallops should be slightly translucent in the center after they're cooked; if they're cooked until the flesh is opaque all the way through, they will be tough.

20 MINUTES

Rinse the scallops in cool water and pat them dry with paper towels. Remove the muscle from each scallop and season both sides of the scallops with kosher salt and freshly ground black pepper.

Heat 2 tablespoons of the oil in a large skillet over high heat for 2 to 3 minutes, until the oil's almost smoking (you will begin to smell the oil at that point). Place half of the scallops in the skillet and sear them for 2 minutes. Turn, reduce the heat to medium, and cook the scallops for another 2 minutes, until they're golden brown and firm to the touch. Transfer the scallops to a plate, wipe out the pan and repeat, heating the remaining 2 tablespoons of oil and cooking the rest of the scallops in the same way. Pour off the oil and discard.

Add the bacon to the skillet you cooked the scallops in, reduce the heat to low, and cook for 4 to 5 minutes, stirring often, until it's cooked through but still chewy, not browned or crispy. Drain off the bacon fat, leaving the bacon in the pan. Add the butter and a pinch of kosher salt and melt the butter over medium heat. Add the corn and edamame and cook for 2 to 3 minutes, swirling the pan often, until the butter browns and the vegetables are warmed through. Add the shallots and pea sprouts and cook, stirring often, for another minute, just long enough to warm the ingredients but not enough to wilt the sprouts, and season with kosher salt.

Divide the scallops evenly among four plates with the first-cooked sides up and drizzle them with the juices from the plate they were resting on. Spoon the vegetables and pan juices over the scallops, squeeze a few drops of fresh lemon juice over each serving, season with sea salt, and sprinkle with the thyme leaves.

16–20 large sea scallops (about 1½ pounds)

Kosher salt and freshly ground black pepper

¼ cup canola oil (or other neutral-flavored oil)

4 strips thick-cut applewood-smoked **bacon,** cut diagonally into ¼-inch pieces

½ stick (¼ cup) unsalted butter

½ cup frozen corn kernels

½ cup frozen shelled edamame

2 medium shallots, grated or minced (about 1 heaping tablespoon)

4 small handfuls of **pea sprouts** (or radish sprouts; about 3 ounces)

Lemon, for squeezing over the scallops

Sea salt

2 teaspoons fresh thyme leaves

Seared Scallops with Sautéed Mushrooms and Aged Sherry Vinegar

My favorite jarred mushrooms are ones that contain a variety of different mushrooms. I think the mix of shapes, textures, and flavors are more interesting than just plain white ones. If the mushrooms you're using for this recipe are packed in oil (some mushrooms are pickled in vinegar), don't add more oil to the pan you sauté them in. And if they're packed with garlic, don't add the garlic in this recipe.

25 MINUTES

Rinse the scallops in cool water and pat them dry with paper towels. Remove the muscle from each scallop and season both sides of the scallops with kosher salt and freshly ground black pepper.

Heat 2 tablespoons of the canola oil in a large skillet over high heat for 2 to 3 minutes, until the oil's almost smoking (you will begin to smell the oil at that point). Place half of the scallops in the skillet and sear them for 2 minutes. Turn, reduce the heat to medium, and cook the scallops for another 2 minutes, until they're golden brown and firm to the touch. Transfer the scallops to a plate, wipe out the pan and repeat, heating the remaining 2 tablespoons of canola oil and cooking the rest of the scallops the same way.

If the mushrooms you're using are not packed in oil, leave the oil in the skillet and heat it up over high heat for 2 to 3 minutes, until it's almost smoking (you will begin to smell the oil at that point). (If the mushrooms are packed in oil, pour out the oil and discard, wipe out the skillet and heat the skillet over high heat for 2 to 3 minutes.) Add the mushrooms and cook them for about 3 minutes, shaking the pan from time to time for even cooking, until they're golden brown. Add the butter, thyme, shallot, garlic (if the mushrooms are not packed with garlic), and a pinch of kosher salt, and sauté for about 1½ minutes, until the shallot's soft and the garlic is soft and fragrant, stirring constantly so the garlic doesn't brown. Stir in the arugula and cook just until it wilts, about 1 minute. Turn off the heat, add 1 tablespoon of water, and stir to release the cooked bits stuck to the bottom of the skillet.

Pile the arugula and mushrooms in the center of each of four plates, dividing them evenly. Place four or five scallops on each plate and drizzle them with the juices from the plate they were resting on. Drizzle a few drops of sherry vinegar and the high-quality olive oil over the scallops and sprinkle them with sea salt.

16–20 large sea scallops (about 1½ pounds)

Kosher salt and freshly ground black pepper

¼ cup canola oil (or other neutral-flavored oil)

4 cups jarred mushrooms (from 2 16-ounce jars), drained and patted dry with paper towels

1½ tablespoons unsalted butter

2 teaspoons fresh thyme leaves

1 small shallot, grated or minced (about 1 teaspoon)

1 large garlic clove, grated or minced (about 1 teaspoon), optional

8 cups loosely packed arugula leaves

Aged sherry vinegar, for drizzling

High-quality extra-virgin olive oil, for drizzling

Sea salt

Clams with Tomato-Basil Broth and Crusty Garlic Toast

This is an especially good dish to make in the summer, when tomatoes are sweet and tasty. When it's not tomato season, either look for Del Cabo organic tomatoes, which are pretty good year-round, or substitute canned Italian tomatoes (preferably San Marzano) for fresh. If you prefer mussels to clams, they would be delicious, but be warned: they take a lot more time to clean than clams do.

30 MINUTES

Adjust the oven rack to the middle position and preheat the oven to 350°F.

Place the bread slices on a baking sheet, brush the tops with olive oil, and bake for 15 to 20 minutes, until they're lightly toasted and golden brown. (You can also toast the bread in a toaster, but *without* the oil. Then brush the toast with oil after they're done.) Rub the oiled side of the toasts with the garlic and set them on your work surface, oiled side up.

Heat the olive oil, shallots, garlic, chile flakes, and kosher salt in a large saucepan over medium-high heat for about 1½ minutes, until the shallots and garlic are soft, stirring constantly so the garlic doesn't brown. Add the tomatoes and cook for about 1 minute. Turn the heat up to high, add the garbanzo beans, wine, basil paste, and thyme, and stir to combine. Bring to a simmer, add the clams, cover the pan, and let the clams steam for about 5 minutes, stirring occasionally to incorporate the flavors, until the clams open.

Divide the clams and the liquid they were cooked in among four large soup plates or bowls. Spoon a dollop of Garlic Mayonnaise on each piece of toast and serve the rest of the mayonnaise on the side.

4 1-inch-thick slices from a large sourdough bread

½ cup **extra-virgin olive oil,** plus more for brushing the bread

1 garlic clove

2 medium shallots, grated or minced (about 1 heaping tablespoon)

2 large garlic cloves, grated or minced (about 2 teaspoons)

½ teaspoon chile flakes

Pinch of kosher salt

48 small, sweet **tomatoes** (scant pint), cut in half, or 24 cherry tomatoes, quartered

1 15-ounce can garbanzo **beans** (or giant white beans or cannellini beans), rinsed and drained (about 1½ cups)

½ cup dry white wine

½ cup **basil paste**

16 fresh thyme sprigs

4 pounds small clams, such as littleneck clams

Garlic Mayonnaise (page 33)

Buttermilk-Fried Oysters with Pickled Vegetables and Chipotle Mayonnaise

I love fried oysters but I really didn't imagine there was any kind of shortcut to shucking them. On one of our many shopping sprees where we picked up bags and bags of weird jarred items, Matt Molina and I came home with, among a million other things, jarred oysters. We liked the way they tasted, but we knew they needed a little something, some kind of textural component to make up for the fact that they weren't fresh-shucked. Matt's idea, a fried buttermilk coating, turned out to be just the thing. Soaking the oysters in the buttermilk helps to neutralize them and also helps the flour coating stick to them. The pickled salad mixtures I found are the perfect contrast to the richness of the oysters.

30 MINUTES

If some of the oysters are much larger than the others, cut them in half. Put the oysters in a medium bowl with the buttermilk to soak briefly while you prepare the other ingredients.

Stir the flour and Old Bay Seasoning together in a small bowl.

Heat ½ cup of the oil in a large skillet over high heat for 2 to 3 minutes, until the oil's almost smoking (you will begin to smell the oil at that point). Dredge half of the oysters in the seasoned flour and carefully lay them in one layer in the oil. Fry the oysters for 2 minutes, until they're golden brown and crispy. Flip the oysters and cook them for another minute, then reduce the heat to medium-high and cook the oysters for a minute more, until the second side is golden brown and crispy. Lift the oysters out of the oil with a slotted spoon and place them on paper towels to drain. Repeat, heating the remaining ¼ cup of oil over high heat and frying the remaining oysters in the same way.

Mound the mixed salad in the center of each of four plates and fill four ramekins (if you have them) with Chipotle Mayonnaise for dipping the oysters. Arrange the oysters around the vegetables and place a ramekin of mayonnaise on the side of each plate; if you don't have ramekins, dollop the mayonnaise on the side.

24 ounces jarred oysters (from 3 8-ounce jars; about 30 oysters), rinsed and drained

1 cup buttermilk

1 cup plus 2 tablespoons all-purpose flour

¼ cup plus 2 tablespoons **Old Bay Seasoning**

¾ cup canola oil (or other neutral-flavored oil)

2 cups **mixed salad,** drained

Chipotle Mayonnaise (page 35)

DESSERTS

It may seem surprising given my background as a baker and a pastry chef, but this was the chapter in the book that I was the most afraid of, and I waited until the very end to work on it. But in fact it was *because* I am a baker that it was so difficult. For my entire career, I've said that fresh-baked was the only way, and now here I am saying, Throw away all my other books and go buy packaged shortbread!

My formula for putting together desserts is similar to how I put entrées together to include contrasting flavors, textures, and temperatures, so it was particularly conducive to the concept of this book. I use ice cream and yogurt to add a cool, creamy component to desserts. Warm fruit, fruit sauces, and chocolate sauce contrast with the temperature of ice cream, and the smooth textures offset the crunchiness of biscuits, cookies, and nuts. With so many different elements going on, even recipes as simple as Strawberries and Ladyfingers with Sour Cream or Raspberry and Lemon Sherbet Sundaes are satisfying—and elegant enough to serve company.

In shopping for this chapter, I found outstanding products to work with: rich, creamy Greek yogurt; premium, high-fat ice cream; delicious, buttery packaged cookies. I tried many different canned, jarred, and frozen fruits and I had a few disappointments, such as slippery, slimy sliced mangoes and apricots. But for the most part, I was pleasantly surprised. Jarred poached pears, which contain essentially the same ingredients as those I would poach myself, didn't suffer at all in terms of texture or flavor. And the quality of frozen berries, especially those from organic producers, was far superior to generic quality fresh berries grown out of season or shipped from South America. (If during their season you want to use fresh fruit in place of any of the fruits to make these recipes, by all means do.)

In fact, the products I found to work with were so good on their own that I didn't need to do much of anything to them. So these desserts are essentially just an assembling of different packaged ingredients. They're nearly instant to make. And in my opinion, they're better than anything you'd be served in most restaurants out there.

Fresh Ricotta with Oat Biscuits, Chestnut Honey, and Candied Walnuts

Fresh ricotta, which you can find at cheese shops and specialty food stores, is a lot more delicate and flavorful than the common varieties sold in grocery stores. If you can find sheep's milk ricotta for this, even better. It has so much more complexity than cow's milk ricotta. Chestnut honey has a rich honey flavor, but it is only faintly sweet. Lately I'm seeing candied spiced walnuts, cooked in sugar syrup, baked, or fried, at the checkout counters of small gourmet food shops across the country. Treat them as you would any packaged item and taste them before using them in a recipe. (If you can't find good candied walnuts, you can refer to my *Sandwich Book* for a really long, involved recipe for making them from scratch!) The cookies I call for are grainy biscuits. I like them because they are not too sweet.

15 MINUTES

Heat the olive oil and balsamic vinegar together in a large skillet over medium-high heat for about 1 minute, until the liquid bubbles. Put the radicchio leaves in the skillet in a single layer and cook them for about 45 seconds on each side, until they're seared and wilted slightly. Season the leaves with a pinch of kosher salt and freshly ground black pepper. Remove them from the skillet and set them aside to cool to room temperature.

If the ricotta you are using is not a spoonable consistency, put it in a small bowl and stir in enough cream or milk to loosen it.

Place two biscuits on each of four plates. Tear the radicchio leaves in half and drape a half over each biscuit, leaving the biscuit partially exposed. Spoon 1 tablespoon of fresh ricotta on top of each piece of radicchio, making sure you can see the radicchio peek through below. Drizzle about 1 teaspoon of honey over each biscuit, sprinkle the crumbled walnuts over the ricotta, and place one candied walnut half on top of each mound of ricotta.

2 teaspoons **extra-virgin olive oil**

2 teaspoons aged **balsamic vinegar**

4 leaves radicchio

Kosher salt and freshly ground black pepper

½ cup fresh **ricotta**

Heavy cream or milk, for thinning the ricotta if necessary

8 Duchy Originals Oaten Biscuits or Carr's Whole Wheat Crackers

Chestnut honey, for drizzling

16 candied walnut halves, or toasted walnuts, broken into small pieces, plus 8 complete halves, for topping the ricotta

Caramelized Pears with Mascarpone Cream, Brandy-Raisin Brown Butter, and Biscotti

Of all the canned fruit I tried, pears were my favorite. Caramelized in butter, they kept a firm consistency. I call for them to be used at room temperature; they're cooked in this recipe for such a short time that a refrigerated pear would still be cold in the center after it's cooked. Not all raisins are created equal. If you have access to specialty food stores or farmers' markets that sell raisins, like ours do in Southern California, buy a few different kinds and see which ones you like best. I like flame raisins, both the black and golden varieties. Look for raisins that are plump and glossy, not dried out and sugary. Mascarpone is a soft, unripened Italian cheese with a mild, delicate flavor. It's just the thing to offset the buttery pears. There are so many biscotti available—those sold individually in coffee bars and packaged domestic and imported Italian brands. Taste them and use your favorites. Carolynn swears by the very authentic Antonio Mattei Biscotti, which you can get at specialty food stores; they come in a bright blue bag.

20 MINUTES

To make the mascarpone cream, combine the mascarpone, cream, and sugar in a medium bowl. Beat the egg in a liquid measuring cup, read the measure, and pour out half to obtain half of an egg. Add the half egg to the bowl and beat the mixture with an electric mixer on high speed or a wire whisk until it forms stiff peaks. Be careful not to overbeat or the mascarpone will become too thick.

Melt the butter with the sugar in a large skillet over high heat and cook. Split the vanilla bean lengthwise with a sharp knife. Using the back of the knife, scrape the seeds into the skillet and stir to combine. (Alternatively, stir in the vanilla extract.) When the butter starts to bubble, add the pears, cut side down, and cook them for 4 to 5 minutes, shaking the pan occasionally, until they're nicely browned. (The butter should brown but not burn. If it begins to burn, lower the heat slightly.) Remove the pears from the skillet and place two pear halves cut side up, side by side, on each of four large soup or dessert plates, leaving the butter in the skillet. (Some of the pear halves may brown sooner than others; remove those that are nicely browned and place them on the dessert plates while you cook the remaining pear halves.)

Add the raisins and brandy to the skillet with the butter and simmer over

FOR THE MASCARPONE CREAM

½ cup mascarpone cheese

¼ cup heavy cream

1½ tablespoons sugar

1 large egg

3 tablespoons unsalted butter

1½ tablespoons sugar

1 vanilla bean (or 2 teaspoons vanilla extract)

8 canned pear halves, at room temperature

½ cup raisins

¼ cup brandy

8 biscotti

low heat for 1 to 2 minutes, until the raisins are plump, and the sauce has thickened slightly. Again, be careful not to burn the butter.

Spoon a dollop of the mascarpone cream over each pear half, dividing it evenly. Spoon the butter-raisin sauce over the mascarpone and serve with a plateful of biscotti in the center of the table.

Easy Apple Turnovers
Gale Gand • Tru, Chicago

Apple butter is very rich because it's made of apples that have been cooked long and slow, until all the water has been cooked out. Using it is a quick and effortless way to spice up the apple filling in these turnovers. The turnovers are much better than anything you could buy in a bakery—especially fresh from the oven—and they're so easy to make. My husband, Jimmy, and I have young twin girls and my job keeps me very busy—but I can get these into the oven for a Saturday morning breakfast treat, no problem. (You do need to think ahead, though, as the puff pastry needs to be defrosted overnight in the refrigerator.) Jimmy, an expert turnover eater, declares these "Great!" The glaze is optional.

25 MINUTES

Adjust the oven rack to the middle position and preheat the oven to 425°F.

Put the chopped apple, applesauce, and apple butter in a small mixing bowl and stir to combine.

Dust a flat work surface lightly with flour and lay out the puff pastry on it. Dust the pastry lightly with flour and use a rolling pin to roll it out into a 10-by-10-inch square. Cut the pastry into four 5-by-5-inch squares. Use a pastry brush to brush the edges of the squares with the beaten egg, reserving the remaining beaten egg for brushing the tops of the turnovers. Dividing it evenly, spoon the apple mixture into the center of each pastry square. Fold the squares over diagonally, pressing the edges to enclose the filling while also working out any air. Press the edges with the tines of a fork to seal them completely and to make decorative hatches.

Place the turnovers on a baking sheet, brush the tops with the remaining beaten egg, and bake them for about 25 minutes, until the tops are dark golden. (The turnovers will be golden after 20 minutes, but they need the extra 5 minutes for the pastry to cook all the way through. If they fall when removed from the oven, they are undercooked.) Remove the turnovers from the oven and place them on a rack to cool slightly.

If you're using the glaze, while the turnovers are baking, stir the confectioners' sugar and milk together in a small bowl until it's smooth. Allow the turnovers to cool slightly before drizzling them with the glaze.

½ Granny Smith apple, peeled, cored, and chopped (½ cup)
¼ cup unsweetened applesauce
2 tablespoons apple butter
Flour, for rolling the puff pastry
1 sheet **puff pastry,** thawed overnight in the refrigerator
1 large egg, beaten

FOR THE GLAZE (OPTIONAL)
¼ cup confectioners' sugar
1 teaspoon whole milk

Strawberries and Ladyfingers with Sour Cream, Muscovado Sugar, and Saba

This dessert was invented one night at a dinner party at my house. One of the guests brought strawberries from the farmers' market that looked so good, Carolynn and I decided on the spur of the moment to turn them into a dessert using whatever I had in the house. This is what we came up with, and it was a big hit. Muscovado sugar is an unrefined brown variety from Africa, made from cane grown in volcanic ash. It has larger crystals than conventional brown sugar and a very strong molasses flavor. It adds another dimension of flavor to a simple dessert like this one that plain sugar wouldn't. You can find it at specialty food stores, but if you don't have any, substitute dark brown sugar. Ladyfingers are small finger-shaped sponge cakes that are most commonly used in tiramisù. I like their light, delicate texture with this simple fruit dessert. They're made of a very plain batter of eggs, flour, and sugar, and are one of the few items where I honestly can't tell the difference between fresh and packaged. Fresh ladyfingers might be slightly softer than packaged, but the flavor doesn't suffer in the packaged version. Just make sure the packaged ladyfingers you buy don't contain any weird ingredients.

10 MINUTES

Place the strawberries in a medium bowl. Drizzle them with the saba and stir to combine.

Mix the sour cream and sugar together in a small bowl to combine.

Spoon the sour cream onto four plates and place two ladyfingers side by side on top. Spoon the strawberries over the ladyfingers and drizzle saba over each serving. Serve with the bottle of saba on the table for extra drizzling.

1 pint ripe strawberries, hulled and cut in half

1½ tablespoons **saba,** plus extra for drizzling and for serving on the table

1 cup sour cream (or **crème fraîche**)

3 tablespoons light brown muscovado sugar

8 ladyfingers

Peppered Balsamic Ice Cream with Fresh Strawberries
Jody Adams • Rialto, Cambridge, Massachusetts

I first tasted the combination of strawberries, balsamic vinegar, and black pepper together about fifteen years ago, in Italy, where it's a classic, and I've been using it in different variations ever since. In this dessert, the balsamic vinegar and pepper are mixed in with the ice cream, which is then refrozen. This recipe calls for just enough strawberries to serve four, but depending on how big your servings are, you may have leftover ice cream. Naturally, I recommend you seek out the tastiest strawberries you can find, preferably organically grown.

20 MINUTES (NOT INCLUDING REFREEZING TIME)

Scoop the ice cream out of the carton and into the bowl of a standing electric mixer or a large bowl, keeping the carton to refreeze the ice cream in. Use the paddle attachment of the mixer to beat the ice cream for about 30 seconds to soften it. With the mixer on, add the freshly ground black pepper, then the balsamic vinegar in a thin, steady stream, taking care not to let it splatter. Continue to mix for about 10 minutes to incorporate the ingredients. (It's okay if the vinegar appears slightly streaky in the ice cream.) Spoon the ice cream back into the carton and return it to the freezer for 45 minutes to 1 hour to refreeze it.

About 20 minutes before serving, remove the stems and hulls from the strawberries and cut them in half. Toss the berries in a bowl with the sugar and set them aside until the sugar dissolves, about 15 minutes.

Scoop one or two scoops of ice cream into each of four small dessert dishes. Divide the berries evenly among the servings and drizzle each serving with balsamic vinegar.

1 pint premium vanilla **ice cream**
½ teaspoon freshly ground black pepper
2 tablespoons aged **balsamic vinegar,** plus extra for drizzling
1 quart ripe strawberries
½ cup sugar

Raspberry and Lemon Sherbet Sundaes

This is a simple sundae made of lemon sherbet topped with lemon curd sauce and raspberry sherbet topped with raspberry sauce. Technically, the difference between a sherbet and a sorbet is that sherbet contains milk products and sorbet doesn't. I call both products "sherbet" because that's what I grew up with and I like the name. Palmiers are flaky French butter cookies made of puff pastry that are rolled in sugar and folded to look like palm leaves. The brand I used was Recette de Champagne, but any palmiers made with real butter will do. Choose a lemon curd that contains only lemon, sugar, egg yolks, and maybe butter.

20 MINUTES

Adjust the oven rack to the middle position and preheat the oven to 325°F. Spread the almonds on a baking sheet and toast them in the oven for 5 to 8 minutes, shaking the pan occasionally for even toasting, until they're lightly browned and fragrant. Remove the nuts from the oven and set them aside to cool.

Combine the raspberries with the sugar in a small bowl and heat them in the microwave for about 30 seconds to warm them through. (Alternatively, combine the berries and sugar in a small ovenproof dish and place them in a 350°F oven for about 6 minutes.)

Whip the cream in the bowl of a free-standing mixer (or handheld mixer or by hand with a wire whisk) until it's just thickened and soft peaks form. Add the crème fraîche and whip until stiff peaks form. Stir in the lemon curd. The acid from the lemon will loosen the cream mixture, bringing it to a more saucelike consistency.

Place two palmiers side by side on each of four dessert plates and for each serving place a scoop of lemon sherbet on one palmier and a scoop of raspberry sherbet on the other. Spoon the lemon sauce over the lemon sherbet servings and spoon the raspberry sauce over the raspberry sherbet servings, dividing the sauces evenly. Scatter the almonds over the sundaes. Pour the confectioners' sugar into a mesh strainer and dust a little over each serving.

1/3 cup sliced almonds, with their skins on

2 ounces frozen raspberries (about 1/2 cup)

1 teaspoon granulated sugar

1/4 cup heavy cream

1/4 cup **crème fraîche** (or sour cream)

1/4 cup lemon curd

8 small (or 4 large) palmiers

4 scoops lemon sherbet (or sorbet)

4 scoops raspberry sherbet (or sorbet)

Confectioners' sugar, for dusting the sundaes

Strawberry Ice Cream Pie with Cinnamon–Black Pepper Strawberry Sauce and Strawberry Sherbet

This dessert is a classic example of how doing just a little something to a packaged ingredient—in this case paddling ice cream and refreezing it—turns an ordinary item into something special and elegant. If you're making this pie when strawberries aren't in season, use frozen ones and don't bother slicing them, as they will break down plenty as they cook. This is a very easy recipe to make—the freezer does most of the work. To save time, you can start with a frozen graham cracker crust. But try to find one made with butter, not shortening. If you want the ice cream to be super-firm, make the pie before dinner and put it in the freezer while you're eating.

MAKES ONE 9-INCH PIE (SERVES 8)   40 MINUTES

Adjust the oven rack to the middle position and preheat the oven to 325°F.

Combine the graham cracker crumbs with the butter, cinnamon, and nutmeg in a medium bowl. Press the crumbs into a 9-inch glass or ceramic pie plate to form an even crust. Bake the crust for about 8 minutes, until it's firm to the touch. Remove the crust from the oven and set it aside (or refrigerate) to cool completely.

Remove the ice cream from the freezer and thaw it at room temperature for 15 to 20 minutes, until it is slightly softened.

Scoop the ice cream into the bowl of a standing electric mixer and use the paddle attachment to beat it until it's very soft but not melted. Spread the softened ice cream into the pie shell and place it in the freezer while you prepare the sauce.

To make the sauce, combine the sugar, cinnamon stick, peppercorns, cloves, and 3 tablespoons of water in a small heavy-bottomed saucepan and bring it to a boil. Boil the mixture for about 10 minutes, until it becomes amber and just starts to smoke, swirling the pan occasionally (but not stirring) so it colors evenly. Remove the pan from the heat and carefully add the wine, standing back as the mixture may splatter. Return the caramel to a boil over medium-high heat and stir until the caramel is melted and syrupy. (It will have solidified slightly when you added the liquid.) Strain the caramel through a fine-mesh strainer into a medium skillet and discard the cinnamon stick, pep-

1 cup graham cracker crumbs or 8 whole graham crackers, finely crushed

½ stick (4 tablespoons) unsalted butter, melted

¼ teaspoon ground cinnamon

Pinch of freshly grated nutmeg

1½ pints premium strawberry **ice cream**

FOR THE SAUCE

¼ cup plus 2 tablespoons sugar

1 cinnamon stick

5 black peppercorns, lightly crushed

2 whole cloves

1½ cups dry red wine

1 pint strawberries, hulled and thinly sliced (about 2 cups)

1 pint strawberry sherbet (or sorbet)

percorns, and cloves. Bring the syrup to a boil over medium-high heat, and add the strawberries and cook them for about 5 minutes, stirring occasionally, until they're softened and syrupy.

Cut the pie into wedges and serve each slice with a small scoop of sherbet on top and a spoonful of strawberry sauce poured over the sherbet and onto the pie.

Dulce de Leche Ice Cream Pie with Hot Fudge Sauce, Cajeta, and Salty Spanish Peanuts

Dulce de leche is a fantastic new ice cream flavor, but if you're one of those people whose favorite is plain old vanilla, that would be delicious here, too. If you want to save time, start with a frozen graham cracker crust; try to find one made with butter, not shortening. Cajeta is Mexico's dulce de leche (caramel); it's made with goat's milk and it has a tangy flavor, one with more character than just straightforward sweetness. You can find it in Hispanic grocery stores and even some regular grocery stores. If you don't find it, any dulce de leche or caramel will work fine.

MAKES ONE 9-INCH PIE (SERVES 8)   20 MINUTES

1 cup graham cracker crumbs or 8 whole graham crackers, finely crushed

½ stick (4 tablespoons) unsalted butter, melted

¼ teaspoon ground cinnamon

Pinch of freshly grated nutmeg

1½ pints premium dulce de leche **ice cream**

1½ cups Spanish peanuts, with their skins on

Peanut oil or canola oil for tossing with the peanuts

Sea salt

1 jar **hot fudge sauce**

1 jar cajeta

Adjust the oven rack to the middle position and preheat the oven to 325°F.

To make the crust, combine the graham cracker crumbs with the butter, cinnamon, and nutmeg in a medium bowl. Press the crumbs into a 9-inch glass or ceramic pie plate to form an even crust. Bake the crust for about 8 minutes, until it is firm to the touch. Remove the crust from the oven and set it aside (or refrigerate) to cool completely.

Remove the ice cream from the freezer and thaw it at room temperature for 15 to 20 minutes, until it is slightly softened.

Spread the peanuts on a baking sheet and toast them in the oven for 8 to 10 minutes, shaking the pan occasionally for even toasting, until the nuts are lightly browned and fragrant. Remove the nuts from the oven, drizzle them with oil, sprinkle them with sea salt, and toss to coat.

Scoop the ice cream into the bowl of a standing electric mixer and use the paddle attachment to beat it until it's very soft but not melted. Spread the softened ice cream into the pie shell and freeze it while you prepare the rest of the components.

Bring a medium pot of water to a boil over high heat. Reduce the heat to a low simmer. Remove the lids from the jars of hot fudge sauce and cajeta and place the jars in the water for about 5 minutes, until the sauces are warmed through, stirring them in the jars occasionally. (Or warm the sauces in the microwave.)

Cut the pie into wedges and serve it with the hot fudge sauce, cajeta, and peanuts on the side for people to use however much they want to of any of them.

Key Lime Custards with Crème Fraîche and Whole-Wheat Crackers
Carolynn Carreño • Writer

When Nancy and I were almost finished writing this book, I suddenly realized that we didn't have any recipes that used sweetened condensed milk. This seemed like sacrilege to me. Sweetened condensed milk is the basis of so many classic American desserts, such as key lime pie and seven-layer cookies. I experienced my first solo baking triumph using a recipe from the back of a can of sweetened condensed milk to make lemon meringue pie. It became my specialty, even after I ordered the recipe booklet from the manufacturer and baked my way from one end of it to the other. When I insisted that we include a recipe using sweetened condensed milk here, Nancy shared her key lime pie recipe with me, which I turned into these custards served with Carr's Whole Wheat Crackers or graham crackers on the side in place of a crust. You can use California limes in place of the key limes, but conventional limes will not work. They just don't have enough of the mouth-puckering lime flavor that makes this dessert special.

15 MINUTES (PLUS CHILLING TIME)

Preheat the oven to 325°F.

Whisk the sweetened condensed milk, egg yolks, and lime juice together in a medium bowl and pour the mixture into four 6-ounce ramekins, dividing it evenly. Place the custards in the oven to bake for 12 minutes, until they're set. Remove them from the oven and set them aside to cool to room temperature, then place them in the refrigerator for 1 hour to chill.

Dollop a tablespoon of crème fraîche on each custard and serve each with two Carr's crackers on the side.

3 1-ounce cans sweetened condensed milk

6 large egg yolks

1⅓ cups fresh key lime juice (or California lime juice)

4 tablespoons **crème fraîche**

8 Carr's Whole Wheat Crackers (or 2 whole sheets graham crackers, each broken into 4 individual segments)

Meringues with Warm Raspberry Compote and Vanilla Ice Cream

Finding good meringues is an easy task. All you have to do is look at the ingredients list and make sure there are only two things in them: egg whites and sugar. To make this compote, rather than cooking the raspberries with sugar I combine them with a caramel. This little bit of extra effort makes the sauce a little thicker and gives it a deeper flavor and brighter color. I add the raspberries at the end so they hold their shape.

15 MINUTES

To make the compote, mix the sugar with ¼ cup water in a small, heavy-bottomed saucepan and bring it to a boil over high heat. Boil the mixture for about 10 minutes, swirling the pan occasionally (but not stirring) so it colors evenly, until it becomes amber and just starts to smoke. Remove the pan from the heat and carefully add the wine and vanilla, standing back as the mixture may splatter. Return the caramel to a boil over medium-high heat and stir until the caramel is melted and syrupy. (It will have solidified slightly when you added the liquid.) Add the raspberries, stir gently to combine, and cook just long enough to warm them through.

Place three meringues in a cluster on each of four plates. Spoon the compote over the meringues, leaving the meringues partially exposed, and nestle a scoop of ice cream next to the meringues.

½ cup sugar

2 tablespoons red wine

½ teaspoon pure vanilla extract

2 cups frozen raspberries (about 6 ounces), thawed in a colander (about ¾ cup)

12 small meringues (about ¾-inch diameter)

4 oval scoops premium vanilla **ice cream**

Warm Brandied Prunes with Vanilla Ice Cream and Butter Wafer Cookies

This dessert is probably my favorite in the book and couldn't be any simpler. Prunes have a maligned reputation, but I love their deep, winy flavor and natural sweetness, both of which are enhanced by the brandy they're cooked in here. I use the common supermarket variety of stewed prunes, Sunsweet. They taste delicious and they don't contain any compromising ingredients so I didn't feel as if I needed to look further. I think everyone should keep a jar of these in their pantry for making this dessert at the last minute. I like those with pits because they hold their shape when they're cooked. The cookies I used were Jules Destrooper Butter Crisps. If you can't find them, any flaky, buttery wafer cookie will work.

20 MINUTES

Combine the prunes with the prune juice and brandy in a heavy-bottomed saucepan and bring to a boil over high heat. Reduce the heat and simmer for 2 to 3 minutes, until the prunes are warmed through. Remove the prunes from the pan with a slotted spoon and divide them among four large soup or dessert plates.

Bring the sauce back to a boil over medium-high heat and cook it for about 8 minutes, until it reduces and thickens.

Place one scoop of ice cream on top of each serving of prunes. Spoon the sauce over the ice cream and serve with the cookies on the side of each plate.

16 stewed prunes (not pitted), plus ½ cup of their juice

3 tablespoons brandy

4 oval scoops premium vanilla **ice cream**

12–16 flaky butter wafer cookies

Creamy Greek Yogurt with Orange Marmalade, Orange Sherbet, and Amaretti

This dessert requires absolutely no preparation. It's assembled from different ingredients that go really well together without your having to do anything to them. Because the dish is so simple, its flavor depends 100 percent on the quality of each component. So go all out and get the best orange marmalade you can find—chunky and tart, such as those labeled "fine cut," which refers to the rind, or Seville orange marmalade. (You can't go wrong with an imported English marmalade or one made by small domestic producers such as June Taylor.) Strained Greek yogurt is the only thing that will work for this; it's thicker and creamier than "normal" plain yogurt, which is what you need since it acts as a bed for the other ingredients. Amaretti are crunchy cookies made with egg whites, sugar, and almond paste, also called Italian macaroons. Look for those that don't have too strong an almond flavor; I like the ones made by Vicenzi.

10 MINUTES

If the marmalade is too thick to release easily from a spoon, put it in a small bowl and stir in enough hot water to loosen it slightly (about 1 tablespoon).

Spoon the yogurt onto four large soup or dessert plates, dividing it evenly. Make three small indentations with the back of a spoon in each mound of yogurt and put a teaspoon of marmalade into each indentation. Lightly swirl the yogurt and marmalade together to combine them slightly. Nestle a scoop of the sherbet next to each serving of yogurt and place two cookies on the side of each plate.

¼ cup orange marmalade

1 cup strained whole-milk **Greek yogurt**

4 oval scoops orange or tropical sherbet (or sorbet)

8 amaretti

Blueberry Pie with Crumb Topping
Ruth Reichl • Editor in Chief, *Gourmet*

I love fruit pies—making them and serving them. Of course, I prefer to make my pies from scratch, but I keep frozen piecrusts in the freezer in case I need to make a quick dessert on the spur of the moment. I find that while frozen crusts tend to be a bit salty, they work beautifully for one-crust creations or, as in this recipe, topped with a homemade crumb. This crumb topping also freezes well, so if you really want to be prepared, double (or quadruple) the recipe and keep it on hand for making last-minute fruit pies or crumbles. The frozen blueberries from Cascadian Farm are so tiny and flavorful that, except at the very height of the local blueberry season, they're better than fresh berries.

•

I love this recipe. It's so simple and its goodness is based on the pure flavor of the blueberries. If you're planning ahead, defrost the blueberries before baking them: it makes their flavor even more concentrated. To defrost the berries, place them in a colander set over a bowl and put them in the refrigerator overnight. —Nancy

MAKES ONE 9-INCH PIE (SERVES 8)   35 MINUTES

Adjust the oven rack to the highest position and preheat the oven to 400°F.

To make the crumb topping, stir the butter and sugar together in a medium bowl. Add the flour, cinnamon, and salt and mix well.

Put the blueberries in the frozen pie shell. Use your fingers to crumble the topping over the berries to cover the pie.

Place the pie on a baking sheet to catch the fruit juices that may boil over the shell and bake the pie for 10 minutes. Reduce the heat to 350°F and bake for another 15 minutes, until the topping is golden. Remove the pie from the oven and place on a wire rack to cool slightly. Serve the pie while it's still a bit warm, with vanilla ice cream.

FOR THE CRUMB TOPPING

1 stick (1/2 cup) unsalted butter, melted
1/2 cup sugar
3/4 cup all-purpose flour
1/4 teaspoon ground cinnamon
1/4 teaspoon salt

3 cups frozen blueberries
1 9-inch frozen pie shell (regular, not deep dish)
Premium vanilla **ice cream**

Hot Chocolate Sundaes with Coffee Ice Cream, Shortbread Cookies, and Hot Fudge Sauce

I use two different jarred chocolate products in this dessert. One is a prepared hot fudge sauce, which contains corn syrup and other ingredients to make the sauce shiny and liquid. The other sauce is almost pure chocolate and it's a solid paste, like a ganache. Scharffen Berger is the only brand I know that makes it. The contrast of the two sauces adds a nice dimension to what is basically just a really good (and really rich!) hot fudge sundae. (If you can't find both sauces, use part straight from the jar and add cream to the other.) I love shortbread cookies, specifically Walkers shortbread. How could you not? They're pure butter! I found that when they're warmed up, the butter in them melts slightly, making them taste freshly made. My son, Oliver, who watched me make this dessert, says nobody will follow my very detailed instructions on how to drizzle the hot fudge. I beg you to prove him wrong.

20 MINUTES

Adjust the oven rack to the middle position and preheat the oven to 325°F.

Spread the almonds on a baking sheet and toast them in the oven for 15 to 20 minutes, shaking the pan occasionally for even toasting, until they're lightly browned and fragrant. Remove the almonds from the oven. Allow them to cool slightly, then coarsely chop them.

While the nuts are toasting, place the shortbread cookies on a baking sheet and warm them in the oven for a few minutes. (Alternatively, place them in the microwave for about 45 seconds.)

Bring a small pot of water to a boil over high heat. Reduce the heat to a low simmer. Remove the lid from the hot fudge sauce and place the jar in the water for about 5 minutes, stirring the sauce in the jar occasionally, until it's warmed through. (Or you can warm the sauce in the microwave.)

Combine the cream and chocolate sauce in a small saucepan over low heat, stirring occasionally, until the chocolate melts and the mixture is combined, about 4 minutes. Be careful not to burn the chocolate or overheat it as it will become bitter. Stir in more cream if necessary to obtain a consistency slightly thicker than heavy cream and the color noticeably lighter than the hot fudge.

Spoon 2 tablespoons of the creamy hot chocolate mixture into the bottom of four large soup plates or bowls. Place one cookie on each pool toward the

1/2 cup whole almonds, with their skins on

4 rectangular shortbread cookies

1/4 cup **hot fudge sauce**

1/4 cup heavy cream, or more as needed

1/4 cup chocolate sauce

Sea salt

4 oval scoops premium coffee **ice cream**

right side of the plate. Spoon 1 tablespoon of the hot fudge over each serving, drizzling some in the creamy chocolate, some over the shortbread, and a bit more on the other side of the shortbread. Sprinkle the hot fudge with a few grains of sea salt, scatter the nuts over the hot fudge, and place a scoop of coffee ice cream on each plate to the left side of the shortbread.

Blackberry-Yogurt Soup with Warm Blackberry Compote, Vanilla Ice Cream, and Buttery Wafer Cookies

Making this compote is one of the rare instances when I use a microwave. I like the microwave for heating the berries because they don't break up. You could accomplish the same thing in the oven, it just takes more time; on the stovetop, the direct heat (and the irresistible impulse to stir!) will cause the berries to break down. I start with the blackberries still frozen because I find they hold their shape better that way. Naturally, you can use fresh berries in place of the frozen if you like. Butter wafer cookies—also known by their Italian name, pizzelle—are thin waffle-shaped wafer cookies. I like them because they're really light and crisp and they don't contain any unnecessary ingredients, just the good stuff: butter, sugar, and flour.

20 MINUTES

To make the soup, combine the yogurt, blackberries, sugar, and honey together in a blender and purée until it's smooth.

To make the compote, gently stir the blackberries and sugar together in a medium bowl and cook them in the microwave until the berries are heated through, about 1½ minutes. (Alternatively, combine the berries and sugar in a small ovenproof dish and place it in a 350°F oven for about 10 minutes.)

Ladle the soup into four large soup or dessert plates, dividing it evenly. Place one cookie on the side of each plate with part of the cookie in the pool of soup. Place 2 scoops of ice cream nestled side by side on top of each cookie and spoon the blackberry compote over the ice cream.

FOR THE SOUP

½ cup plus 2 tablespoons strained whole-milk **Greek yogurt**

4 ounces frozen blackberries (about ½ cup)

3 tablespoons sugar

2 teaspoons honey

FOR THE COMPOTE

4 ounces frozen blackberries (about 1 cup)

¾ teaspoon sugar

4 large butter wafer cookies

8 oval scoops premium vanilla **ice cream**

TWIST ESSENTIALS

During the process of developing the recipes for this book, I tasted many wonderful products and had many great surprises. I've introduced you to a number of these products in the head notes to the recipes in which they're used. The items listed here are those that I use repeatedly throughout the book. They range from the basics, like bacon, breadcrumbs, and tomatoes, to more unusual essentials such as jarred onions and beets.

While I've mentioned the brands of certain products I can vouch for, I do this just to help you make your shopping decisions. I want this book to be a household staple, and over time there are going to be certain brands that phase out and new ones that come in. Every year the products seem to be getting better and better. Choose those that you like and that are available to you. And remember to look at the ingredients list—and taste it—before using a product.

Anchovy fillets come two ways, salt-packed, which are found in large tins (or sold in bulk, by the pound, in deli cases), and packed in oil in tins or jars. I definitely prefer salt-packed anchovies, but they require a bit of time to prepare—you have to rinse them and then remove the bone from each fish. With oil-packed anchovy fillets, you just pull them from the jar and that's it. They're so soft from having marinated in the oil that you don't even need to chop them—just smash them with the flat side of a knife or break them up when they're in the pan. If you do use oil-packed anchovies, I recommend you buy those packed in olive oil, not soybean oil.

Arbol chiles are small, elongated spicy red peppers that are used to add heat to soups and stews or to infuse oils. They're widely available.

Artichoke hearts: Marinated artichoke hearts are readily available jarred. The quality varies so much, I suggest tasting a jar before you stock up. If you can find them in the deli case of your local supermarket or Italian grocer, buy those. My favorites are the Roman-style artichoke hearts, which come with their long (edible) stems attached. Note that one of these is the equivalent of four standard-size artichoke hearts.

Bacon: I like to cook bacon until it's just done, not crispy, so I buy only thick-sliced bacon. I also look for brands that are applewood smoked (also sometimes called "apple smoked"). And I use only nitrate-free bacon. My very favorite is a brand from Wisconsin, Nueske's. I also like the bacon produced by Niman Ranch. Both of these are available from their Web sites in addition to specialty food stores.

Bagna cauda is a very simple sauce of anchovies, garlic, lemon, olive oil, and, often, butter. I found it easier to make my own than to find a decent one in a jar, but after tasting many, I found one made by Retrivo that I would use in place of homemade if I were in a hurry.

Balsamic vinegar: True balsamic vinegar comes from Modena or Reggio Emilia in Italy, and it is always aged. When I call for aged balsamic vinegar, I'm specifically referring to balsamic vinegar that's been aged for at least twelve years. Balsamic vinegar that is aged longer can run upwards of $100. You don't need to buy this quality for the purpose of this book—although it certainly wouldn't hurt to add a few drops where aged balsamic is called for! What you don't want when I call for aged balsamic vinegar is the really cheap stuff you find at grocery stores, which is very acidic and not even close to what real balsamic vinegar tastes like. The only time I use this is when I'm going to reduce the vinegar.

Basil paste is different from pesto in that it doesn't contain nuts or cheese, just basil, olive oil, garlic, and salt. I use it when I don't want the cheese, such as when I'm serving it with seafood. I always use the one made by Rustichella d'Abruzzo. The same company makes a product called Green Sauce, which is essentially a parsley paste. It can be used in place of basil pesto if you like.

Basil pesto: I was surprised by how difficult it was to find a pesto that I liked. There are so many brands out there, but most of them tasted rancid or just "off." I knew I had to stand by pesto since it's such a popular jarred item, so I kept tasting, and eventually found a few brands, including Rustichella d'Abruzzo, La Bella Angiolina, and Pesto Ligure, that make pesto true to the flavor of homemade. All are available in specialty food stores.

Beans play a big role in this book. I found so many jarred and canned varieties that were delicious and almost completely uncompromised in terms of flavor and texture that I wanted to find different ways to use them. In fact, I found them perfectly cooked and creamy, as opposed to the chalky, under-cooked beans served at many restaurants. In addition to standards such as garbanzo beans, cannellini beans, navy beans, kidney beans, black beans, lima beans, and pinto beans, I found some unusual varieties from organic and arti-sanal producers, such as Radici of Tuscany Tuscan White Beans, Matiz Navarro Tender Broad Beans, and Annalisa Brown Beans. If you're buying more common, supermarket brands, look for those that are organic and/or low sodium and contain no artificial flavorings or preservatives.

Beets are one of those vegetables that most of us grew up eating *only* from a can. It wasn't until I was introduced to fresh beets as an adult that I learned to like them, so it's ironic that for this book I set myself to the task of trying to find a good alternative to fresh ones. I prefer jarred beets to those from a can, which tend to pick up a tinny taste. When dressed as they are in this book, Aunt Nellie's Whole Ruby Red Beets were almost indistinguishable from fresh.

Black olives vary so much in flavor, and there are so many different kinds, which you choose to use is really a matter of personal preference. Many supermarkets have an olive bar where you can taste the olives before buying them. This is the ideal opportunity to try different varieties to find out which you like. My preferred varieties are Niçoise, Saracen, or taggiasche, all of which are very small and oftentimes come pitted. If you can't find a good-quality pitted olive, use another good black olive, such as Moroccan oil-cured or kalamata olives. I don't mind pits, but if you do, you can easily remove the pits of some olives. If the olives you use are large, you may want to cut them in half.

Breadcrumbs: I find the common supermarket varieties of breadcrumbs terrible. They all taste stale. If that is all that is available to you, substitute crushed saltine crackers. I recently discovered a brand of packaged bread-crumbs that I love: Artesian Baked Breadcrumbs by Heaven Scent, sold at Whole Foods. They are full of flavor and don't taste stale. If you are lucky enough to live by a neighborhood bakery that sells freshly made breadcrumbs that's the best way to go.

Broth: For both chicken and vegetable broth, I've found that the best-tasting ones come in boxes, not cans. I specifically like Trader Joe's Free-Range Chicken Broth. Generally speaking, look for those that are labeled low-sodium and that contain no colorings or MSG (monosodium glutamate) in the ingredients list.

Capers: I prefer salt-packed capers, which are available at Italian and specialty food stores, to those packed in brine, which are available in regular grocery stores. Salt-packed capers are more flavorful, but can also be a little harder to find, and they need to be rinsed and drained before using them in recipes. Caper paste, which comes in a tube, is what I consider a perfect product in that the ingredients list is totally pure: just capers, vinegar, and salt. Although I didn't use it in this book, it's an easy way to add caper flavor to dishes when you don't need the texture of the whole capers.

Caperberries are the actual fruits of the caper plant, of which capers are the buds. They have a similar taste to capers but they aren't as pungent, so you can use them in different ways than you would capers. I like the flavor of the two together. You can find them in jars, shelved next to the capers, or in the deli section of specialty food stores, sold in bulk with the olives.

Celery root, also called celeriac, is the root of the celery plant. It has a wonderful, subtle flavor that's best known for the role it plays in celery root rémoulade, which is how I use it in this book. I was pleasantly surprised to find a jarred brand imported from France, Maitre Provi, that maintained the crunchy texture necessary to stand up to the creamy mayonnaise-based dressing.

Chestnut honey is sometimes referred to as a "savory" or "bitter" honey. It has a rich honey taste, but it's only faintly sweet and even a bit bitter. It's used differently than conventional honeys and is most often drizzled over cheese. It's sold in specialty shops and cheese stores. If you can't find it, use buckwheat honey in its place.

Chipotle peppers are roasted jalapeño peppers. The roasting changes their nature entirely—they become a deep reddish brown color and take on a rich, smoky flavor. Chipotle peppers are available both dried and canned in adobo sauce made from vinegar, tomato, and paprika. The canned variety is so readily available and so easy to work with—you can just dump the entire contents in a blender and purée—that I never bother with the dried.

Chunky red pepper spread is made from roasted peppers that are sweet, not spicy. It has more texture than red pepper paste or red pepper sauce. I like the one made by Aiello. If you can't find it, substitute finely chopped roasted Piquillo peppers.

Cornichons are small pickled cucumbers often served with French paté. You can find them in most grocery stores under their American name, gherkins.

Crème fraîche is French-style aged cultured cream, which is similar to sour cream but thicker and with a tangier, more buttery flavor. You can find it in specialty food stores either in the dairy or cheese case. I look for brands made by domestic producers such as Bellwether Farms, Vermont Butter & Cheese Company, or Sadie Kendal. If you can't find crème fraîche, you can make your own by stirring 1 tablespoon of buttermilk into 1 cup of heavy cream. Cover the bowl with plastic and let it sit at room temperature overnight, until it's thickened.

Demi-glace, most commonly used to make rich sauces and in sautéing, is stock, usually chicken or veal, that has been reduced until it's rich and concentrated. It used to be something reserved for chefs, who could afford the time and ingredients it took to make it. Today, there are a few really good ready-made demi-glaces out there, including good ones made by Vatel. You'll usually find them frozen, or in small containers in the meat department of specialty food stores.

Dried oregano is one of the few dried herbs I use. I prefer the kind imported from Greece or Italy, which is more flavorful and aromatic than the bottled stuff. It usually comes in the form of a whole branch of the dried herb in a plastic bag. You pinch the oregano off the branch as you need it.

Eggplant appetizer, such as the one I found from ZerGüt, is a simple purée of eggplant seasoned with ingredients including onion, garlic, and parsley. It has a really delicious, pure eggplant flavor, which is what I want when I call for eggplant appetizer. I don't recommend that you use the products labeled eggplant "dip" or "pesto," which contain all sorts of ingredients that I wouldn't add to eggplant—they tend to taste funky.

Extra-virgin olive oil is a mainstay of this book. I use two different grades: a common, inexpensive one for cooking and a more expensive variety for drizzling on salads and finished dishes. Olive oil really varies in flavor, so taste it before you buy it, and have a few on hand to use in different dishes.

Fennel pollen, which is the flower of the top of wild fennel after it's gone to seed, is something I discovered very recently. Wild fennel grows all over Italy and in parts of California. It has a more concentrated, earthier flavor than conventional fennel. Fennel pollen is the closest I've found to imitating the intense flavor of wild fennel.

Feta: I'm sure there are many good varieties of feta cheese, but the one I use almost exclusively is a French brand, Valbreso. It has a moist, creamy texture and a lot of flavor without being too salty. I also like Bulgarian feta cheese. Whatever you choose, I recommend you avoid buying feta that comes already crumbled, which tends to be low quality and very salty.

Ghee is clarified butter used in Indian cooking. After the butter is melted, it's strained and the milk solids are removed. Because it doesn't contain milk solids, it can be heated to the smoking point without burning the way butter does. I use it when I want the flavor of butter but want to cook at a high temperature. You can find it in ethnic stores and specialty food stores in jars. Plugrá makes a clarified butter that you can use in place of ghee.

Greek yogurt is much creamier than any other yogurt. I used to have to go to Greek or Middle Eastern stores to find it, but now a brand called Fage Total is available in many grocery and health food stores and at Trader Joe's. The Greek yogurt I call for in these recipes is strained, which means it's thicker and creamier than "regular" yogurt. (Fage Total Greek yogurt is strained.) I only use whole-milk yogurt, but even low-fat Greek yogurt is thicker and creamier than the whole-milk yogurt of other brands.

Green chile salsa is made with tomatillos, small green tomato-like vegetables used in Mexican cooking. The tomatillos give it a unique tangy, almost lemony flavor. This salsa makes an ideal addition to black beans because it contains the very same ingredients—onions, garlic, and jalapeño peppers—that I would cook the beans with if I were making them from scratch. I found a few brands I like, such as Mark Miller's Coyote Cocina New Mexico Green Chile

Salsa, Rick Bayless's Frontera Tomatillo Salsa, and Whole Foods Roasted Green Chile Salsa.

Green masala paste is an Indian curry paste that gets its color from fresh mint and cilantro leaves. I use Classic Ashoka Madras Green Masala Paste, which is available in standard grocery stores.

Green olives: My two favorite varieties of green olives, both French and both fairly small, are Lucques and picholine. Anchovy-stuffed green olives are another product altogether. Produced in Spain, they come canned and are fairly easy to find in specialty food stores. If you can't find them, use plain green olives instead.

Harissa is a red chile pepper paste used in North African, particularly Tunisian and Moroccan, cooking. The chiles are pounded together with other seasonings such as coriander, caraway, garlic, and salt. The brands that I found with the purest ingredients came in a jar. Harissa also comes in tubes, but those brands also contain "fillers," such as carrots, turnips, and beets.

Hot fudge sauce contains ingredients such as corn syrup that make the sauce shiny and liquid. There are so many superb chocolatiers in America and many good brands imported from Europe that it's almost impossible to pick favorites among them. Fran's Dark Chocolate Sauce and The King's Cupboard Bittersweet Chocolate Sauce are two brands that are widely available.

Ice cream: I call for only premium ice cream in this book—and that's all I ever eat or use. Premium ice cream is higher in fat and less airy than conventional brands, and it also contains high-quality ingredients, such as pure vanilla extract, and no fillers or stabilizers. In addition to the big producers whose ice cream you find in grocery stores, look for those made by small boutique producers, such as McConnell's of Santa Barbara, Graeter's, or a local producer in your area.

Lemon-infused olive oil is a wonderful product for drizzling over seafood dishes, soups, and salads. My favorite brand is Agrumato, imported by Manacaretti. Make sure you buy a good-quality one made with extra-virgin olive oil and real lemon—and nothing else. Otherwise, the lemon flavor can taste rancid or synthetic. If you can't find or don't want to invest in a separate bottle of high-quality lemon-infused oil, rather than buy a poor-quality one you're better off grating some fresh lemon zest into a good olive oil and using that.

Lentils are the one legume I never would have thought to use from a can before working on this book. Initially I sought out unusual varieties of canned lentils and found some that had great texture and flavor, such as black beluga lentils from an organic producer, Westbrae Natural. But in an effort to find something more easily accessible, I tried Progresso Lentil Soup and was amazed—after the liquid is drained off, the lentils are remarkably intact and the seasoning is just right.

Mayonnaise: I tried a lot of different brands of mayonnaise for this book. I really wanted to find one that was organic or made by a small producer. But after all of the tasting, I went back to my old favorite: Best Foods (called Hellmann's on the East Coast). Its taste just says "mayonnaise" to me.

Meat rubs are spice mixtures usually sold for use on a specific meat or fish or chicken. I was surprised to find how much I liked the various rubs I used in this book, such as those made by Tulocay's Made in Napa Valley. As a quick and easy solution for seasoning, they were much better than any of the store-bought marinades I tried, all of which tasted synthetic.

Mexican crema, which is Mexican sour cream, is tangier and more pungent than American sour cream. It's also much more liquid, so it's ideal when you want to drizzle the cream rather than spoon it. It comes jarred and is available in many supermarkets or in Latin American grocery stores. If you can't find it, use sour cream in its place.

Mixed salad, a mix of jarred shredded crunchy cabbage; onions; green, red, and yellow peppers; carrots; and pickles, was one of the real surprises I found when writing this book. The vegetables stay remarkably crunchy in the brine and are the perfect tangy accompaniment, straight from the jar, to go with fried oysters. There are many producers, but the two brands I can vouch for are Bende and Adro.

Mozzarella is a creamy fresh cheese usually available in 8-ounce balls. Look for it in your local cheese store or the cheese counter of a specialty food store. It's usually made from cow's milk in this country. Occasionally you can find imported buffalo milk mozzarella, which is a real delicacy and worth the extra expense if you do find it. **Bocconcini** are small bite-size balls of the cheese whose name means "little mouthfuls." **Burrata** is cream-filled mozzarella. You can find imported burrata at cheese shops, and a few domestic producers are starting to make it. In Los Angeles, we're fortunate to get fresh burrata and mozzarella from a local company, Gioia. If you can't find burrata, substitute mozzarella. With any mozzarella, freshness is key, so if you have access to a cheese store, that's the best place to buy it. Ideally, it will have been made the same day or within a few days of using it. What you definitely don't want are the rubbery balls wrapped in plastic sold at grocery stores—the low-moisture mozzarella used on the kind of pizza that we all grew up with.

Mushrooms: Good-quality marinated mushrooms are available in jars, and sold in bulk from a deli case. If you do opt for jarred mushrooms, look for the imported ones from Italy that contain a variety. The varying flavors, textures, and shapes make any dish more interesting. And note that when I call for mushrooms, I never mean *canned* mushrooms.

Mustard is such a convenient seasoning to use in vinaigrettes, marinades, and sauces. I always have a few kinds on hand. I like whole-grain mustard when I want the look and texture of the mustard seeds. Otherwise I use an imported Dijon mustard. I'm not a big flavored mustard person, but if you are, you might want to keep some on hand, such as tarragon mustard. Just be sure that there are no weird ingredients added.

Old Bay Seasoning is a classic spice mix from Maryland. It's traditionally used to add flavor to simple steamed and boiled seafood dishes. I'd heard of it, but never used it before working on this book. I was intrigued by the ingredients list (celery salt, mustard, red pepper, bay leaves, cloves, allspice, ginger, mace, cardamom, cinnamon, and paprika) and found that it was a wonderful blend to boost the flavor of some seafood dishes. You can find it at the seafood counter of grocery stores or at fish markets.

Olive tapenade and **olive paté** are similar products. Products labeled tapenade generally contain other ingredients, such as roasted peppers and capers. Paté is usually just black olives, puréed with a little olive oil and salt. My favorites are the ones from my favorite importers—Manacaretti (Rustichella d'Abruzzo) and K. L. Keller. But I also found one by Olive Harvest and another, called Chunky Olive Spread, by Aiello that I liked. In general, a tapenade or paté shouldn't contain anything you wouldn't put in it if you made it from scratch, such as food coloring or preservatives, and should be made with olive oil, not vegetable oil.

Onions, which I used exclusively from a jar for this book, were an invaluable resource. The time saved in terms of peeling, chopping, and sautéing or roasting really helped to keep cooking times down in these recipes. I found that all jarred onions contained at least a little bit of sugar, but not enough to detract from their flavor. I do, however, prefer those that don't taste too pickled, like martini onions. I found many brands that I liked, including Patsy's Roasted Onions, Aunt Nellie's Whole Holland-Style Onions, Valbona Cipolline, and Valbona Organic Grilled Onions. Some cipolline onions, such as Roland Sweet Italian Onions in Balsamic Vinegar and those found in the deli section of Italian and specialty food stores, are a different product—they have a sweet balsamic vinegar taste—and shouldn't be used interchangeably with regular onions.

Pancetta is pork belly that is cured with salt but not smoked, as American bacon is. Pancetta is sold rolled up and sliced. You can find it at Italian delis and in the deli section of specialty food stores. Thick-sliced bacon can be used as a substitute.

Panko are Japanese breadcrumbs often used to coat tempura and other fried foods. Their coarse texture makes for a crunchier crust than you would get with conventional dried breadcrumbs. It used to be that you could find panko only in Japanese and other specialty food stores, but lately, I've seen them stocked with the breadcrumbs in regular grocery stores. If you can't find panko, substitute regular unseasoned breadcrumbs.

Paprika: Paprika can have such a nice flavor if you get a good one. I like smoked Spanish paprika, in particular one made by Pimenton de la Vera, which is from the La Vera region of Spain, a famous paprika-producing region. It imparts a hint of deep smoky flavor to dishes along with the heat of the pepper. It comes in *picante* (spicy) and *dulce* (sweet). I like the spicy one.

Paprika paste is made from whole puréed paprika peppers. The one I used was a Turkish brand, Mis, which I found at an import store and which is also available from several online sources. I like the sweet, smoky flavor it imparts. If you can't find it, substitute red pepper paste mixed with smoked Spanish paprika.

Parmigiano-Reggiano: There are many cheap imitations of Parmesan cheese, none of which have the intense nutty, sweet, and salty flavor and grainy texture of real Parmesan. Called Parmigiano-Reggiano, it's made only in certain regions in northern Italy: Modena, Parma, Reggio Emilia, and parts of Bologna and Mantua. You can recognize it by the stamp that's impressed into the large wheel and that can be found on the outside edges of the small chunks you buy in stores. I always keep a wedge of Parmesan in my refrigerator for shaving and grating. I never buy pregrated Parmesan cheese, which tends to be dried out. Grating the cheese is such a simple step; it's not worth the time saved in terms of the compromise in freshness and flavor. To keep the wedge from drying out, wrap it tightly in a fresh sheet of plastic wrap after every use.

Passato means "passed" in Italian. The name refers to the process by which tomatoes are passed through a simple home kitchen tool, a *pasa pomodoro* ("tomato passer" or tomato mill), which separates the tomato juice from the seeds and skin. In Italy, tomatoes bottled in this way are stored in the larder and are a mainstay of home cooks year-round. You can buy passato in bottles at Italian and specialty food stores. If you can't find passato, use canned, peeled San Marzano tomatoes, crushed between your fingers, instead.

Pasta sauce: There probably isn't any cook—or at least no mother of small children—who hasn't relied on jarred pasta sauce at one time or another. I think most people have a favorite brand. My favorite is Rustichella d'Abruzzo, imported by Manacaretti. Use what you like.

Patak's is one of the few brands I call for by name in this book. I felt justified in doing so because their products, in addition to being good quality and made with no compromising ingredients, are widely available in standard grocery stores. That said, I also really like Maya Kaimal's simmer sauces, which we sell at La Brea and are also available at Whole Foods (sold in the refrigerator case). If you have access to those and want to use them in place of the curries in this book, they're wonderful.

Pea sprouts have the sweet taste of peas and the crunchy texture of sprouts. I can sometimes find them at farmers' markets in Los Angeles, but I can count on finding them year-round in supermarkets, packaged in clear plastic boxes. If you can't find them, substitute pea shoots in season, or live watercress or pepper cress.

Petite peas, which are younger and smaller than regular frozen peas, are just as easy to find and tend to be much sweeter. If you can find organic brands, even better. I also love canned peas. There are many imported French brands that are good (some are bottled, so you can see the small peas inside). And there's one domestic brand, LeSueur, whose peas are so good I could almost eat them from the can.

Pickled garlic: I never use jarred chopped garlic. It tastes so bitter and rancid that it ruins any dish you add it to. But I found another product, Delicias garlic cloves, which are whole pickled garlic cloves that I do like. The pickling stops the garlic from oxidizing, so it doesn't discolor or turn bitter.

Pickled jalapeño peppers are the canned or jarred peppers you probably saw for the first time on a nacho cheese platter. (I did.) I wouldn't use them in place of fresh, because the pickling taste is really prevalent. But as an item in themselves, when I want to add heat and a little bit of acidity to a dish, I love them.

Pickled red cabbage is a pretty common jarred item, one you'll find in any conventional grocery store. Because it's pickled, the quality of the cabbage doesn't suffer at all from being jarred.

Piquillo peppers are a delicacy from Spain. On a visit to the farm where the peppers are grown, I was told that you should never put a knife to a Piquillo pepper. I've always respected that, which is why I call for them to be torn, not chopped, in these recipes. They're more expensive than conventional roasted peppers, but the difference in flavor is absolutely worth the difference in price.

Polenta: For an Italian home cook or a chef in an upscale restaurant, instant polenta would be the ultimate cop-out. But regular polenta takes at least an hour of nearly constant stirring to cook, so it was just not feasible for this book. While instant polenta may not have quite the same toothsome texture as slow-cooked polenta, when you need to get dinner on the table, it's worth the slight compromise for the time saved.

Pomegranate molasses is pomegranate juice that has been reduced to a thick, dark, sweet syrup. It's available at Middle Eastern markets and specialty food stores.

Potatoes from a can or jar are one of the victories of this book. I found a few good brands, such as Roland and Gefen, available in regular grocery stores.

Prepared horseradish often contains sour cream, but I was able to find some that contain only horseradish and vinegar, which is what I prefer for the recipes in this book.

Preserved lemon is a staple in traditional Moroccan cuisine. The whole lemons are brined in a mixture of salt water and sugar (and sometimes spices) until the skins break down and the peel is tender enough to eat on its own. In fact, the peel, not the pulp, is the only part of preserved lemons that is used. It imparts a lemon flavor that is more intense and exotic than just lemon juice or zest. You can find it in specialty food stores or from Bella Cucina.

Prosciutto is salt-cured Italian ham. It has a delicate flavor and is usually eaten very thinly sliced. Genuine prosciutto is made in the province of Parma, in Emilia-Romagna. Thus, when you ask for prosciutto di Parma, you are getting the best. Prosciutto di San Daniele is also a good product and is less expensive. Most important, when you're buying prosciutto, you want to buy it from a deli where it's sliced right in front of you. Avoid the presliced stuff that's sold vacuum-packed in plastic in grocery stores.

Puff pastry: The thing to remember when buying puff pastry is summed up in one word: *butter*! Look at the ingredients list and make sure to buy one made with butter, such as the Dufour or Indo-European brands, not oil.

Pumpkin seed oil is an almost black, intensely flavored oil extracted from pumpkin seeds. It is used to finish a dish, never to cook with. It goes rancid very quickly, so it should be stored in the refrigerator and tasted before each use.

Red pepper paste: I used red pepper paste and red pepper sauce in many of the recipes in this book because they add not just heat, but the rich, sweet flavor of the peppers. I found many brands I like, such as ZerGüt Hot or Mild Ajvar (available in grocery and import stores or online), Trader Joe's Red Pepper Spread, Rustichella d'Abruzzo's Red Pepper Pesto, and Crema di Peperoni from A.G. Ferrari. Alternatively, you could use a jarred romesco sauce, such as La Masia, in its place. Many come in spicy or mild varieties. I prefer spicy. Use what you like.

Ricotta: Fresh ricotta is a delicacy in Italy, where it's prized for its subtle flavor, and always eaten the day it's made. In Los Angeles, we're lucky enough to have access to fresh ricotta from a local producer, Gioia. In New York, Di Palos cow's milk ricotta is the most common, but if you find sheep's milk, you're in for a treat. That said, the supermarket stuff will do in a pinch if that's what you have access to.

Roasted chicken: I always have a roasted chicken in my refrigerator. It lasts at least five days, and it's so handy for making last-minute meals. Roasted chicken is available these days at just about every supermarket across the country. But not all roasted chicken is created equal. Seek out organic, free-range birds, and look at the ingredients list to see that they're seasoned with only natural ingredients. My favorite roasted chickens are those cooked over an oak fire, like the ones I get from a Peruvian place, Pollo alla Brasa, near my house in Los Angeles. They have a nice crispy skin and moist, flavorful meat. If you can find flame-roasted chicken, it's worth the effort to get it.

Roasted eggplant, such as Patsy's Roasted Eggplant, or fried eggplant, such as ZerGüt Fried Eggplant, is different from any product labeled "eggplant appetizer" in that the eggplant is in chunks or slices, not pureed. If you can't find roasted eggplant jarred, you'll probably find it in an Italian deli case.

Saba is grape must that has been reduced to a syrup. It is available only at the most high-end specialty stores or at Italian import Web sites, such as A.G. Ferrari. It has a similar taste to and is used in the same way as good aged balsamic vinegar, which can be used in its place if you can't find saba.

Salsify is a root vegetable that looks similar to a long, white carrot but is less sweet and much earthier tasting than a carrot. It's often braised and it's always fully cooked. The canned salsify I found, imported from France, has a very similar texture to braised fresh salsify.

Saltine crackers: Using saltines to make breadcrumbs saves you the step of toasting bread. Each saltine yields about 1 tablespoon of breadcrumbs. My aim in using them was to avoid using the packaged toasted breadcrumbs that taste synthetic and stale. If you can find a good alternate brand (see "Breadcrumbs," page 240), use it.

San Marzano tomatoes, a variety grown in the San Marzano region of Italy, are said to be the best canned tomatoes there are. Any time you're using a canned or bottled tomato product, including passato, if you see some labeled "San Marzano," choose those. San Marzano tomatoes are not hard to find in specialty food stores, but you're guaranteed to find them at Italian markets.

Sauerkraut, finely chopped, fermented white cabbage, is available in conventional supermarkets. Seek out one with the fewest ingredients—ideally just cabbage, water, and salt—and from small or organic producers, such as Bubbies, which is sold at Whole Foods.

Sherry vinegar has a slightly sweet, complex taste that gives a nice finish to dishes, especially fish and beans. The best quality sherry vinegar comes from Jerez, the sherry-producing region of Spain. I use only the aged varieties, which, like aged balsamic vinegar, are less acidic and have a deeper, more interesting flavor than the stuff that is not aged.

Smoked salmon fillet: The smoked salmon that I call for in this book are chunky smoked salmon fillets that come vacuum-packed in plastic, not the thinly sliced salmon you'd put on a bagel. My favorite brand is Blue Hill Bay Salmon with Cracked Pepper. They also sell smoked trout. Your fishmonger might sell chunks of smoked salmon and you might also want to seek out products from small smokehouses across the country.

Soup that comes in boxes generally tastes better to me than canned soups. Those I chose for this book—corn, roasted red pepper and tomato, and butternut squash—were all made of the very same ingredients I would use to make the soup. My two favorite brands are Trader Joe's and Imagine.

Stock, like demi-glace, was once reserved for professional chefs who had the time to simmer meat bones for hours on end. Today, we're fortunate as home cooks to have available to us products such as Vatel's fish and veal stocks. You'll usually find these quality stocks at the fish counter or meat counter, though there are some good frozen stocks available also.

Sun-dried tomatoes: I don't use a lot of sun-dried tomatoes, and I am very particular about those I do use. I look for those that are plump and deep red in color, not shriveled and brown. **Semi-dried tomatoes** are something I'm seeing more and more in ethnic markets. I like them because they're not overly dried. Again, look for those that are red, not brown.

Tahini is a sesame-seed butter. You can find it both canned and jarred, though I've only ever used jarred. Buy it from a source that turns over their product quickly, and taste it before you use it to make sure it's not rancid.

Tandoori paste is a classic Indian paste used to flavor meats before they are grilled—and to give tandoori meats their signature bright-red color. I used Classic Ashoka Madras Tandoori Paste, which has the two ideal qualities of being widely available and tasting great.

Tabasco: A vinegar-based spicy pepper sauce. A few drops goes a long way.

Tomatoes: I use a lot of small tomatoes in this book for a reason: when tomatoes are out of season, it's a lot easier to find good small tomatoes than good big tomatoes, which I would never use out of season. Del Cabo, an organic producer at the southern tip of Baja California, grows really good small, sweet tomatoes, including Sweet 100s, an heirloom variety, and grape tomatoes, year-round. I don't know how they do it, but I've been to the farm and there are no greenhouses; all the tomatoes are grown outdoors.

Tuna: I may use water-packed tuna when I'm making tuna salad for sandwiches, but for anything else, I use only olive oil–packed tuna from a tin or a jar. I prefer those imported from Italy and Spain because I think the olive oil they're packed in tends to be of better quality. The best tuna you can buy is ventresca, which is tuna belly marinated in olive oil. It is a delicacy in Spain and Italy, prized for its rich flavor and tenderness. It is very expensive. A good olive oil–packed tuna can be used in its place.

Walnut oil has a very distinct flavor that works really nicely to finish certain vegetables, such as beets, or to add another component of walnut flavor to dishes in which walnuts are used. It goes rancid very quickly, so I recommend that you store it in the refrigerator and always taste it before using it. My favorite is a French producer, Huilerie J. Leblanc, which you can buy at La Brea Bakery, among other places.

Verjus is the unfermented juice of unripe wine grapes. You use it as you would vinegar or lemon juice—to add acidity to a dish, though verjus is sweeter. I look for verjus made by winemakers. I also like one made by Maggie Beer, a well-known Australian cook. If you don't have verjus, you can use champagne or white vinegar or white wine in its place.

Vinegar: In these recipes, you can use apple cider, wine, and champagne vinegar interchangeably if you don't have the vinegar I specify. The most important thing about the vinegar you use is to look for those made by small producers. They're often labeled by the variety of grape from which they're made, such as "chardonnay vinegar" or "cabernet vinegar." You can find nice vinegars at specialty food stores and cheese shops. At La Brea Bakery, we sell a red and white wine vinegar made by Le Vinaigre Artisanal that I think is superb.

ACKNOWLEDGMENTS

My thanks go to the following:

To my *Twist of the Wrist* collaborator, Matt Molina, who was by my side at every supermarket exploration and tasted his way through the good and the not-so-good cans, jars, bags, and boxes. He took my ideas—as well as his— and transformed them into recipe after amazing recipe. He always knew what I wanted.

To my co-writer, Carolynn Carreño, whom I didn't know before our mutual agent got us together. Not only does she have a knack for turning my half-thoughts into full sentences, she became a good and lasting friend. (I thought we would never put that glossary to rest.)

To Marcella Capasso, who taught me by example that if you hire an expert recipe tester and food stylist, you get a professional result.

To Amy Neunsinger whose simple, lyrical style of photography always brings my food to life.

To Nicolas Beckman, who constantly kept my shelves well stocked with all my favorite jarred items at La Brea Bakery.

To my agent, Janis Donnaud, who always looks after me, and to my editor and steadfast supporter, Peter Gethers, and his hard-working assistant, Shilpa Nadhan. And thanks to Leyla Aker for her attention to detail in editing this book. Thanks also to the diligent, hard-working copy editors, art directors, and production staff at Knopf.

To all of the chef friends, who, when I asked for a not-from-scratch recipe, didn't hesitate to reveal the truth about how they occasionally cook at home.

To my hilarious best friend, Margy Rochlin, who, in part, inspired this book by asking me to help her test recipes for an article she was writing about a cookbook that championed the use of all things jarred, tinned, and premade. We laughed as hard during the baking phase as we did at the sand-textured, preservative-flavored results. After that, I *knew* that I could do a better job, that that kind of food could be made quickly and taste good, too.

SOURCES

Acme Smoked Fish
(718) 383-8585
3056 Gem Street
Brooklyn, NY 11222
www.acmesmokedfish.com

A.G. Ferrari Foods
(877) 878-2783
www.agferrari.com
They have thirteen stores throughout
northern California.

Amazon
www.amazon.com

Bella Cucina
(800) 580-5674
www.bellacucina.com

The Cheese Store of Beverly Hills
(310) 278-2855
419 N. Beverly Drive
Beverly Hills, CA 90210
www.cheesestorebh.com

Central Market
www.centralmarket.com
There are seven store locations,
all in Texas.

Chef Shop
(877) 337-2491
www.chefshop.com

CyberCucina
www.cybercucina.com

Dean & DeLuca
(800) 221-7714
560 Broadway
New York, NY 10012
www.deandeluca.com
There are store locations in
New York, California, Kansas,
North Carolina, and the District
of Columbia.

Formaggio Kitchen
(888) 212-3224
244 Huron Avenue
Cambridge, MA 02138
(617) 350-6996
268 Shawmut Avenue
Boston, MA 02118
www.formaggiokitchen.com

Fox & Obel
(312) 410-7301
401 E. Illinois
Chicago, IL 60611
www.foxandobel.com

igourmet
(877) 446-8763
www.igourmet.com

Jons Marketplace
www.jonsmarketplace.com
There are seventeen locations,
all in Southern California.

Kalustyan's
(212) 685-3451
123 Lexington Avenue
New York, NY 10016
www.kalustyans.com

La Brea Bakery
(323) 939-6813
624 South La Brea Avenue
Los Angeles, CA 90036
www.labreabakery.com

Parthenon Foods
(877) 301-5522
www.parthenonfoods.com

The Pasta Shop
(510) 547-4005
5655 College Avenue
Oakland, CA 94618
www.rockridgemarkethall.com/
pastashop/index_pasta.html
(510) 528-1786
1786 Fourth Street
Berkeley, CA 94710
www.4thstreetshop.com/pages/pasta
_shop.html

The Spanish Table
(206) 682-2827
1427 Western Avenue
Seattle, WA 98101

The Spanish Table 2
(510) 548-1383
1814 San Pablo Avenue
Berkeley, CA 94702

The Spanish Table 3
(505) 986-0243
109 North Guadalupe Street
Santa Fe, NM 87501

The Spanish Table 4
(415) 388-5043
123 Strawberry Village
Mill Valley, CA 94941
www.spanishtable.com

**Surfas Restaurant Supply
and Gourmet Food**
(310) 559-4770
8825 National Boulevard
Culver City, CA 90232
www.surfasonline.com

Trader Joe's
www.traderjoes.com
There are store locations
all over the United States.

Whole Foods
www.wholefoods.com
There are store locations
all over the United States.

Zabar's
(800) 697-6301
2245 Broadway
New York, NY 10024
www.zabars.com

Zingerman's
(888) 636-8162
www.zingermans.com
Zingerman's Deli
(734) 663-3354
422 Detroit Street
Ann Arbor, MI 48104

INDEX

Page references in *Italic* refer to illustrations.

A Note About the Authors

Nancy Silverton is the author of *Nancy Silverton's Pastries from the La Brea Bakery* (recipient of a *Food & Wine* Best Cookbook Award in 2000), *Nancy Silverton's Breads from the La Brea Bakery* (nominated for Julia Child and James Beard Cookbook Awards) and *Desserts.* She will soon be opening a new restaurant in Los Angeles, Mozza, with Mario Batali. She lives in Los Angeles.

Carolynn Carreño is a James Beard Award–winning journalist and the coauthor of *100 Ways to Be Pasta* (with Wanda and Giovanna Tornabene), *Fresh Every Day* (with Sara Foster) and *Once Upon a Tart* (with Frank Mentesana and Jerome Audureau). She lives in Los Angeles and New York.

A Note on the Type

This book was typeset in a font named Gotham, designed by Tobias Frere-Jones at Hoefler Type Foundry in New York.

Frere-Jones wanted Gotham to exhibit the "mathematical reasoning of a drafts-man" rather than the instincts of a type designer.

In 2000, Tobias Frere-Jones undertook a study of building lettering in New York, inspiring the design of Gotham. It is an honest and straightforward font that is neutral without being clinical, authorita-tive without being impersonal, and friendly without being folksy.

Composed by

North Market Street Graphics,
Lancaster, Pennsylvania

Printed and Bound by

SNP Leefung, China

Designed by

Iris Weinstein